W9-BUT-307

✦✦✦

Counseling Today's Families

✦✦✦

Counseling Today's Families

Herbert Goldenberg
California State University, Los Angeles

Irene Goldenberg
University of California, Los Angeles

Brooks/Cole Publishing Company
Pacific Grove, California

Brooks/Cole Publishing Company
A Division of Wadsworth, Inc.

© 1990 by Wadsworth, Inc., Belmont, California 94002. All rights reserved. No part of this book may be reproduced, stored in a retrieval system, or transcribed, in any form or by any means—electronic, mechanical, photocopying, recording, or otherwise—without the prior written permission of the publisher, Brooks/Cole Publishing Company, Pacific Grove, California 93950, a division of Wadsworth, Inc.

Printed in the United States of America

10   9   8   7   6   5   4   3   2   1

Library of Congress Cataloging in Publication Data
Goldenberg, Herbert.
   Counseling today's families / by Herbert Goldenberg and
Irene Goldenberg.
      p. cm.
   Bibliography: p.
   Includes indexes.
   ISBN 0-534-11934-4
   1. Family social work—United States. 2. Problem families-
-Counseling of—United States. 3. Family—United States–
–Psychological aspects. 4. Behavioral assessment.   I. Goldenberg,
Irene. II. Title.
HV699.G65   1989
362.82'86'0973—dc20   89-984
                                                         CIP

Sponsoring Editor: Claire Verduin
Editorial Assistant: Gay Bond
Production Editor: Linda Loba
Interior Design: Linda Loba
Cover Design: Flora Pomeroy
Manuscript Editor: Lorraine Anderson
Permissions Editor: Carline Haga
Printing and Binding: Malloy Lithographing, Inc.

For each other: To continuity and change

84819

◆◆◆

Preface

The birth of this book has occurred only after a prolonged gestation period. The process began nearly a decade ago, when we independently became aware that the families who sought our professional help were struggling with issues that often superceded the problems clients from intact families brought us. While occasional journal articles were beginning to document the increased diversity of family forms and living arrangements, particularly following analysis of the 1980 U.S. Census data, no textbook seemed yet to address the inevitable implications for counselors or other members of the helping professions that such societal changes were bringing. We decided such a book was needed, and set ourselves the task of exploring what special problems such "non-traditional" families faced, and what counseling procedures might be of greatest benefit to them.

Early on in our research, however, we realized that we were hardly dealing with a new phenomenon, nor, correspondingly, were the variant family forms we were seeing particularly "non-traditional." Single-parent households, for example, have always existed; while they were likely to be formed as a result of death or desertion by a spouse in the past, today they far more frequently come about through divorce or births to unwed mothers. The phenomenon of single parenthood is unchanged, but the psychosocial consequences to the single parent (usually female) of dealing with her life situation have been immeasurably altered. Together, we decided to refocus our attention on just what such repercussions were for families as they are organized today.

Today we are witnessing profound changes in the everyday living experiences of a significant portion of our population. A large number of adults and children alike must learn to redefine themselves as part of a remarried or step-family, struggling together to achieve an identity as a family unit. Others must learn to cope with complicated custody and visitation arrangements; children in particular are handed the difficult task of functioning, simultaneously, as part of each of their biological parents' household systems. Unmarried couples, of the same or of opposite sexes, must decide whether they wish to live together openly, in defiance of convention, and in the process attempt to cope with possible sitgmatization and estrangement from family and the larger social system. Couples in dual-career marriages must attempt to juggle family and career demands if both wish to pursue equally active roles outside the home.

What must a counselor understand before attempting to help? Answering that question is essentially our purpose in writing this book.

All of the family forms described in this text have by now become sufficiently familiar—even commonplace in some circumstances—that researchers and clinicians alike have begun to ferret out significant distinguishing characteristics. We have attempted to elaborate on these characteristics from a family systems perspective, meaning that we adopt a relationship frame of reference in conceptualizing what transpires within a family. Throughout the book, we have attempted to maintain a primary focus on the family context, attending especially to the transactional patterns and processes currently taking place as the family tries to cope with its transitions and developments. At the same time, we have taken care not to neglect the fact that the family is itself part of a larger system (made up of schools, child care facilities, health establishments, job opportunities), and its experiences (and levels of stress) are frequently effected by its involvements with this larger social context.

A major goal in writing this text is to help counselors prepare to deal effectively with families they are likely to encounter today. To do so skillfully and effectively, we believe, the counselor needs an appreciation of how a family functions as a social system, how dysfunction may come about, how to tap into family strengths, how to utilize community resources where available, and so forth. Although we wish to make it clear that we believe each family presents the counselor with a unique configuration and distinctive set of relationship patterns, we nevertheless would argue that the counselor is better prepared if aware of which common interpersonal patterns to possibly expect with each family structure. While the family living arrangements described throughout the book may not appeal to every reader, nor are we necessarily endorsing any, we do believe we have provided an objective look at what life outside of the traditional nuclear family is like today, and a representational sample of what counselors might expect in their daily work.

To the extent that such information is currently available, we have offered our readers sets of guidelines for assessing different types of families and planning effective intervention strategies. We wish to emphasize our belief that while each family configuration we discuss may have its unique pattern of potential problems or vulnerabilities, each also has certain inherent strengths, something a counselor must not overlook. To facilitate the learning process, we have included numerous case studies throughout the book, both to illustrate typical problems in a particular family's organization as well as describe particular coping styles and strategies. We hope, by this pedagogical technique, to shed some light on how a counselor might proceed in various situations and with differing family types.

In trying to make this text as up to date and as readable as possible, we have had the able assistance of a number of our academic as well as counseling colleagues. We wish particularly to thank: Dr. James H. Bray, Baylor College of Medicine, Houston, Texas; Dr. Roberta Driscoll, University of Central Florida; Dr. Norma Gilbert, Denton, Texas; Dr. Susan Hendrick, Texas Tech University; Dr. Janine Roberts, University of Massachusetts; and Dr. Thomas Smith, University of Wisconsin-Milwaukee.

Once again we wish to acknowledge our gratitude to our many friends at Brooks/Cole, who never seem to stop believing in our ability to reach the goal line by finishing a book, even if we ourselves occasionally stumble and temporarily need team support. Claire Verduin has provided her usual assistance and encouragement, and Linda Loba has made the task of turning a manuscript into a book a relatively painless task.

Herbert Goldenberg
Irene Goldenberg

Contents

Part I

♦♦♦

Families in Transition

Chapter 1

◆◆◆

The Changing American Family

We live today in a complex and increasingly varied society. The family, no less than other institutions, is undergoing rapid and dramatic changes in form, composition, and structure. Nontraditional families (led by **single parents,**[1] for example) are becoming more commonplace and the traditional **nuclear family** (with the male as sole breadwinner and the female as full-time homemaker, wife, and mother remaining together in an intact marriage 'til death do them part) less and less the American norm. Skyrocketing divorce rates (one in seven marriages ended in divorce in 1920; one in two dissolved by divorce in 1980), the surge of women into the work force, marriage postponement, stepfamilies, single people living alone or with a partner of the same or opposite sex, childless families, mothers with out-of-wedlock children—these are just some of the realities of contemporary American life.

1 Terms printed in **boldface** are defined in the Glossary at the back of the book.

Not surprisingly, counselors today are being confronted with new sets and combinations of clients, presenting new sets of attitudes, lifestyles, and relationship problems. Customary diagnostic categories designed for individual clients do not adequately describe a breakdown in a family's transactional patterns. While individual candidates for long-term psychotherapy continue to receive such treatment for their personal maladaptive or problematic behavior, today's counselor must also be prepared to deal with couples, entire families, or combinations thereof, as well as clients who come individually to seek help for their relationship woes. As Barth (1988) observes, faced with varying types of couples seeking help to decide whether they should remain together or separate, today's counselor is often hard pressed to decide if marriage counseling, divorce counseling, family counseling, or individual counseling is called for.

Moreover, today's counselor is likely to confront client misfortunes that arise from circumstances that were once relatively uncommon, such as growing up in a fatherless home or one where **custody** was shared between divorced parents and the youngster moved from household to household every three or four days. Or conceivably the problems arise from an alternative family life pattern in which two unmarried adults share an intimate living arrangement but struggle over differences in their sense of commitment to the future of their relationship. Or perhaps conflict exists between children from separate parents joined together in a **stepfamily**. Today's counselor is more likely than at any time in the past to be called upon to help two-career couples work out conflicts between career demands and personal or family demands.

Counselors need to alert themselves to the general problems (and strengths) inherent in each of today's many family structures, in addition to grasping the interplay in each specific situation. Beyond that, they need to become familiar with current counseling strategies for dealing with these new developments in family life. In this book, we describe five contemporary family structures: single-parent-led families, remarried families, cohabiting heterosexual couples, gay male and lesbian female couples, and dual-career families. For each family configuration, we develop a format for assessing their situations and counseling needs, and offer suggestions (along with excerpts from sessions) for delivering effective therapeutic intervention.

A FAMILY COUNSELING SAMPLER

Consider the following brief descriptions from a typical caseload of today's counselor:

Mr. and Mrs. Brown, married six months, after having each been in marriages ending in divorce, referred themselves for counseling. [Self-referral is actually fairly common with stepfamilies, since one or both parents have had earlier unhappy experiences in marriage and want to avoid a repetition of that trauma.] Both were computer scientists who met as graduate students at a midwestern university. Since both were married at the time, and both were expressing considerable despair about their deteriorating marriages, they found solace in one another, and soon were having a sexual affair. Immediately after graduation, Mr. Brown divorced his wife, left his two preteenage children with their mother, and departed for a job on the West Coast. His wife-to-be shortly thereafter left her husband, took their 6-year-old daughter, and by prearrangement joined Mr. Brown. Within one year, they were married, both employed in rewarding jobs, and living happily with her young daughter in a large urban community. Mr. Brown talked by telephone with his own children on occasion, but saw them rarely, only when he had business in the town where they lived.

Unfortunately, the Brown's honeymoon period was short-lived. For one thing, each of them had been married to people of the same ethnic and social class background as themselves before, and they now experienced some rift as a result of her Baptist and his Jewish background. (Her effort during their first Christmas to maintain a family custom by reading aloud from the New Testament did not go over well with him!) Even more disrupting was the sudden appearance of his daughter, now 13, who had been struggling with her mother and decided to come out, unannounced, to live with her father. Within a short period, during which Mrs. Brown was determined to make her stepdaughter feel at home, conflict erupted in the household. Mrs. Brown was especially upset at what she viewed as her husband's overindulgent and overly permissive child-rearing actions, which she believed led to undisciplined and uncontrolled behavior. In addition, she disliked her stepdaughter's intrusiveness—using her perfume, wearing some of her clothes, behaving as though she had proprietary rights over her father. Mr. Brown, caught in the middle, felt concerned about his wife's increasing unhappiness, but also believed he needed to indulge his daughter or she would feel neglected and rejected. One major worry and source of guilt feelings was that his daughter might begin to believe he favored his stepdaughter over his own child. Finally, when conflict in the household had reached an unacceptable level, the Browns contacted a family counselor, who suggested over the telephone that the parents and both children come together for family sessions.

Andrea and John could not make up their minds about living together, although they had been having an ongoing (and tempestuous) love affair for five years. Both single, in their late 20s, and both employed as salespeople at the same department store where they met, each claimed to be having too much fun to settle down with one person. More likely, however, each had pervasive fears of an intimate relationship as well as some sense that each would have problems sustaining such closeness over any length of time. Despite these misgivings, and after a long series of on-again, off-again decisions, they determined that they would try living together, and decide once and for all whether they should marry or split up permanently. John gave up his apartment and, doubts aside, moved in with Andrea.

It seemed within a month that their worst fears were confirmed. Andrea felt her territory, which she had carefully and lovingly decorated with objects very personal and meaningful to her, was being invaded. John felt very critical of Andrea's way of doing things—cooking, stacking dishes after they were washed, caring for her car, spending money. Accustomed to straight, direct talk—he had been raised in a large family where get-togethers often became free-for-alls—he could not understand Andrea's long silences and quiet weeping. She, on the other hand, an only child raised by a doting mother (who herself had little if any relationship with an increasingly ostracized father), could not understand why John had so many complaints about her if, as he claimed, he loved her so much. After living together two months, both were depressed and confused, and at the suggestion of a fellow employee, sought professional help.

Glenn and Carl had been lovers more than two years, and had moved into Glenn's house together about a year and a half before their conflicts led them to seek counseling as a couple. Glenn was a Ph.D. historian, graduate of a prestigious university and himself a university professor, while Carl had had a sporadic education, worked as a bookstore clerk, and was currently taking evening classes at a community college. Glenn had been in individual psychotherapy with a gay psychologist even before living with Carl, and had continued to go after they were together. It was that psychologist who first suggested to Glenn that he was in the midst of a highly intense and disturbing relationship that required the help of a counselor who worked with couples, something that psychologist was not trained to do.

When both partners decided to live together, they believed the relationship would be more or less permanent. Each of them had had experiences with various men—Glenn in relatively long-term relationships, Carl in brief affairs, usually of the pickup, one-night variety. Each was sexually sophisticated about the gay life; each knew how to please the other. In Glenn's case, he had moved from being the more passive, more dependent member in the past to his current situation with Carl of being more active and dominant. Carl had always enjoyed adopting a passive role with other men and continued to do so with Glenn.

Several long-standing issues and certain immediate ones had led to their current crisis. Among the former was Glenn's critical and meticulous behavior; for example, constantly carping about a dirty spot on the sofa or the fact that Carl did not empty ashtrays after each use. Carl's reaction was typically to become increasingly defiant and sloppy. There were additional struggles over status differences, Glenn never failing to remind Carl of the latter's low-level work and the fact that he, Glenn, had lived before with higher-status individuals such as "a physician, a novelist, and a hospital administrator." Perhaps the most acute problem, however, was Carl's return to "cruising" gay bars and being promiscuous, despite (or perhaps because of) Glenn's terror of contacting AIDS.

Mrs. Taylor, 42, called a male counselor in near panic, indicating she wanted help for Lois, her 15-year-old daughter, an only child. Mrs. Taylor revealed that she had been in individual counseling with a social worker for three years, since shortly after her husband died, but mainly appeared to be receiving support to resume her life; the matter of dealing with Lois, increasingly a problem, had been a secondary issue until recently. Now, however, the pressures of being a single parent of an adolescent girl were mounting. The school had called several times to report that Lois was not attending class, and when she was present seemed to be disinterested and uninvolved. What appeared to trigger the call to the counselor, however, was a rare confrontation between mother and daughter in which Lois blurted out that she had visited a clinic to get birth control pills and was having a sexual relationship with Tom, 20, a sometimes student at a local junior college. Mrs. Taylor wanted a male counselor in particular because she felt most of her family problems could be traced to the loss of her husband and her subsequent efforts "to be both mother and father to Lois."

As is often the case with adolescents, especially when seeing a counselor because of a parent's prodding, an individual session with Lois proved of limited value. Although the counselor and Lois hit it off well enough, Lois was guarded and sulky; she was willing to answer questions, and seemed to do so honestly, but she volunteered little information and gave most of her responses in as brief a form as possible. She did acknowledge her sexual activity, insisting it was her business alone and that her mother—and now the counselor—were intruding into her life. She was willing to continue the sessions to pacify her mother, but, frankly, she felt the problem was her mother's and not hers. The counselor did persuade her to return for a joint session with her mother the following week.

In person, Mrs. Taylor gave the impression of a passive-dependent, uncertain, frightened, and depressed woman. Not knowing how to deal with Lois, and especially her budding sexuality, she had adopted a laissez-faire attitude, abdicating any responsibility for providing guidance for her daughter. She herself barely managed to hold onto a part-time job as a bank teller, and essentially led a fairly solitary and joyless life. Her living standard, now far below what her husband had provided as a self-employed accountant, left her with few options for travel or other social activities she had known in the past. At some level—although she refused to deal with the issue at first—she felt competitive with her young daughter, and resentful of the romance in the latter's life.

Joel, born and raised in a small town and relatively innocent about the outside world, did not stray far from home until he was 18 and went off to college in a nearby state. Lindsay, by contrast, had been brought up in the college town, and was sophisticated, brainy, and beautiful. What this "college queen" ever saw in Joel never ceased to amaze him, since she had a choice of dozens of more attractive men, or so it seemed to him. In any case, choose him she did, and in their last year of school they were married.

Joel completed his premed training, Lindsay continued working on her elementary teaching credential, and their dual-career relationship seemed to flourish. All through his medical school, internship, and residency years, Joel worked hard, continuing to be the high achiever he had been since his earliest school years. Lindsay got a job as a teacher, discovered it was rewarding but demanding, and although she saw herself as a career person, seemed to welcome Joel's urging that she stop working and have a baby. Within two years, they had another child, Joel was busy establishing his practice in internal medicine, and Lindsay, like many another woman in a dual-career marriage, was trying to decide whether to return to work part-time or on a substitute teacher basis while their preschool children still needed her attention. Intent on resuming her career, with aspirations toward becoming a school psychologist, Lindsay nevertheless was torn between the needs of her children and the requirements of a demanding profession. She was unable to find satisfactory child care for her two children, and rather than return to teaching and take evening classes to obtain an advanced degree and school psychologist credential, Lindsay decided to interrupt her career somewhat longer until the children were more self-sufficient or more fully grown.

Increasingly, however, Lindsay began experiencing periods of depression and feelings of worthlessness. Bored and dissatisfied at home, she tried a variety of part-time jobs: secretary in a large office, assistant to a book publisher, private tutor. None challenged her intellectually. She felt despondent over not living up to her career potential and resentful that Joel was gaining recognition and her career aspirations were stalled. Typically, when morose, she would return home, have dinner with the family (Joel had picked up the children from the day-care center near his office and prepared dinner), spend a brief period with the children, and go to bed. Weekends were similar: Joel playing the role of mother and father, taking the children shopping for clothes, to the movies, or to kiddyland activities, preparing dinner, and getting them to bed.

During this time, Lindsay stayed in bed most of the day, slept on and off, hardly seemed to notice the comings and goings of people around her. More and more, the children turned to Joel as a single parent; more and more, they shared his unexpressed contempt and rage at Lindsay's behavior. After some initial fruitless attempts to get Lindsay to seek professional help, little changed in this family pattern for two years. By then, however, Joel was receiving enough satisfaction from his martyrdom that he no longer allowed Lindsay to share in raising the children, even at those times when she expressed a desire to do so. Curiously, despite Joel's self-righteousness and Lindsay's escapist behavior, their sex life seemed to continue and give pleasure to both of them. Whether such physical intimacy represented the exchange of true affection or simply the seeking of comfort and reassurance of two needy, dependent people was never considered. However even this tentative effort to reach out to one another ultimately dwindled, and, as a last resort before filing for divorce, they contacted a family counselor.

TODAY'S FAMILIES: SOME DEMOGRAPHIC NOTES

American life has changed drastically in the past two decades, and that change is reflected in the workplace, in male-female relationships, and, inevitably, in the family. Women now account for approximately half of the total work force, in sharp contrast with times as recent as the early 1960s, when they accounted for perhaps one third of those employed. Within the professions, the number of women employed equals the number of men (although most women are still clustered in the less-prestigious and lower-salaried professions of teaching and nursing), according to a recent survey (ABC News, 1986). Eighteen percent of all lawyers are now women, up 14 percent in 14 years; 17 percent of American physicians are women, compared to 10 percent in 1972; one out of four of today's MBAs is female.

Clearly, these statistics reveal significant changes in our attitudes and expectations, and profoundly affect the number and kind of decisions faced by today's woman of marriageable age. She is more likely than ever before to have obtained a higher level of education, and her options are more varied than ever before. She must decide if and when to marry; what kind of work to devote herself to; whether to have children and when to do so; the economic feasibility of being a divorced woman, should a marriage be unsuccessful; whether to remarry; and so on. Her having far greater sexual freedom than her counterpart of two decades ago, more career options, and increased economic power have together helped alter man-woman relationships in ways that the mothers of today's women would likely find incomprehensible. With new choices have come increased uncertainty and, in many cases, role confusion, as today's young women (as well as the men with whom they interact) grapple with changing ideals and evolving notions of personal and interpersonal fulfillment.

Nowhere is the social upheaval of the last two decades more apparent than in family patterns and relationships. As demographer Peter Morrison (1986) points out:

> Fewer and fewer American families conform to traditional stereotypes. They are more diverse and less stable now than ever before. More children are born to unmarried mothers, and more childhood years are spent in fatherless families. Couples marry later and are quicker to divorce. Fully 54 percent of wives with preschool-age children are now in the work force (only 30 percent were in 1970). (p. 2)

Figure 1.1 illustrates some of the changes that have already occurred as well as those projected for 1990 in types of American households. Note especially the jump in numbers of childless married couples, single men and women living alone, and female-headed households over the thirty-year period. Between 1960 and 1975 alone, according to Gullotta, Adams, and Alexander (1986), 8 million more married couples were counted; however, 7.1 million were couples without children at home, primarily young childless families. In addition, substantial increases were found in female-headed families. (This phenomenon, along with its implications for today's counselors, is discussed more fully in Chapter 4.)

From a contemporary perspective, it no longer makes sense to refer to what is "typical" when speaking of American family life. More accurately, we need to consider varying types of families—with diverse organizational patterns, styles of living, and living arrangements. America's idealized and nostalgic portrait of the nuclear family— the carefree family with a suburban residence, sole-provider father and homemaker mother, both parents dedicated to childrearing, remaining together as an intact family for life, children obtaining an education in a neighborhood school, trips to church together on Sunday, plenty of money, supportive grandparents—is the stuff of television make-believe and not reality today for the vast majority of the population (if, indeed, such a picture-postcard family ever existed).

Consider the following facts and forecasts (Gullotta, Adams, & Alexander,1986; Masnick & Bane, 1980; Morrison, 1986):

- Half the marriages made this year in the United States will probably end in divorce.
- One out of five children is now born to an unwed mother; the number of teenage unwed mothers is at an all-time high, but so is the number of unwed mature women, economically self-sufficient, with a stronger desire for a child than for a husband.
- Today's teenage mother is opting increasingly to keep her child, launching another single-parent household.
- Married couples are divorcing earlier in marriage than ever before, and thus younger children are more and more likely to be affected by divorce.

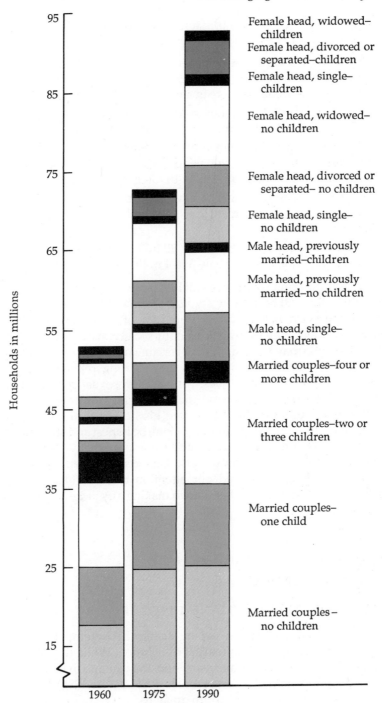

Figure 1.1.   Types of households, 1960, 1975, and 1990
Source: Gullotta, Adams, & Alexander, 1986, p. 302.

- Fully three-fifths of all children born today will spend at least part of their childhood in a single-parent family.
- Single-parent families, 90 percent of which are headed by women, now represent more than one out of five families with children. More than half of all black children live in a one-parent household.
- Single people living alone now make up one-fourth of U.S. households, reflecting decisions to remain single or postpone marriage.
- There has been a 90 percent jump in one-person households in the last 15 years, representing single people who have never married as well as those living alone as a result of divorce or widowhood.
- Women are waiting longer to have children and are having fewer of them. As many as 15 percent of women in their childbearing years will remain childless.
- By 1990, it is expected that of the 20 million new households formed during the prior 15 years, only 3 to 4 million will be married couples.

None of the family forms we will be describing in detail in the remainder of this book will be entirely atypical or unfamiliar to the reader. What is new is the sharp increase in the proportion of such alternative lifestyles today, as well as their partial acceptance by society. We recognize that there are readers who may be disdainful of certain patterns (for example, working mothers) and readers who may have strong religious or political objections to others (gay couples, young heterosexual couples living together outside of marriage). Before undertaking any clinical work with such families, the counselor should explore his or her feelings regarding a particular lifestyle, and if there is a problem, be honest and straightforward with the clients. It has been our clinical experience that all these lifestyles face certain serious problems, but also have certain internal strengths. In this book we have addressed our attention to the understanding and resolution of these issues rather than to making any judgment or endorsement of a lifestyle.

CHANGING TIMES: MARRIAGE, DIVORCE, REMARRIAGE

PATTERNS OF MARRIAGE AND DIVORCE

A central determinant of the sweeping changes in contemporary American family life is the high rate of marital dissolution. While the marriage rate has remained stable in recent years, and the rate of divorce has in fact dropped slightly (National Center for Health Statistics,1985), it is nevertheless true that the marriages of approximately 50 percent of today's couples will eventually terminate in divorce. Figure 1.2 illustrates both marriage and divorce trends over the last half century in the United States.

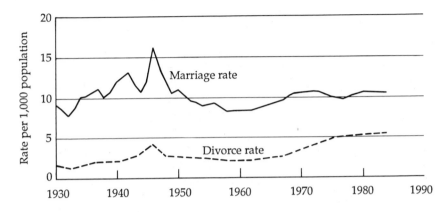

Figure 1.2. Marriage and divorce rates, 1930–1984.
Source: National Center for Health Statistics, 1985, p. 4.

The reasons for marrying are, of course, varied and complex, and not surprisingly, the answer to what went wrong in any specific marriage is correspondingly difficult to pinpoint. Acknowledging the myriad of factors that may influence a couple's decision to separate and perhaps eventually divorce, Bornstein and Bornstein (1986) offer a three-part classification of possible reasons: social, personal, and relationship issues.

Socially, these authors contend, changes in marital and family relations are but a reflection of the period of rapid change in our society, in which values, beliefs, and customs are continuously being challenged. The complexity and impersonalization of society at large contributes to a further sense of isolation and distrust. Alternative lifestyles (**open marriage, non-marital cohabitation, gay couples**, sexually active singles, remarriage), increasingly common and socially acceptable in an increasing number of circles, offer a wider range of relationship choices than ever before. Such an expansion of lifestyle options means that an individual may choose to leave a traditional marriage not simply because it is terribly dissatisfying, but perhaps because other options, not formerly available, appear to be more attractive. The increasing "respectability" (or at least social acceptability) of divorce as well as the ease with which it may be obtained may help facilitate the decision to end the marriage.

As Levinger (1976) contends, people remain in a marriage on the basis of an unconscious accounting to themselves of three factors: (1) the extent of their attraction to the relationship; (2) the barriers they perceive to obtaining a divorce; and (3) comparisons they make between what they have in their current marriage and the alternatives they sense are available outside. In the event that their marriage has eroded to the point that the first two factors are perceived as weak arguments for remaining in the light of possible alternative attractions, then the likely consequence is the breakup of the marriage.

Bornstein and Bornstein (1986) also identify a number of personal factors that contribute to marital unhappiness. Unrealistic expectations (for example, that one's spouse will always try to please, never be angry, always be open and honest) based on romantic dreams and false hopes—inevitably unfulfilled—may lead to disappointment and ultimately to despair. Happiness may seem elusive to some partners, who may then withdraw from the relationship and perhaps seek satisfactions in work-related activities or extramarital affairs.

Inevitably, too, people change as they mature, and a couple (particularly if they married at an early age) may discover a growing divergence in interests and values to the point of "irreconcilable differences." Some partners may find that their parents provided poor role models for a successful marriage; others may find themselves too uncomfortable trying to sustain an intimate relationship; still others may become stressed to the point of dysfunction when called upon to care for a newborn child. Serious psychological problems in one or both partners may become exacerbated in the process of living as husband and wife.

Disillusionment with the relationship, a feeling that one's emotional and physical needs remain unmet, and a sense of growing in different directions may build over time, until a precipitating event—the "last straw"—or an accumulation of unfulfilled expectations provides the momentum behind the decision to divorce (Milne, 1988).

Beyond personal factors, interpersonal issues are at the core of most marital breakups:

Ineffective communication patterns;

Sexual incompatibilities;

Anxiety over making and/or maintaining a long-term commitment;

Fewer shared activities ;

Reduced exchange of affection;

Infidelity;

Lack of sensitivity or indifference to a partner's feelings or wishes;

Conflicts over power and control;

Underdeveloped problem-solving skills;

Conflicts over money, independence, in-laws, or children;

Physical abuse;

An inability to respond positively to changing role demands such as those brought about by the birth of a first child or the return to paid work by one partner.

Typically, several of these episodes, transactions, or transition-point experiences, repeated without resolution over a period of time, escalate the growing marital dissatisfaction of one or both partners. In effect, once a partner concludes that the costs of staying together outweigh the benefits, then the marriage is in jeopardy.

SUCCESSFUL MARRIAGE

A healthy marriage is able, flexibly and even synergistically, to adapt to the individual growth of each partner, while a dysfunctional one often is strained by the developmental changes that inevitably occur in each partner (Rice & Rice, 1986b). As individuals grow apart, there are often resented accommodations to one's spouse and self-denial of opportunity for self-growth in an effort to cling to the marriage. Ultimately such compromises become too personally costly, work against the relationship, and stifle the growth of the marriage.

By way of contrast, Beavers (1988) contends that healthy couples by and large respect the other's perceptions; they negotiate, and occasionally fight without necessarily struggling for a one-up position over the other. They tend to believe in the trustworthiness of their spouse, accepting occasional conflict as inevitable but without fearing abandonment as the result. They tolerate sporadic outbursts of unpleasant or angry feelings from spouse and children without using such experiences to "prove" the others have evil intent.

Their accommodation to one another allows for more equal overt power without hostile competition and continuous rivalry. Whether their quarrels are loud or quiet, open or covert, intense or emotionally subdued, distancing or embroiling, rationally presented or passionately expressed, they tend to end up, when the smoke lifts, with a clear sense of boundaries (knowing where one person ends and the other begins, recognizing the difference between one person's feelings and wishes and the other's), making productive resolution of the conflict possible. Healthy couples operate mainly in the present, according to Beavers, aware of the past without being its prisoner or driven repeatedly to behave as in their childhood. Healthy couples, too, respect each other's individual opinions and choices (that is, without viewing a difference as an expression of the other's willfulness, selfishness, stubbornness, or ignorance). All of these attributes outlined by Beavers help couples negotiate solutions to problems or opportunities that meet the needs of both partners.

THE PROCESS OF DIVORCE

Separation and divorce are procedures that occur over time and in stages; the entire process usually involves a great deal of stress, ambivalence, indecision, self-doubt, and uncertainty, even when both partners agree to the action. Although they cannot be fully aware of what lies in store for them, in most cases, they are about to undergo a painful, disruptive process from which, more likely than not, it may take much time to recover. Kressel (1985) goes so far as to characterize the process of divorce negotiation as "one of the more demanding tasks that rational beings are expected to perform" (p.4).

In most cases, one person initiates the process, although the other may be feeling the same urge but be less able or less willing, financially or emotionally, to act; in far fewer cases, the non-initiating person is taken by surprise, although probably because he or she did not want to know and thus denied what was taking place prior to the initiating act. It is the exceptional couple who mutually and simultaneously reach the decision to divorce (Milne, 1988).

However the decision is reached, or by whom, the counselor seeing the couple at any point in the marriage/separation/divorce continuum must be attuned to the blow to self-esteem separation and divorce inevitably bring. To have invested time, effort, personal resources, youthfulness, all for naught is to experience a personal feeling of failure and the sense that perhaps one does not possess the necessary traits to ever achieve or maintain a satisfying marriage. Moreover, marriage bestows a sense of identity, maturity, acceptance, respectability in most segments of society. For many people, then, despite a veneer of sophistication, to have failed at marriage is to have failed as an adult. Yet, divorce also has a positive potential—offering a new beginning as much as an ending—important for the counselor to impart to the divorcing pair.

Divorce, even a relatively amicable one, rarely occurs abruptly. More likely, couples undergo a series of events together before both partners can let go and begin to lead separate lives. A useful framework for conceptualizing the divorce process has been offered by Paul Bohannan (1970; 1984), who views the entire circumstance as usually requiring six overlapping stages before such disengagement can be accomplished. While these stages do not necessarily occur in an invariant sequence, nor do all persons involved feel the same anguish at each phase, Kaslow (1988) argues that each stage must be experienced and its stumbling blocks removed before a sense of well-being can be achieved by both mates.

First comes the **emotional divorce** which may or may not involve physical separation, during which, often at the instigation of one, both partners finally recognize that the marriage is deteriorating. This period may be brief or prolonged, but whatever its length the couple must deal with the decline of the relationship. If one person gives voice to his or her dissatisfaction or disillusionment before the other, the latter may become alarmed, even agitated, and try to cajole or seduce the initiator back into the marraige. Promises to change, declarations of good intentions, desperate pleas, threats of suicide, even a willingness to begin counseling (if previously resisted) may be offered as inducements to stay. Another common scenario is for both marital partners to use this opportunity to hurl criticisms and invectives at each other, each defending his or her own behavior and denouncing the actions, past or present, of the other.

Kessler (1975) has further divided this stage into three phases—disillusionment, erosion, and detachment—during which couples focus on each other's weaknesses and deficiencies and each partner blames the other for the marital unhappiness. Destructive verbal and nonverbal exchanges, avoidance, lack of attention, withdrawal, perhaps self-pity characterize behavior at this point, as one or both mates prepares to cope with the future, sometimes by seeking solace through outside sexual contacts or affairs (Woody, 1983).

Kaslow (1988) believes that couples who enter conjoint marital counseling at this point—resolving frustrations, ventilating and understanding their suppressed anger, perhaps working on improving the relationship now that it is in jeopardy—are more likely to work out their marital conflict than by one or both entering individual counseling or psychotherapy. Table 1.1 (pp. 18 – 19) offers a useful description of what a counselor might expect in the form of feelings or actions of divorcing couples at each of Bohannan's (1970) stages of the divorce process.

Returning to Bohannan's stages, next comes the **legal divorce**, during which one partner contacts an attorney, serves legal notice on the other, and begins the judicial process. Until a decade ago, it was necessary in most states to justify the action by alleging some grounds—adultery, mental cruelty—but today almost all states allow partners to terminate the marriage without a presumption of fault by either party. While still adversarial, "no-fault " legislation can be interpreted as an encouraging move toward normalizing divorce in our society (Ahrons & Rodgers, 1987). Increasingly, as Rice and Rice (1986a) note, divorce has come to be seen as a predictable phenomenon and life cycle stage, particularly for a segment of society that places great value on individual fulfillment and independence. In Bohannan's view (1984), today divorce is as much a societal institution as marriage.

The **economic divorce** follows as decisions are made by the divorcing pair regarding the redistribution of assets, property, child support payments, possible alimony payments, and so forth, usually with the help of attorneys, sometimes in conjunction with mental health workers. **Divorce mediation** (Coogler, 1978; Folberg & Milne, 1988; Kressel, 1985), an alternative to traditional legal intervention, is a relatively recent innovative attempt to facilitate the negotiation of these emotion-arousing issues by taking into account the affective as well as the legal dimensions of the marital dissolution. As we discuss later in this chapter, divorce mediation is a nonadversarial approach in which professionals (mental health workers, lawyers, or both working together) help a couple arrive at an acceptable and mutually beneficial settlement based on their own agreed-upon choices. By helping the couple reach their own decisions with the aid of a

Table 1.1 Common Client Feelings, Actions, Therapeutic Interventions, and Mediation Strategies at Six Stages of the Divorce Process

Divorce stage	Station[a]	Stage	Feelings	Actions and tasks	Therapeutic interventions	Mediation
	I. Emotional divorce	A	Disillusionment Dissatisfaction Alienation Anxiety Disbelief	Avoiding the issue Sulking and/or crying Confronting partner Quarreling	Marital Therapy (one couple) Couples group therapy	
Predivorce A time of deliberation and despair		B	Despair Dread Anguish Ambivalence Shock Emptiness Anger Chaos Inadequacy Low self-esteem Loss	Denial Withdrawal (physical and emotional) Pretending all is okay Attempting to win back affection Asking friends, family, clergy for advice	Marital therapy (one couple) Divorce therapy Couples group therapy	
	II. Legal divorce	C	Depression Detachment Anger Hopelessness Self-pity Helplessness	Bargaining Screaming Threatening Attempting suicide Consulting an attorney or mediator	Family therapy Individual adult therapy Child therapy	Set the stage for mediation Ascertain parties' understanding of the process and its appropriateness for them
During divorce A time of legal involvement	III. Economic divorce	D	Confusion Fury Sadness Loneliness Relief Vindictiveness	Separating physically Filing for legal divorce Considering economic arrangements Considering custody arrangements	Children of divorce group therapy Child therapy Adult therapy	Define the rules of mediation Identify the issues & separate therapeutic issues from mediation issues

(continued)

Source: Kaslow, 1988, pp. 88-89.
[a]These stations are taken from the work of Bohannan (1970)

Table 1.1 (continued)

Divorce stage	Station[a]	Stage	Feelings	Actions and tasks	Therapeutic interventions	Mediation
	IV. Coparental divorce and the problems of custody	E	Concern for children Ambivalence Numbness Uncertainty	Grieving and mourning Telling relatives and friends Reentering work world (unemployed woman) Feeling empowered to make choices	Same as above plus network family therapy	Negotiate & process the issues & choices Reach agreement Analyze & formalize agreement
	V. Community divorce	F	Indecisiveness Optimism Resignation Excitement Curiosity Regret Sadness	Finalizing divorce Begin reaching out to new friends Undertaking new activities Stablizing new life-style and daily routine for children Exploring new interests and possibly taking new job	Adults Individual therapy Singles group therapy Children Child play therapy Children's group therapy	
Postdivorce A time of exploration and reequilibration	VI. Psychic divorce	G	Acceptance Self-confidence Energetic Self-worth Wholeness Exhilaration Independence Autonomy	Resynthesis of identity Completing psychic divorce Seeking new love object and making a commitment to some permanency Becoming comfortable with new lifestyle and friends Helping children accept finality of parents' divorce and their continuing relationship with both parents	Parent-child therapy Family therapy Group therapies Children's activity group therapy	Return to mediation when changed circumstances require a renegotiation of the agreement

neutral party, divorce mediation is likely to diminish or remove altogether the emotional intensity and blaming behavior commonly associated with adversarial actions.

During Bohannan's fourth stage, that of **coparental divorce**, child custody and visitation rights are hammered out. While custody has traditionally been awarded to the mother, based on the assumption that a young child's interests are best served by his or her mother, that tradition is being increasingly challenged today. More and more fathers are awarded sole custody now, and shared custody or **joint custody**, in which both parents retain legal custody, is more the norm. One parent may retain **physical custody**, they may take turns caring for the child, or each parent may be granted custody of one or more children. Ahrons and Rodgers (1987) argue that while marriages may be ended, families (especially with children) continue, even if the parents reside in separate households. These authors prefer the term **binuclear families** to *single parent* or *broken* families, in order to emphasize that the two households form one family system. (We'll return to these issues in Chapter 4.)

The former partners must next redefine their separate places in the community as single individuals, and must also reestablish relations with family and friends; this all occurs during the stage of **community divorce**. In many cases, as Weiss (1975) observes, decisions to separate (and especially to divorce) may have been postponed for lengthy periods because of reluctance to face friends and family and make the divorce public. Now, relations with others must be reestablished and new lifestyles attempted. Young divorced persons may find it necessary for a variety of reasons (help with child care, finances, feelings of isolation and despair) to move back with their parents, perhaps triggering old parent-child conflicts.

The final stage, for many the most trying, calls for **psychic divorce**, as each former mate must accept the fact of permanent separation, redefine himself or herself as a single and unattached person, and begin the often painful process of seeking and being open to new relationships.

The entire event is a process with roots in the past, before divorce is contemplated, and carries with it effects that extend into the future. As Ahrons and Rodgers (1987) point out, every family member, children as well as adults, will be profoundly affected; as family reorganization results, each person must redefine himself or herself as part of a divorced family and must learn new ways of coping with society at large as well as with each other. Feelings of abandonment, betrayal, loneliness, anxiety, rage, inadequacy, disillusionment, continued attachment to the person who has left, desperation at feeling unloved (and thus, unlovable), mourning—all are likely to appear in some form (Kessler, 1975). Depression, hostility, and bitterness may continue for many divorced persons, who may persist in struggling with an ex-spouse and/or develop dysfunctional parent-child relationships. Others may rush prematurely into new attachments in an effort to reassure themselves of their worth and attractiveness, or to cope with feeling inadequate or fearful of being alone.

LIFE AFTER DIVORCE: SINGLE PARENTHOOD AND REMARRIAGE

Beyond the high divorce rates is the even more disturbing fact that younger couples not only divorce more readily, but also do so at an earlier age than ever before. Figure 1.3 reveals that whereas one-quarter of the women currently in their mid-50s, for example, had become divorced by the time they reached age 43, younger woman are divorcing much earlier: one-quarter of those now in their mid-30s had been in a broken marriage by age 29. The point is that by age 43, middle-aged mothers are likely to have grown children, while younger divorced mothers have younger children and therefore such children, today, are affected by marital disruption much earlier in their lives (Morrison, 1986). Far more than in the past, today's youngsters are spending part of their youth in single-parent families, and perhaps in stepfamilies.

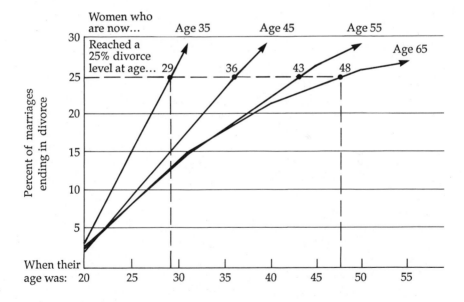

Figure 1.3.   Trends toward earlier divorce among today's younger women.
Source: Morrison, 1986, p. 3. Adapted from Schoen et al., 1985.

Men are consistently more likely to remarry than are women, for several reasons: they are more apt to marry someone not previously married, and they tend to marry younger women and thus have a larger pool of potential partners than do divorced women (Glick, 1984a). Divorced women, as a group, typically with physical custody of their young children, have far less chance of remarriage. Census data as analyzed by Glick, a distinguished demographer, indicate that among women in their 30s who have divorced, the likelihood of remarriage declines, too, with increasing levels of education. While divorced women with no college education are likely to remarry rather quickly, other things being equal, those with more education are not, perhaps choosing to enter marriage more deliberately or deciding to remain unmarried. (These data suggest that, generally speaking, the more economically independent a divorced woman feels, the more choices she has and the less attractive remarriage may appear to her.) In either case, divorced mothers increasingly are heading single-parent households. Widowed and divorced women with custody of their children were about equally numerous in 1960; but by 1983, divorced mothers outnumbered widowed mothers by five to one (Glick, 1984b). Divorce, separation, and the leap in premarital births have doubled the proportion of single-parent-led families in the last 20 years, from 10.1 percent of all American families in 1965 to 22.2 percent in 1985 (*The Wall Street Journal*, 1986).

CHANGING FAMILIES, CHANGING RELATIONSHIPS

FROM BABY BOOM TO BABY BUST

Baby boomers—those persons born between 1946 and 1964, the most fertile period in U.S. history—are now in their prime childbearing years, and thus might be expected, themselves, to be producing a bumper crop of children. The facts, however, are otherwise. Whether delayed marriages, career priorities, decisions to remain single, the high cost of child rearing, fear of bringing children into an unstable world, more reliable contraceptive methods, the reluctance to have children in a risky marriage, or simply the desire to enjoy freedom unencumbered by too many family responsibilities is most responsible—and, clearly, different couples have different reasons—the percentage of couples today without children is at the highest point in 50 years.

Consider the options available 50 years ago in order to better understand the dramatic changes in traditional life-cycle events. Then, for the most part, people lived with parents until married; most married by 21; they began to have children almost immediately, as a rule; childbearing typically was over by age 31; marriages remained intact until the death of one of the spouses; widowhood followed by the mid-60s, and, since remarriage at that point was uncommon, men and women both lived out their remaining ten years or so alone. Now, after living with parents, they may live alone, live with a roommate of the same sex, cohabit with an adult of the opposite sex, perhaps marry, have children (in or out of wedlock), get divorced, live alone again or with a lover of the same or opposite sex, remarry, become stepparents, perhaps become widowed or divorced a second time, marry for the third time, and so forth.

Today's Americans are experiencing transition points in their lives unknown to previous generations. People no longer marry in order to start a family; more single women are having babies than ever before and many married women are choosing to remain childless or delay childbearing until their late 30s (Morrison, 1986). Childlessness has become a more socially acceptable option for married women, who no longer have to be embarrassed or become defensive or otherwise justify such a choice, their parents' disapproval notwithstanding.

LIVING IN TODAY'S NONTRADITIONAL FAMILIES

We are once again experiencing important changes in American family life, as we have done repeatedly over the last two centuries. As Hareven (1982), an historian, notes, contemporary lifestyles (cohabiting heterosexual couples, homosexual partners, dual-career families, single-parent-led households, and so on) are not necessarily new inventions, but rather have become more visible as society becomes more tolerant of change and alternative living arrangements. She argues that we are now witnessing not a fragmentation of traditional family patterns, but an emergence of an acceptance of pluralism in family lifestyles.

Recent trends indicate that the proportion of adults living alone or in a nonmarital twosome arrangement has been growing, while the proportion living together as married couples has been declining (Glick, 1984a). Table 1.2 reveals that the total number of U.S. households rose by 58 percent between 1960 and 1983, as the overall population has increased, with nontraditional household patterns accounting for most of that increase. Note that while the number of households containing married couples with children younger than 18 rose only 4 percent during that entire period of nearly a quarter century, one-parent households increased by 175 percent; one-person households by 173 percent; and households composed of unmarried couples a staggering 331 percent!

The face of the American family has been altered remarkably over the past several decades, during which profound social and demographic changes have taken place. Thriving marriages, successful child rearing, the ability to build and maintain a mature and intimate relationship with another, commitment—none of these have ever been easy to come by, and are probably more difficult than ever today. Conger (1981, p. 1483) calls particular attention to the increased strains on couples, as well as increased challenges:

> Changing sex roles; the rapid increase in women's participation in the work force; the pressure of two-job families; generational differences in values and outlook; continued geographic mobility; relative isolation of

Table 1.2   Number of U.S. Households, and Percentage Distribution of Households by Type, 1960, 1970, and 1983; and Percentage Change in Number of Households, 1960-1983

Measure	No. and % distribution			% change in no. of households		
				1960-1970	1970-1983	1960-1983
	1960	1970	1983			
No. of households (in 000s)	53,019	63,401	83,918	20	32	58
Household type						
With own children under 18	48	45	37	10	7	18
With no own children under 18	52	55	63	29	53	97
Married-couple households	75	70	59	13	12	26
With own children under 18	44	40	29	9	-5	4
With no own children under 18	31	30	30	19	33	58
One-parent households	4	5	8	36	102	175
Mother-child groups	4	4	7	40	100	180
Father-child groups	*	1	1	13	116	145
Living alone	13	17	23	54	80	173
Women	8	11	14	65	63	166
Men	5	6	9	34	116	184
Unmarried-couple households	1	1	2	19	262	331
Female householder	1	*	1	-11	188	157
Male householder	*	*	1	76	333	662
Other households	7	7	8	17	56	83
Female householder	6	5	5	71	114	271
Male householder	1	2	3	5	37	45
Total	100	100	100	na	na	na

Note: *Fewer than 0.5 percent. Na = not applicable.

Source: Glick, 1984a, p. 206. This table is based on data published in the U.S. census reports for 1960 and 1970 and in the Census Bureau's *Current Population Reports* for March 1960, 1970, and 1983.

the nuclear family; continued age segregation; extremely rapid social, economic, and technological changes and the uncertainty about the future that they create; the economic penalties of parenthood in today's world compared to earlier generations—all of these realities have added to the stresses of marriage and parenthood, as well as to their challenges and exciting opportunities.

IMPLICATIONS FOR TODAY'S COUNSELORS

Family counselors today can expect to deal with at least some of the following situations: married couples attempting in one final way, through joint counseling sessions, to hold a deteriorating relationship together; divorcing couples (see the following section); single parents, usually women, experiencing the emotional and financial hardship of raising children alone (Chapter 4); stepfamilies desperate to work out an arrangement so that they might live together in some degree of harmony despite major differences in background, experiences, and values (Chapter 5); young people in a nonmarital cohabitation living arrangement, knowing they need to make some decisions about their future but panicked over what a long-term commitment to another person means giving up (Chapter 6); homosexual couples experiencing the agony of breaking up a long-term love relationship; overloaded dual-career couples attempting to juggle career and family while seeking to achieve equity in their relationship (Chapter 8).

DIVORCE COUNSELING

Considering the prevalence of divorce and the fact that counselors must deal with this issue repeatedly in their practices, it is curious that until the last decade few published guidelines existed for this form of family intervention. In recent years, however, a spate of books has appeared (Everett, 1987; Isaacs, Montalvo, & Abelsohn, 1986; Kaslow & Schwartz, 1987; Rice & Rice, 1986b; Sprenkle, 1985), generally offering a systems outlook for conducting conjoint sessions of divorce counseling. We should note here that in some cases—an unwilling or untrusting or geographically unavailable spouse, an angry or violent spouse, a spouse resistant to further contact with an ex-mate—the counselor may be forced to work with only one member of the dyad, although continuing to view the dissolution of the marriage in systems terms may still be appropriate.

While the term *divorce counseling* may technically be presumed to mean that the decision has been made to terminate the marriage, so that the procedure focuses on disengaging the couple as easily as the situation permits, in reality the circumstances are rarely so clear-cut. More likely, marriage and divorce counseling are segments of the same continuum, and where the former ends and the latter begins not readily demarcated.

Married couples enter counseling together with a variety of expectations and hopes, to say nothing of varying degrees of commitment to remaining together. One or both may have concluded earlier that the marriage is no longer satisfying, although they nevertheless are prepared to engage briefly in the counseling process as a last resort or perhaps to give the appearance of making a final effort before separating and filing for divorce. Others may be badgered into coming by an insistent spouse, denying their internal sense of hopelessness about the future of the relationship, and remaining fearful even about saying the word *divorce* publicly. Still others think of divorce as a personal failure, or perhaps as something that occurs to other people but not themselves or their families.

Finally, some couples enter counseling together hoping to improve the relationship—a good possibility, as we have noted earlier, especially if too much damage has not yet been done and they still wish to strengthen their marital bond. On the other hand, marriage counseling may force them to face the fact that their differences are irreconcilable, their goals unrealistic, their future together unpromising despite positive changes each has attempted. In these instances, divorce may be the most feasible alternative for resolving their relationship conflicts.

Divorce counseling, then, may be the sequence of earlier efforts at trying one last time to save the marriage. Or, under other circumstances, divorce counseling may follow the legal divorce proceedings, as ex-mates, individually or conjointly, attempt to cope with unfinished or continuing conflict (for example, over visitation rights with the children). In the former case in particular, in which the couple seeking to repair their marriage are forced to conclude it cannot be done, counseling need not be finished once that decision is reached. Rather, even if the decision to divorce has been agreed upon, the counselor must help educate both spouses about a number of unfinished tasks: understanding why the relationship failed (as insurance against future failure); how best to disengage (and not continue or escalate their conflictual relationship); how to cope with the sense of loss, acute stress, and perhaps temporary disorganization in personal functioning (in one or both); how best to deal with other members of the family system (children, parents, and others); how to foster autonomy and personal development for each as individual persons (Rice & Rice, 1986b).

The decision to divorce is never made lightly, even in mutually destructive marriages, and is almost always accompanied by feelings of anguish, despair, shock, and disbelief that this is actually happening. Frequently the couple vacillates between trying one more time to salvage the marriage and wishing to dissolve it. The counselor may find himself or herself alternating between doing marital and divorce counseling during this period, and must be especially vigilant to avoid becoming entrapped or triangled into taking sides in the middle of the conflict, as one mate insists on leaving and proceeding with the divorce while the other begs for another chance. It is the counselor's task to help the couple consider all options at this pre-divorce decision-making stage, being careful not to be maneuvered into deciding for them whether or not to remain together.

Great care, too, must be exercised by the counselor not to become impatient or intolerant with the vacillation and thereby force a premature decision. As Turner (1985) points out, the counselor can expect puzzling decisional behavior at this stage, often marked by seeming irrationality, a great deal of ambivalence, regressive behavior, impulsivity, and frequent decisional reversals.

Granvold (1983) recommends the possibility of a planned structured separation for couples at an impasse, especially if they continue to be doubtful about whether divorce is the best alternative. The therapeutic purpose here is to interrupt the heated marital conflict in order to facilitate a more measured, rational decision. Such separation also provides both parties with a glimpse of independent living, a period of value reassessment, and an opportunity for experimentation with other lifestyles. A written contract outlining the length of separation (say, three months) as well as its ground rules (dating others, outside sexual relationships, visits with the children) is common under these circumstances. Typically, the nature and frequency of the partners' contacts with one another is spelled out during this "cooling off" period, and conjoint counseling on a regular basis is continued.

The counselor needs to be particularly attuned to the stage of the individual, marital, and family life cycle, and to the stage of the divorce process (see Table 1.1) of the presenting clients. Grief, mourning for the failed relationship that once held so much promise, and despair at ever weathering the crisis and going on alone are all to be expected. Denial, feelings of anger and frustration, vengeance, rage, fear of abandonment— these too are familiar to any counselor dealing with a divorcing couple, especially in the early phases of the marital dissolution. Later, sadness, resignation, regret, and remorse are more common. Rice and Rice (1986b) suggest that the counselor, in addition to offering support, be prepared to teach social, interpersonal, and even assertiveness techniques to help individuals regain confidence and learn effective coping skills as a single person.

Particularly when children are involved, the parents have the additional task of learning to deal cooperatively with one another, even if their personal contact is minimal. In the following case, a couple has separated but are stalled in the divorce process. What appears to be a request for counseling directed at reaching decisions regarding their 3-year-old child turns out to be an effort to finish up their divorce.

Harry and Lola, separated for six months, called a counselor for help in making joint decisions regarding Meredith, their 3-year-old daughter. They asked to come in together as a couple, without the child, and while the counselor suspected more was involved between them than was apparent, she agreed to their plan, hoping that without Meredith they might more readily deal with what was blocking their proceeding with the divorce.

As expected, the presenting problems—arrangements regarding visitation, overnight stays for Meredith, vacation plans for her stay with each parent—were indeed easily resolved, the couple spending less than one session on deciding these issues. Later in the first counseling session, however, the counselor began to wonder aloud about the reasons their marriage had failed, observing that Harry and Lola showed little awareness or insight into their relationship. It was soon clear to the counselor that they were covering up a number of unresolved issues between them, and that their inability to deal with those conflicts kept them from moving ahead with the divorce. The counselor suggested that they seemed to have some unfinished business between them, and invited them to explore those areas for a session or two. They quickly agreed, and set up the additional meetings with the counselor for the forthcoming week.

As Harry and Lola spoke of their backgrounds, it became clear that they had come a long way, socially, culturally, intellectually, financially, from their working-class beginnings. Now both successful architects, they had met at school, drawn together by similarities in religion and the shared experience of growing up poor and being the first in each of their families to attend college. Both were ambitious and fiercely determined to get ahead in their profession. They married soon after graduation, struggled together to succeed, and put off having a child until they were closer to their professional goals—academic careers as professors of architecture and urban planning at a major university.

Meredith was born when the couple was in their early 30s, and they both adored her right from the start. However, aside from their devotion to her, they seemed less and less to have their earlier closeness and affection for one another. During the previous decade, each had emphasized work, career, success, and without acknowledging it had become highly competitive with the other. While each rarely if ever expressed unhappiness or dissatisfaction to the other, both partners nevertheless realized that something was amiss. Sex between them had become infrequent, and while they blamed it on fatigue, busy schedules, and preoccupations with careers, both had a sense—never put into words—that they had lost much interest in each other over the years. Instead, they viewed their lives as filled with obligations and responsibilities from which they drew little pleasure.

Under these circumstances, it was hardly surprising that Harry met Celeste, a young instructor, and was immediately drawn to her. Astonished by the intensity of his feelings, he became all the more aware of the emptiness in his life at home. Despite a renewed effort to reach out to Lola, he found himself still unable to speak to her about any of his feelings of discontent, nor was she able to do so to him. Thus immobilized in any effort to become more intimate, each pulled further and further away from the painful marital situation. Finally, overwhelmed with guilt—although he and Celeste had not become sexually involved with one another—Harry moved out. Typically, finding himself unable to face Lola, he left behind a note, indicating his unhappiness and despair, and blamed his upset on his "mid-life crisis." Dismayed, dumbfounded, internally enraged, Lola nevertheless accepted Harry's decision with outward calm.

The couple continued a civil relationship, especially in regard to their daughter. No anger ever got expressed directly, no bitterness ever shown by either partner. However, their underlying rage at their failed marriage did manifest itself in their inability to agree to the simplest arrangements regarding Meredith. While they never brought up what went wrong or what was missing in the marriage, they continuously disagreed about every detail (school, clothes, activities, lessons) of Meredith's life. While the counselor agreed that the rift between them had gotten too great to be breached, she noted that if they wanted to help Meredith, which they did, that they would have to learn to express feelings more directly to one another (and by implication, to any future person with whom each wished to pursue a serious relationship). The block in their ability to communicate angry or hurt feelings was holding up each of them in moving on with their lives.

Straight talk was alien to their personal styles or cultural backgrounds. Each had been carefully raised only to speak of pleasant things, and to say nothing if one could not say something nice. Nevertheless, the counselor pressed them to get in touch with their feelings, insisting that they learn to put into words what each was experiencing internally and expressing nonverbally through their oppositional behavior. As they did so, the problems they initially presented regarding their daughter were more easily resolved.

The couple terminated counseling after three sessions, as they had originally planned. They continued to practice a more open exchange of feelings, and while it did not seem to come naturally, they did make progress. After two months, they returned, having moved along sufficiently that they were ready to see an attorney and reach decisions regarding child custody and the division of their assets. The counselor encouraged their greater openness, and helped each overcome feelings of anger, sadness, and disappointment. Each seemed more ready to move on in their lives as separate persons who continued to have a relationship because of their child as well as their common profession.

They divorced a month later. On the day of their court date, and within five minutes of one another, each separately called the counselor to indicate what had transpired and to say they were pleased and relieved. Together they had shared a meaningful experience with the counselor, toward whom they both felt close. Each independently reported that Meredith seemed happy and that the ex-spouses were getting better at working their differences out. Within two years both were happily remarried.

--- ◆◆◆ ---

DIVORCE MEDIATION

Assuming a couple has decided to divorce, there remain a multitude of practical problems to face, disputes to be resolved, differences inherent in the marriage dissolution to be negotiated. As Stier (1986) reminds us, after the divorcing couple has mourned together in divorce counseling, worked through their feelings of disappointment and anger, perhaps explored their separate fears and hopes about the future apart, the immediate need exists to work out the terms of their dissolution agreement and their postdivorce family relationship. Divorce mediation with the aid of a specially trained, nonpartisan third party is intended to provide precisely such an opportunity.

Traditionally, during the legal stage of the divorce process, the spouses separately seek the counsel of attorneys and embark on the adversarial procedures of a litigated divorce. Each lawyer sets out to serve the best interests of his or her client, retaining or obtaining as much as possible for that client. While attempting to portray one's client in a most favorable light, each attorney assumes that the other spouse's interests will be similarly represented by opposing legal counsel. Negotiations are thus primarily in the hands of attorneys, or should they fail to arrive at an agreement, settled by a judge. As Kaslow (1988) observes, the resulting fray sometimes becomes a destructive free-for-all, resulting in "long-term embattlement and embitterment in which relatives and friends take sides, children are victimized by the continuing strife, and everyone is left depleted and feeling like a loser" (p. 87).

On the other hand, divorce mediation, which arose in the mid-1970s, offers an alternative route to resolving potential disputes over custody, visitation rights, the distribution of family assets, and other such issues. Here the assumption is that the couple themselves are the experts in their own divorce, and they know better than anyone else what they need for a satisfactory postdivorce working relationship. Much as in labor mediation, the divorce mediator, knowledgeable about the substantive issues involved in marital dissolution and trained to provide impartial mediation services, acts as a facilitator aiding the couple to arrive at a calmer, more equitable, and ultimately more humane set of joint decisions.

The mediator's role, according to Stier (1986), a psychologist-lawyer, is to help reorient the disputing parties toward each other, not by imposing rules but by helping them achieve a shared perception of the situation and of their relationship. Ideally, if mediation is successful, the new perception will redirect their attitudes and dispositions toward each other.

Most divorce mediation can be accomplished in six to twelve hour-long sessions. Despite the possible examination together of the couple's disputing patterns, particularly as they hamper progress in the mediation process, the approach is not the same as divorce counseling. It does not focus on the interpersonal problems that led to the breakup nor does the approach seek to modify existing individual personality patterns. Although insights and stress reduction may occur, these are fringe benefits, not the major purpose of mediation. Divorce mediation does, however, provide for an airing of emotional issues, something rarely occurring in court proceedings, and thus may help resolve them and avoid their resurfacing later in the form of postdivorce litigation (Folberg & Milne, 1988).

Divorce mediation is a multistage, conflict-managing or resolving process with a continued focus on the family system rather than the interests of a particular family member. The impartial mediator (or team of mediators) helps the couple identify disputed issues, develop and consider options, and make choices, in order to reach consensual agreements that will realistically meet the needs and concerns of the family. Taylor (1988) distinguishes the following seven stages:

Stage 1. *Creating structure and trust:* The mediator develops rapport with the couple and begins to gather relevant information about each partner's perceptions of conflicts as well as their goals and expectations; the participants begin to understand the nature of the mediating process.

Stage 2. *Fact-finding and isolation of the issues:* The underlying conflict areas, their duration and intensity, as well as the expressed and perceived rigidity of positions are identified.

Stage 3. *Creation of options and alternatives:* Both parties are actively involved in assigning priorities to the remaining disagreements, locating stumbling blocks, and together developing new options that may be more satisfactory to both participants.

Stage 4. *Negotiation and decision making:* The couple is encouraged to take the risky step of making choices, accepting compromises, bargaining; the couple is directed from a competitive negotiation to a more cooperative interaction.

Stage 5. *Clarification—writing a plan:* A document outlining the participants' intentions and decisions is produced and is agreed to in writing by both parties.

Stage 6. *Legal review and processing:* The family system is connected to larger watchdog social systems and institutions, such as private attorneys or judges, in order to verify the agreement's completeness, fairness, and feasibility.

Stage 7. *Implementation, review, and revision:* Outside the confines of the mediation sessions, a follow-up is conducted on the participants' ability to match intentions with agreed-upon action and behavior.

Animosity and rancor are typically reduced as a result of the mediation experience, allowing both partners to separate peacefully so that each might begin building a new life. While the mediation process is not acceptable to all divorcing couples, nor necessarily effective under all circumstances for those willing to participate, it does hold promise for many as a way of lightening the pain of divorce, not only for the spouses but for their children as well.

Before we look at the makeup, common problems, and counseling needs of many of today's families, however, we need to provide a theoretical framework for understanding how families function and how and why some become dysfunctional. We turn, therefore, in the next chapter to a view of the family as a social system.

SUMMARY

In today's changing society, the nuclear family is less common and certain nontraditional family forms are becoming more evident. The high divorce rate; the rapid increase of women in the professional work force; the choice of singlehood over marriage or the delay of marriage by many Americans; the sharp rise in the number of childless couples, illegitimate children, single-parent-led households, and stepfamilies—these contemporary phenomena have, together, forced counselors to deal with new sets of lifestyles and family relationship problems.

Approximately half of those couples who marry today can expect to become divorced, for a variety of social, personal, and interpersonal reasons; relationship problems are probably the major cause of most marital breakups. The process of divorce typically extends over time and goes through certain predictable stages before each of the ex-mates can resume separate lives. Because couples are divorcing at an earlier age than ever before, it is increasingly common for young children today to live with a single parent and perhaps, later, in a stepfamily.

Today's counselors can expect to deal with a variety of family styles in addition to nuclear families. Single-parent-led families, stepfamilies, cohabiting heterosexual couples, gay male and lesbian couples, and dual-career families are increasingly common.

Divorce counseling, an increasingly practiced form of family intervention, may be the end segment of an effort at marital counseling or may follow the legal divorce proceedings as former spouses attempt to cope with unfinished or continuing family conflict. A newer technique, divorce mediation, offers a nonadversarial attempt by mediators, trained in mental health as well as the law, to help divorcing couples together to reach agreements, avoid future conflict, and, ideally, to separate without recrimination so that all family members, children included, may go on with building new lives.

Part II

✦✦✦

Outlook and Approaches in Family Counseling

Chapter 2

♦♦♦

The Family as a Social System

Historically, efforts by counselors and other clinicians to conceptualize the origins and meaning of problematic or dysfunctional behaviors have turned to explanations that focus on the individual, particularly the person's intrapsychic conflicts. Correspondingly, therapeutic endeavors were, for many years, directed at penetrating as deeply as possible into the individual's psyche—that mysterious "black box"—in order to extract those repressed memories, wishes, or thoughts that were, presumably, at the core of the current behavioral or emotional difficulties.

Beginning in the 1950s, however, an alternate view of human problems and their alleviation began to emerge. In part, the shift in thinking reflected a growing dissatisfaction with mechanical or analytical explanations then occurring in various branches of science and mathematics. Within the social sciences, more specifically, a number of counselors and other therapists began looking beyond the past for explanations of current, ongoing behavior. Just as their counterparts in biology, for example, were beginning to comprehend the complex ecological system in which different forms of life (people, animals, plants, birds, air, soil) share a common environment, affecting each other so intimately that it would be foolish to consider them separately, so clinicians began to wonder if it might be useful to consider an individual as existing in a similar kind of ecological system, namely his or her family (Segal & Bavelas, 1983). Within such a framework, they reasoned, perhaps the individual can be better understood, and more effectively treated, when the disturbed behavior (anxiety, depression, alcoholism, an eating disorder) is seen as representative of a **system** that is faulty. That person's current difficulties might then be viewed in the context of a family social system in disequilibrium (Minuchin, 1974), rather than as symptoms of some internal conflict.

GENERAL SYSTEMS THEORY

The systems view has come to dominate much of scientific thinking in the second half of the 20th century, as researchers and theory builders in various disciplines are recognizing the commonality of their efforts. Many have come to appreciate that a common thread interweaves much of their work, and that the rules and regulations of one discipline may have counterparts in others. Some scientists from related disciplines such as Bertalanffy (1968) from biology and Miller (1978) from psychology have proposed that general principles are sufficiently discernible to hazard developing an integrative theory that underlies a multitude of scientific disciplines. While it is still too early to suggest that systems thinking is applicable to all sciences in equal measure or even that the systems perspective is entirely relevant to understanding the intricate transactions within a family, it is a fact that its impact on both the scientific and clinical communities has been significant.

Largely the result of the efforts of Ludwig von Bertalanffy, although by no means his alone, since scientists in various fields were developing similar perspectives, General Systems Theory emerged in the 1940s as a new way of conceptualizing seemingly unrelated phenomena and understanding how together they represent interrelated components of a larger system. As Bertalanffy (1968) later elaborated, a system represents a complex of component parts or interacting elements that may together form an entity. To fully comprehend how the entire unit operates, we must look beyond a mechanistic view of the functioning of the separate parts; indeed, it is precisely the relationship, the interfunctioning, of the parts that make up the whole that requires our attention. The wholeness of the system, how it's organized, the rules underlying how its component parts relate to one another, its repetitive patterns—these are the system's vital signs.

What is the relevance of the systems view to better comprehending what occurs within a family? As Andolfi (1979) notes, family members are studied in terms of their interactions and not merely their intrinsic personal characteristics. More than the sum of what each family member adds to the whole, it is the ongoing relationship between and among the members that requires our attention. Such a global view calls for the examination of established patterns; families form patterns over time and it is this patterning over time that is the essence of the family system (Segal & Bavelas, 1983). As Constantine (1986) points out, the family is a good example of the organized complexity for the study of which the systems view is most appropriate. What, then, constitutes a "problem family" likely to be seen in a counseling situation? According to Constantine, the determining factor is neither the number nor severity of a family's problems but rather their response to the problems and the extent to which their problems disable the way their family system operates.

LINEAR AND CIRCULAR CAUSALITY

Pre-systems theories—those which for the most part we have labeled as mechanistic—tended to be reductionistic. That is, they explained complex phenomena by breaking the whole down and analyzing the separate, simpler parts. Thus, ever-smaller units were investigated in order to get a fix on the causes of larger events. In this simple Newtonian view of the physical universe, it made sense to think of causality in **linear** terms: A causes B, which acts upon C, causing D to occur.

Within psychological theory, such an outlook took the form of stimulus-response explanations for complex human behavior. From this perspective, all current behavior is seen as the result of a series of outside forces that build upon one another in sequence and ultimately produce the behavior in question. To the psychoanalyst, such forces are likely the result of childhood experiences; to the behaviorally inclined, the causes are more apt to be found in past and present learning experiences. By focusing on the individual, however, both viewpoints fail to examine the context in which, as well as the process by which, the current behavior occurs. Thus, they fail to understand fully the complexity of what transpires within a family system.

The systems view, by comparison, more holistic and better attuned to tangled interpersonal relationships, stresses the reciprocity of behaviors between people. **Circular causality** emphasizes that forces do not simply move in one direction, each event caused by a previous event, but rather become part of a causal chain, each influencing and being influenced by the other.

Goldenberg and Goldenberg (1985) offer the following contrast between statements based on linear and circular analysis:

Linear: A bad mother produces sick children.

Implication: Mother's emotional problems cause similar problems in others.

Circular: An unhappy middle-aged woman, struggling with an inattentive husband who feels peripheral to and excluded from the family, attaches herself to her 20-year-old son for male companionship, excluding her adolescent daughter. The daughter, in turn, feeling rejected and unloved, engages in flagrant sexually promiscuous behavior, to the considerable distress of her parents. The son, fearful of leaving home and becoming independent, insists he must remain at home because his mother needs his attention. The mother becomes depressed because her children do not seem to be like other "normal" children, and blames their dysfunctional behavior on her husband, whom she labels an "absentee father." He in turn becomes angry and defensive, and their sexual relationship suffers. The children respond to the ensuing coldness between the parents in different ways: the son by withdrawing from friends completely and remaining at home with his mother as much as possible, and the daughter by having indiscriminant sexual encounters with one man after another but carefully avoiding intimacy with any of them.

Implication: Behavior has as least as much to do with the interactional context in which it occurs as with the inner mental processes or emotional problems of any of the players. (p. 6)

Gregory Bateson (1979), a cultural anthropologist by training but with broad interest in **cybernetics** (the study of methods of feedback control within a system) provided many of the theoretical underpinnings for the application of systems thinking to human relationships. He labeled the stimulus-response paradigm as a "billiard ball" model—a model that describes a force as moving in only one direction and affecting objects in its path—and called instead for a focus on the ongoing process and the development of a new descriptive language that emphasized the relationship between parts and their effect on one another. While A may evoke B, it is also true that B evokes A, as we have just seen. A marital counselor is likely to hear the following exchange in a quarreling couple, where each partner feels put upon and blames the other for his or her feelings of unhappiness:

Wife: You never seem to talk to me and let me know that you notice I exist.

Husband: It's true. You become so heated and intense at times that you frighten me and I clam up.

Wife: You don't get it! The reason I become so upset is that I get frustrated by your withdrawing behavior. The more frustrated I become, the more persistent I become.

Husband: You're the one who doesn't get it! The more you persist, the more intimidated I get and the more I withdraw.

A counselor working with an entire family, many of whose members blame their woes on one another, is even more likely to confront such a circular situation. These examples illustrate the causal chains that tie together family behavior and communication. Shifting to a perspective that emphasizes circular causality helps us conceptualize a family's collective behavior in current transactional terms—as a network of circular loops in which every member's behavior impacts on everyone else.

FEEDBACK, CONTROL, AND HOMEOSTASIS

One of the pioneers in cybernetics, mathematician Norbert Wiener (1967), defined **feedback** as a method of controlling a system by reinserting into it the results of its past performance. Stated another way, information about how a system is functioning is looped back (fed back) from the output to the input, thus modifying subsequent input signals. **Feedback loops**, then, are circular mechanisms whose purpose is to reintroduce information about a system's output back to its input in order to alter, correct, or ultimately govern the system's functioning.

One frequently cited example of such a system is the familiar home furnace. Setting the thermostat at a desired 70° F programs the system so that when the temperature drops below that point, that information is fed back and activates the furnace. When the desired temperature is reached again, that new information, once again fed back, alters the ongoing state by deactivating the system until such time as reactivation is needed to warm up the house again and keep the temperature stable. Balance is achieved by the inclination of the system to maintain a dynamic equilibrium around some set point and to undertake operations to restore equilibrium whenever it is threatened. This tendency toward a stable state of equilibrium, called **homeostasis**, is achieved with the help of what cyberneticists call servomechanisms; in a self-regulating system, the servomechanisms are feedback loops that return information in order to activate the internal interactional processes that maintain stability and ensure a dynamic but steady state.

The example just cited illustrates **negative feedback**,[1] or the use of attenuating feedback loops in order to maintain aspects of the system's functioning within prescribed limits. As depicted in Figure 2.1, negative

---

1 Although *negative feedback* and *positive feedback* are terms commonly used in systems literature, some critics have argued that these terms may suggest value judgements concerning undesired versus desired outcomes, and therefore may prove misleading. Kantor and Lehr (1975) suggest that we substitute *constancy feedback loops* (loops that promote equilibrium) for *negative feedback*, and *variety feedback loops* (loops that promote change) for *positive feedback*. In a similar vein, Constantine (1986) offers *attenuating loops* versus *amplifying loops*. We have adopted the latter suggestion.

feedback is corrective, adjusting the input so that the system returns to its preset, steady state. All of us are familiar with such error-activated causal events in our daily lives. The attentive driver does not simply hold the steering wheel steady, but actually continuously makes slight corrections to keep the car travelling in a predetermined direction. Automobiles with cruise control devices allow the driver to set a desired speed; if a temporary problem arises, say a sudden sharp incline, causing a momentary reduction in speed, that information activates the system, acceleration follows, and the preset speed is once again achieved.

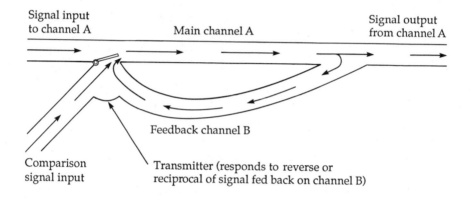

Signal input to channel A

Main channel A

Signal output from channel A

Feedback channel B

Comparison signal input

Transmitter (responds to reverse or reciprocal of signal fed back on channel B)

Figure 2.1. In this illustration of negative feedback, part of a system's output is reintroduced into the system as information about the output, thus governing and correcting the process. A negative signal from channel A, fed back to the sender through channel B, alters the signal in A. Feedback loops characterize all interpersonal relationships.
Source: Miller, 1978, p. 36.

Positive feedback (the use of amplifying feedback loops) has the opposite effect: it causes further change by augmenting or accelerating the initial deviation. In some cases it may reach runaway proportions, forcing the system beyond its limits to the point of self-destruction. The furnace explodes; the car is oversteered and goes out of control; the cruise control continues to accelerate to ever-higher speeds and disastrous consequences.

Both negative and positive feedback loops abound in families. Negative feedback may occur with a remarried couple like this:

Husband: I'm upset at the way you talked to that man at the party tonight, especially the way you seemed to be hanging on every word he said.

Wife: Don't be silly! You're the one I care about. He said he had just come back from a trip you and I had talked about going on and I was interested in what he could tell me about the place.

Husband: OK. But please don't do that again without telling me. You know I'm touchy on the subject because of what Gina [ex-wife] used to do at parties with other men that drove me crazy.

Wife: Sorry, I hadn't thought about that. I'll try to remember next time. In the meantime, you try to remember that you're married to me now and I don't want you to be jealous.

In a less-blissful situation, positive feedback may occur:

Husband: I'm upset at the way you talked to that man at the party tonight, especially the way you seemed to be hanging on every word he said.

Wife: One thing I don't appreciate is you spying on me.

Husband: Spying? That's a funny word to use. You must be getting paranoid in your old age. Or maybe you have something to hide.

Wife: As a matter of fact, I was talking to him about a trip he took that we had talked about, but I don"t suppose you'd believe that. Talk about paranoid!

Husband: I give up on women! You're no different from Gina, and I suppose all other women.

Wife: With an attitude like that, I'm starting to see why Gina walked out on you.

While most transactions can probably be characterized by the predominance of one of these two loops—one attenuating a possible conflict, the other amplifying it—both may occur between the same players under different conditions or at different points in their relationship. Despite the potentially escalating impact of the runaway system described in the second example above, not all positive feedback need be considered damaging. Counselors may at times encourage positive feedback to motivate clients to break out of existing, but stultifying, family behavior patterns, such as using one member as a scapegoat in order to hide or obscure other more pressing but unresolved family issues.

Theorists such as Maruyama (1968) and Dell (1982) have suggested that at times it may be advantageous to push a system with untenable behavior patterns beyond its previous homeostatic level. Rather than restore equilibrium, it may be more therapeutic in the long run to encourage family members to make those breakthrough changes that will help the family system function at a new level. The counselor needs to determine whether to help the family return to its former level of functioning (from which they may have deviated because of a temporary stress) or to seize an opportunity to help promote discontinuity and newness.

OPEN AND CLOSED SYSTEMS

Systems may be relatively open or closed, depending upon the degree to which they are organized to interact with the outside environment. An **open system** receives input—matter, energy, information—from its surroundings and discharges output back into those surroundings. Theoretically, **closed systems** are not able to participate in such transactions; in point of fact, however, systems are rarely if ever completely isolated or closed off from the outside, hard as laboratory researchers may try to create such a sterile test-tube environment.

Theoretically, for a family truly to be operating as a closed system, all outside transactions and communications would have to cease, hardly a likely prospect.[2] Nevertheless, some families such as recent immigrants or members of insular ethnic groups do exist in relative isolation, communicating only among themselves, suspicious of outsiders, fostering dependence on the family. Children may be warned only to trust family members and nobody else. Characterized by Constantine (1986) as regulated predominantly by deviation-attenuating (negative) feedback, such families seek to hold onto the traditions and conventionalities of the past and avoid change.

In their extreme form, such families may attempt to impose rigid and unchanging behavior patterns, sealing themselves off from exchanges with the outside world. These closed systems tend toward **entropy**—gradually regressing, decaying because of insufficient input, possibly becoming disorganized and destined for eventual disorder. Sauber (1983) describes such families as maintaining strict taboos regarding who and what should be admitted into the house, limiting the introduction of news and certain forms of music, screening visitors, and so on. Beavers (1977) offers this example of an entropic family: the parents have a daughter late in life; out of touch with what parent-adolescent relationships are like today, they may prevent their teenage daughter from behaving as she claims her friends behave. By insisting that she follow rules as they were taught by their parents, without discussion, the parents are inviting family conflict (to which the daughter will no doubt also contribute).

---

2 Some religious cults do attempt to close out the world beyond their borders, specifically to halt the flow of information. Those countries that do not permit foreign newspapers or radio or television broadcasts are also deliberately closed systems, in order to better control the behavior of their citizens.

New ideas, new information, new outlooks are seen as threatening to the status quo in closed systems. As Kantor and Lehr (1975) describe them, closed family systems impose strict rules and a hierarchical power structure that force individual members to subordinate their needs to the welfare of the group. Family loyalty is paramount, rules are absolute, tradition must be observed, any deviation in behavior can only lead to chaos. As White (1978) portrays closed family systems, parents see to it that doors are kept locked, family reading matter and television programs are screened, children are expected to report their comings and goings scrupulously, rigid daily schedules are kept as closely as possible. Stability in such an arrangement is achieved though the maintenance of tradition.

Open systems use both negative (attenuating) and positive (amplifying) feedback loops. Thus, they are considered to be operating on the systems principle of **equifinality**, meaning that the same end state may be reached from a variety of starting points. (Closed systems, by way of contrast, do not have the property of equifinality and thus their final state is determined solely by their initial conditions.) Within open systems, the same result may be achieved from different initial conditions, and the same initial state may produce different results. The major point here is that to appreciate how a family functions, we must study the organization of the family system—the group's interactive process—rather than search for either the origins or outcomes of those interactions.

In open systems, where a variety of inputs are possible, as we are about to see, the family's feedback process is an overriding determinant of how it functions. Since a number of pathways lead to the same destination, there is no single "correct" way to raise children, to insure a happy marriage, and so on. Uncertain beginnings do not necessarily doom a relationship; a shaky start, perhaps as a result of an early marriage, may be compensated for by the introduction of corrective feedback as the relationship matures. By the same token, an apparently congenial marriage of many years may become stale or turn sour for a variety of reasons. As we saw in our discussion of causality, a linear description of A inevitably leading to B overlooks the central role played by the intervening family interactive process. The concept of equifinality allows the counselor to intervene with a family at any of several points or through a number of different counseling techniques to obtain the same desired end results.

Open systems are characterized by their members having the freedom to move in and out of interactions with one another, with extended family members (such as grandparents, aunts, uncles, cousins), or with extrafamilial systems such as the school, church, neighbors, or teachers. The family has an impact on the outside environment; the outside environment impacts the family. In contrast to the relatively closed family system, where continuity and tradition are held in high regard, open family systems tend to stress adaptability to unfamiliar situations, particularly if it enables greater effectiveness in serving a purpose or reaching a goal the family finds worthwhile. Because an open and honest dialogue both within and outside the family is prized, disagreement and dissent may be common, and not a threat to the ongoing functioning of the family. Negotiation, communication, flexibility in shifting roles, interdependence, authenticity—these are the signs of an open system.

Some individuals find relatively closed family systems safe and secure and never stray too far, physically or psychologically, from their families. Members may on occasion be called upon to sacrifice their individual needs for the good of the family, but in the long run may get most of their important needs met through participation in the family group. One problem, of course, is that a closed structure may become rigid; family members may run away or otherwise rebel. Or families may feel isolated, as in the case of a young never-married mother, alienated from her unaccepting parents, with little opportunity for exchange with the outside world except with her baby. Open family systems, desirable as they may appear to be, run the risk of having free expression turn ugly and, perhaps, divide the family into warring factions. Incompatibilities may surface, say within a stepfamily, over discipline, and excessive strains may result.

In gauging the degree of openness of a family system, the counselor needs to evaluate how (and how well) the family deals with new information, particularly if that new input provokes a family crisis (for example, discovering a teenager's drug addiction). To what extent do the family members realistically perceive and appraise the problem? How well are they able to delay closure until sufficient information has been sought and discussed and a family plan formulated? To what degree are they able to coordinate their individual responses so that the best possible family action can be undertaken in this unfamiliar situation?

In systems terms, open systems are said to have **negentropy**—they are organized to be adaptable, open to new experiences, able to alter patterns and discard those that are inappropriate to the present situation. Through their exchanges outside their own system boundaries, open systems increase their chances of becoming more highly organized and developing resources to repair minor or temporary breakdowns in efficiency (Nichols & Everett, 1986). The lack of such exchanges in closed systems decreases their competence to deal with stress. Limited or perhaps nonexistent contact with others outside the family may lead to fearful, confused, and ineffective responses to a crisis situation. In extreme cases of rigid systems and/or persistent stress, chaos and anarchy within the family may follow.

SUBSYSTEMS AND BOUNDARIES

Subsystems are the parts of an overall system assigned to carry out particular functions or processes within that system, in order to maintain and sustain the system as a whole. Every family has a number of such coexisting subdivisions, formed by generation, gender, interest, or role and function within the family (Minuchin, 1974). The most enduring are the spousal, the parent-child, and the sibling subsystems.

The spousal (husband-wife) unit is basic; it is central to the life of the family in its early years, and continues to play a major role over the life span of the family. There is little doubt that the overall success of any family is to a large extent dependent upon the ability of the husband and wife to work out a successful relationship with one another. (The absence of one parent, more and more common, may have a particularly damaging effect on the remaining parent as well as the children, as we shall see in subsequent chapters.) Any dysfunction in this subsystem is bound to reverberate throughout the family, scapegoating certain children, co-opting others into alliances with one parent against the other, and so on. The way spouses together make decisions, manage conflict, plan the family's future, meet each other's sexual and dependency needs, and much more, provides a model of male-female interaction and husband-wife intimacy that will surely affect the children's future relationships.

The parent-child subsystem teaches children about child rearing; nurturance, guidance, limit setting, socialization experiences are all crucial here. Through interaction with the parents, children learn to deal with people of greater authority, developing in the process a strengthened or weakened capacity for decision making and self-direction. Problems in this subsystem—serious intergenerational conflicts involving rebelliousness, symptomatic children, runaways, and so on—reflect underlying family disorganization or instability. The following case reflects dysfunctional behavior extending over several generations:

Jill Clemmons, now 40, had a history of unstable relationships with men. An only child, lonely and unhappy, she lived in poverty with her mother, herself bitter at having been deserted by her husband a decade earlier. Finally feeling unable to bear the boredom and frustration of her life, Jill (with the tacit encouragement of her mother) ran off at 16 and married her high school boyfriend. Their marriage—stormy, without much affection or intimacy, filled with daily fighting—lasted several months, before Jill met and ran off with Dave, an older single man of 40, whom Jill was sure would take care of her. Divorced at 17, she married Dave immediately. However, their marriage soon proved to be a nightmare: Dave was verbally and physically abusive, and occasionally beat her severely, especially when he came home drunk. On some nights, he would bring home a man he had met at a bar, often insisting Jill have sexual intercourse with the stranger while Dave watched. Jill finally managed to escape after three years, even though she had no place to go.

Drifting from one menial job to the next, Jill managed to survive and live a relatively uneventful life for several years. She dated on and off, and when she met Tom, at 27, she thought her life had finally turned around. He seemed intelligent, caring, and sensitive to her needs. They married after a brief time together, and for a while the relationship was the best Jill had ever known. They had two children together, and seemed to be living a relatively tranquil and conventional existence for several years. However, Jill found herself feeling bored and restless having to stay home with her youngsters. She had few child-rearing skills, her mother had been such a poor model, and more and more began to view the children as a burden. Correspondingly, as the children grew into adolescents, their conflicts with their parents (especially Jill) increased sharply. Jill and Tom, too, found less and less to do or talk about together; all they seemed to agree about was that something needed to be done about the children, although neither one knew exactly what. Neither had the ability or the experience to work out problems together, nor did they consider getting professional help.

Soon Tom and Jill realized that there was nothing to stay together for, and they separated. Nora, 16, and Tom Jr., 14, remained with their father, and Jill moved to another state to "start life again." However, Nora found that she could not get along with her father and brother, and, like her mother earlier, she ran off, ultimately finding her mother and moving in with her. Although she had considerable misgivings, Jill still believed she and her daughter could work things out. Not surprisingly, they could not, and within four months Nora had run away from home and begun living with a series of men in a nearby city, contacting her mother only in emergencies. Occasionally, when Jill was at work, her daughter would return to the house for some clothes or food or whatever money she could find.

The parent-child subsystem, beginning with the wife's pregnancy, expands the boundaries of the previous husband-wife spousal subsystem. The arrival of children vastly complicates family life, particularly when a first child is involved. With subsequent children, as the family expands, the system multiplies in complexity. Alliances, coalitions, some along age lines, some by sex, some by personality characteristics or attitudes, may make an impact on the spousal subsystem, sometimes to the point of threatening its existence, as parents may experience their own conflicts about growing up and taking responsibilities. The relatively sudden shift to child-related issues, as Nichols and Everett (1986) point out, may be especially taxing on young-adult marriages, challenging each spouse's own degree of individuation and dependency. A facilitating effect may result, consolidating their parenting efforts; on the other hand, some may retreat back into alliances with their own parents, or perhaps out of the marriage.

Siblings represent a child's first peer group. Through participation in this sibling subsystem, a child may develop patterns of negotiation, cooperation, competition, mutual support, and later attachment to friends. Interpersonal skills are honed here, and, if successful, may develop further in school experiences and later in the workplace. Although the future impact of this subsystem is not always clearly discernible when the children are young, its influence on overall family functioning is to a great extent dependent on how viable the other subsystems are. Especially noteworthy for overall family functioning is the extent to which alliances and intergenerational coalitions exist in the family.

Other subsystems, most less durable than those just described, exist in all families. Father-daughter, mother-son, father-oldest son, mother-youngest child are only some of the common transitional alliances that can develop within a family group. The overdevelopment or protracted duration of any of these to the detriment of the spousal subsystem should signal to the counselor that instability and potential disorganization exist within the system.

Goldenberg (1977) illustrates the possible impact of a father-daughter alliance on family functioning. In this case, the coalition between the two has destructive results for all family members:

Lisa Ash, a 5-foot, 260-pound, 13-year-old girl, was brought to a mental hospital by a distraught mother who complained that she couldn't control her daughter's eating habits and was alarmed about the danger to her health. Lisa, a junior high school student, was the oldest of three daughters in a middle-class Jewish family. Both the father, a moderately successful shoe store owner, and his wife, a housewife, were overweight, as were various other uncles, aunts, and to a lesser extent, Lisa's two younger sisters.

The mother-daughter conflict was evident from the intake interview. In particular, both agreed that they battled frequently over discipline or any restrictions imposed by Mrs. Ash on Lisa's eating behavior. Whenever this occurred, Lisa would lock herself in her room, wait for her father to come home, and then tell him how "cruel" the mother had been to her. Usually, without inquiring further or getting the mother's story, he would side with Lisa and countermand the mother's orders. Occasionally he would invite Lisa out for a pizza or other "snack."

Needless to say, the mother-father relationship was poor. They had not had sexual intercourse for several years, and Mrs. Ash assumed that her husband was impotent, although she was too embarrassed to ask him. She had become increasingly unhappy and had seen a psychiatric social worker a year earlier for several sessions, although then, as now, her husband refused to participate in counseling. He also opposed Lisa's hospitalization and for several months would not speak to any member of the hospital staff about his daughter's progress.[3]

Lisa was placed on the adolescent open ward of the hospital and attended the special school within the hospital complex, remaining there for 12 months. During that period, four coordinated therapeutic programs were introduced: nutritional control (including a careful watch on caloric intake), individual psychotherapy twice weekly, family counseling (which, after much resistance, Mr. Ash agreed to attend), and ward milieu therapy. The picture that emerged was of an emotionally intense and chaotic family existence in which Lisa often screamed, hit, swore, and threatened to break household objects if she didn't get her "sweets." There was no regular mealtime at the Ash house; each member ate when and what he or she wanted. Lisa would regularly visit her father's store after school, and they would go out together for an ice cream soda or sundae. Finally acknowledging, during one family counseling session, that the situation had gotten out of hand, Mr. Ash defended his actions by saying that he could never get himself to say no to Lisa for fear of losing her love. Mrs. Ash quickly conceded her resentment of her husband's relationship with Lisa, her own feelings of isolation, and her sense of helplessness; she was finally able to separate the two by hospitalizing her daughter.

The program of caloric restriction was immediately successful. After 2 months, Lisa had lost 35 pounds, after 7 months, 80 pounds, and by 10 months, a full 100 pounds. Family counseling was less immediately successful. Mr. Ash and Lisa continued to play seductive games with each other; he called her on the telephone frequently, sent her flowers, and even visited her with a box of candy on her birthday, and she deliberately delayed coming to the telephone or lobby, to make her ultimate appearance more appealing. Finally, Lisa put an end to this kind of transaction, to Mrs. Ash's relief; Lisa learned limits on her behavior largely from milieu therapy on her ward. Eventually, Mr. Ash was able to give up his seductive and overprotective behavior, realizing that if he really wanted to help his daughter, he should limit her self-indulgent, self-destructive behavior rather than encourage it.

Upon her discharge from the hospital, Lisa weighed 140 pounds, had some insight into her eating behavior, and had dealt with a number of other preadolescent problems. She agreed to undergo weekly individual psychotherapy for a while so that she would not regress to her former ways once she was home. A two-year follow-up found her able to control her eating and generally proud that she could take care of herself successfully. (pp. 350–351)

---

3 The detrimental effect of the flawed spousal subsystem on the parent-child subsystem should be clear to the reader here, as should be the similar impact of the latter on the former. For the sake of brevity, we have omitted a description of the influence of both on the other children and the sibling subsystems in general, although the reader can assume that both have a powerfully negative effect on all concerned.

Lisa's recovery and her parents' being forced to examine their deteriorated marriage were two of the beneficial results of their entering counseling as a family. Strengthening the parental coalition resulted in more clear delineation of boundaries and a greatly diminished need for parent-child alliances. Lisa's eating behavior was no longer used by all family members to avoid the real issues between the parents. As communication was reestablished between the parents, they were more open to looking at what had led to their deteriorating relationship, of which the lack of a sexual life was but one manifestation. Ultimately, they learned new ways of problem solving and instituted the necessary changes to break out of their old destructive patterns.

Before leaving the general topic of subsystems, we should note that all members participate in several subsystems simultaneously within the family. For example, a 22-year-old woman may be a new stepmother of three, pregnant with her first child, trying at the same time to build a satisfactory marriage, learning to cope with her "instant" family, looking to her own mother for guidance, remembering to check on her aging grandmother and to encourage her younger sister to go to college, and lots more. From a subsystems vantage point, she is at one and the same time a wife, a prospective mother, a stepmother, a daughter, a granddaughter, and an older sister, engaging in perpetual exchanges with those around her, participating in various alliances (with greater or lesser success), and playing different roles in each. Ascendant in one, she may be submissive in another; fulfilled in one, she may be utterly frustrated by her lack of success in another; feeling competent in one, she may feel defeated in another. All the subsystems in which she takes part are interrelated and all perform vital routines necessary for the whole—the family—to grow and change in order to keep the system balanced.

Subsystems within a family stand in dynamic relationship with one another, both influencing and being influenced by the others. All are organized to perform the functions necessary to allow the family as a whole to go about its tasks smoothly and efficiently.

Family interaction is governed by rules, for the most part unstated, typically developed and modified through trial and error over a period of time. Such rules (for example, who has the right to say and do what to whom; what is expected of males versus females, adults versus children) determine what is permitted and what is forbidden within a family, and thus serve the necessary function of regulating each member's behavior toward one another. The origin of such rules is buried in years of explicit and implicit negotiation among family members; the rules themselves become so fine tuned in most cases that they are taken for granted by all and only draw attention when an effort is made by a member (an early adolescent in many cases) to change the long-standing "regulations."

An essential way in which the family maintains itself as a self-regulating system is through the constant exchange of information fed back into the system, automatically triggering any necessary changes (for example, extending late night privileges to the adolescent) to keep the system fluid and functional. In systems terms, feedback loops (circles of response from which there is a return flow of information into the system) are operating and information is being processed through the system.

Boundaries are invisible lines of demarcation that separate the family from the outside, nonfamily environment; they circumscribe and protect the integrity of the system and thus determine who is considered inside and who remains outside. Within the family itself, boundaries differentiate subsystems; they help achieve and define the separate subunits of the total system. As Minuchin (1974) notes, they must be sufficiently well defined to allow subsystem members to carry out their functions without undue interference. At the same time, they must be open enough to permit contact between the members of the subsystem and others.

For example, firm but flexible boundaries between parents and children allow for closeness when necessary, while at the same time ensuring that individuality will be honored and protected. Information can be exchanged across permeable boundaries as needed. At the same time, each subsystem is free to carry out its own tasks and responsibilities. Boundaries thus help safeguard each subsystem's autonomy while maintaining the interdependence of all of the family's subsystems.

The clarity of the subsystem boundaries is actually more important than who performs what function. As an illustration, the parent-child subsystem may at times be flexible enough to include a grandparent (or, under special circumstances, an oldest child pressed into service) when both parents are temporarily unavailable, so long as the lines of responsibility and authority remain clear. However, a grandmother who interferes with her daughter's management of a child in ways that undermine the parent-child subsystem (and perhaps the spousal subsystem as well) is overstepping her authority, being intrusive, and damaging family boundary lines. Thus, while boundaries between family members may vary in their degree of permeability, they need to be clearly drawn and apparent to all members. If they are too blurred or too rigid, they invite confusion and increase the likelihood of family dysfunction.

Deviation from subsystem boundaries may occur in one of two ways: through **enmeshment** or through **disengagement**. In the former, the boundary is too permeable, and thus family members become overinvolved and entwined in each other's lives (opening each other's mail, looking in each other's drawers, knowing each other's secrets). The latter involves overly rigid boundaries, with family members sharing a home but operating as separate units, with little interaction or exchange of feelings or sense of connection to one another. Little support, concern, or family loyalty is evident in disengaged families. At their extremes, enmeshed families run the risk of forbidding separation by viewing it as an act of betrayal, thus making autonomy impossible; disengaged families whose members remain oblivious to the effects of their actions on each other may thus preclude their members from ever developing caring relationships with others.

Boundaries, then, are useful, if arbitrary, metaphors for defining the overall system as a functioning unit, an entity. They exist around the family as a whole, around its subsystems, and around individual family members. Without them, there would be no progressive differentiation of functions in individuals or in the separate subsystems and, hence, as Umbarger (1983) contends, no system complexity. Without such complexity, a family's ability to create and maintain an adaptive stance in society is weakened. Adaptability is essential if the system is to avoid the forces of entropy and ultimate decay.

SYSTEMS THEORY AND FAMILY COUNSELING

For an ongoing living system, such as a family, to maintain its continuity, it must be able to tolerate change. Evolution is a normal and necessary part of every family's experience as it goes through its life cycle. However, as Nichols and Everett (1986) observe, a crucial question facing any system is how much change it can tolerate and still survive. Systems theorists use the concepts of **morphostasis** and **morphogenesis** to describe a system's ability to remain stable in the context of change and, conversely, to change in the context of stability. In well-functioning systems, both processes are necessary. A tightrope walker must continually sway in order to remain balanced. Remaining balanced while standing in a canoe calls for making it rock.

Within each system, tension inevitably exists between forces seeking constancy and the maintenance of the status quo, on the one hand, and opposing forces demanding change on the other. Morphostasis calls for a family to emphasize interactions involving negative or deviation-attenuating feedback; it refers to the system's tendency toward stability or a state of dynamic equilibrium. Morphogenesis demands positive or deviation-amplifying feedback in order to encourage growth, innovation, and change.

Systems theorists such as Maruyama (1968) and Hoffman (1981) point out that the survival of any living system depends on the interaction of these two key processes—morphostasis (seeking constancy in a system's basic structure in the face of environmental changes) and morphogenesis (seeking changes in the structure in order to adapt to changing environmental conditions). Unlike homeostasis, which is the maintenance of behavioral constancy in a system, morphostatic mechanisms operate to maintain the system's structural constancy. Morphogenetic mechanisms, on the other hand, seek to push the system toward new levels of functioning, allowing it to adapt to changing conditions. The satisfactory ongoing functioning of a couple or family requires a suitable balance between the two processes—maintaining stability, accommodating change.

Umbarger (1983) stresses the importance of both processes for effective family functioning. That is, both stability and change are necessary for the continuity of any family. Family stability is actually rooted in change. A family must maintain enough regularity and balance to maintain adaptability and preserve a sense of order and sameness; at the same time, it must subtly promote change and growth within its members and the system as a whole.

Thus, a family is continually subject to inner pressures from the developmental changes in its members (for example, from young child to adolescent; from middle-aged parent to older adult). At the same time, accommodation to changing conditions outside the family (for example, necessitating return of the housewife to paid work, or necessitating a school or job transfer) is demanded. Minuchin (1974), focusing on the family's structural components, notes that responding to these pressures calls for "a constant transformation of the position of family members in relation to one another, so they can grow while the family system maintains continuity" (p. 60). He argues that family dysfunction results from rigidity of its transactional patterns and boundaries when faced with stress, and the corresponding resistance to exploring alternative solutions. Minuchin contends that families that function effectively adapt to life's inevitable stresses in ways that preserve continuity while facilitating family restructuring as needed.

If a family system is as self-regulating as we have been asserting, then what could make it go out of balance for such a long time or to such a degree that the family seeks professional help? Several causes are possible. Operating at either extreme of the morphostatic/morphogenetic continuum may lead to family dysfunction; inflexibility may prevent rule changes, or changes may occur in too rapid or haphazard a fashion. Perhaps the family has achieved equilibrium only as a consequence of a member developing a symptom (for example, **anorexia** or **delinquency**) unacceptable to them or society, compelling them to seek help.

Fishman (1985) asserts that every symptom, regardless of its name, serves a function in maintaining family homeostasis; if the problem did not do something useful for the family organization, it would not be maintained.[4] As an example, he offers the following case:

---

4 As we note in the following chapter, the view that maintaining symptoms in one family member thus "protects" the other members and the family organization as a whole, is not necessarily supported by all family counselors. In the view of some researchers, the mismanaged solution attempted by the family ultimately becomes "the problem."

Anorexia is a good example. A family is in crisis. Brother just got married. The identified patient, Bonnie, is a 14-year-old girl who is having trouble with her peers (even though her grades are very good). Mother has just been promoted and now earns more than her husband, who is a truck driver. Husband and wife are fighting a great deal. The system is unstable. Bonnie stays out too long after school and comes home with "pot" on her breath. The parents scold her and continue to fight. A few weeks later, at dinner, Bonnie refuses to eat. The parents are very upset. In this Italian family, food is very important. Furthermore, mother works in a laboratory and is very concerned with health issues. The parents are very preoccupied with the girl's refusal to eat. The more they focus on the problem the more power the symptom has in diffusing the ambient tension in the house. Thus the symptom emerges as the point of family crisis and is maintained by the system. (p. 8)

Symptoms, in family systems terms, develop to help balance or alleviate stress between the family members. As Friesen (1985) puts it, when a family member's behavior exceeds the normal range of behavior as defined by family rules, a crisis occurs and homeostatic mechanisms are introduced into the system to reestablish equilibrium. Symptoms are one example of such stabilizing devices used to relieve stress and bring the family back into the normal range of its customary behavior. As illustration, Friesen presents a case of husband-wife conflict in which one son begins to act delinquent (see Figure 2.2). His behavior turns the attention of the parents away from themselves, relieving the stress in their relationship but increasing the stress on the son. They rally together to help with his problem. As he improves, the husband-wife relationship once again becomes stressful, retriggering the son's delinquent behavior.

The appearance of symptoms is often linked to life cycle transitions, periods when changes are called for in how a family operates (for example, in the case of forced retirement) (Hansen, 1983). Such transition periods cause a temporary disequilibrium in the family system, during which family stability and continuity may be threatened by demands for change. At the same time, the members may be experiencing a sense of loss, confusion, and anxiety (Walsh, 1983). Depending on the effectiveness of their problem-solving style, their flexibility and openness to change, the strength and persistence of the stress(es), and other such factors, they may become dysfunctional or reorganize and make a successful adaptation.

A symptom may be precipitated by a number of events, some external, some from within the family. As Papp (1983) explains, a symptom may be triggered by a change in a larger system (for example, an economic depression leading to the unemployment of the primary breadwinner). As part of

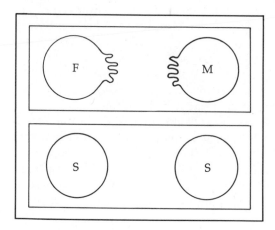

Parents in conflict

Children observe the conflict
and become stressed.

A conflictual spouse system

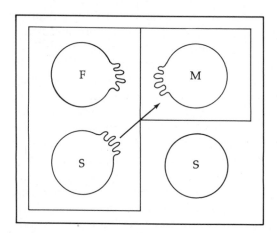

Father and son form coalition
against mother.

Youngest son is isolated
and becomes delinquent.

Parent–child triangulation

*Figure 2.2. A stressful family relationship in which conflict in
the spousal subsystem (upper diagram) leads to the creation of
family coalitions (lower diagram) and the manifestation of symptomatic behavior in a family member.*
Source: Friesen, 1985, p. 46.

a cybernetic circuit, the whole family may be affected, and the teenage daughter, for example, may develop an eating problem. Or perhaps some internal family event (for example, birth of a handicapped infant, death of a grandparent) shatters the family's customary coping patterns, and a symptom develops as a means of establishing a new pattern. In any case, the symptom now becomes part of the family's ongoing transactions, either as the focus of every member's concern or as an unacknowledged factor that nevertheless insinuates itself on all transactions.

The family seeking to eliminate some problematic, maladaptive, or symptomatic behavior in one of its members (or in relationships between several of its members) may ultimately feel sufficiently distressed to seek help. Viewing the disturbing symptom of one member not as an isolated event but as part of a larger family context, the counselor attempts to alter the broader family system by transforming its structures and customary transactional patterns.

Merely eliminating an individual's symptoms (a mechanism for maintaining self-regulation within the system) may throw the entire family system into disarray; one part cannot be altered without the whole undergoing change. Instead, the counselor attempts to unbalance the family's established equilibrium and change the overall family context so changes in individual behavior can transpire. Effective intervention, as we shall see in forthcoming chapters, helps a dysfunctional family to reorganize and create more satisfying interactive patterns as they attain a new equilibrium.

SUMMARY

The systems view of dysfunctional behavior in an individual looks to disequilibrium in the family system of which that person is a part. General Systems Theory, an increasingly prominent influence in modern scientific thinking, defines a system as a complex of component parts or interacting elements that together form an interdependent entity. A system's wholeness, organization, and patterns are its crucial characteristics; in family terms, ongoing relationships and enduring transactional patterns represent its essential aspects.

Systems thinking stresses circular causality, the cybernetic idea that each element in a system influences and is influenced by every other. Dynamic equilibrium or homeostasis is maintained in a system through a series of feedback loops, which reintroduce information into the system. Negative feedback attenuates deviation and thus maintains the stability of a system; positive feedback amplifies deviation and thus causes change.

Families can be differentiated by their degree of openness to the outside world. Open systems interact with the outside environment; closed systems do not. Closed family systems, which hold onto the traditions of the past and avoid change, are in danger of becoming rigid and isolated. The prospects for open family systems is better, since they stress adaptability, but they too may show strain and break down if open expression results in incompatibilities.

Systems are composed of interacting subsystems, and within a family such subsystems carry out separate functions that together sustain the whole. All family members participate in several subsystems simultaneously, playing different roles in each. Boundaries differentiate these subsystems and have differing degrees of permeability. In enmeshed families, the boundaries are too loosely defined and members may become too entwined in each other's lives. Disengaged families have overly rigid boundaries. The former makes separation from the family difficult; the latter may preclude learning to develop caring relationships with others.

Families frequently seek professional help because of the appearance of symptomatic behavior in a member. Such symptoms reflect a disturbance in the overall family system, as a result of changes either in the larger system of the external world or caused by an internal family event. Symptoms become incorporated into the family's transactional patterns; merely helping eliminate them may disrupt the ongoing functioning of the family system. Dysfunctional families need to reorganize and learn new interactive patterns to attain a new equilibrium.

Chapter 3

◆◆◆

Appraising Family Functioning

From a systems perspective, an individual's personal as well as interpersonal problems must be viewed in the context of the family system of which that person is a part. The family counselor regards any set of presenting problems or symptoms not merely as the manifestation of individual **psychopathology**, but as indicative of a disturbance in the family's relationship patterns. The **identified patient** is thus seen as signaling the presence of family pain or distress.

As we noted in the previous chapter, to attempt to relieve the symptom without helping repair the family system of which the individual (and his or her symptom) is a part, is to ignore that the symptom may serve to keep the family stable and functioning. (The teenage girl who develops a drug habit may rally her divided parents into uniting in their concern over her welfare, rather than allow them to go through with the divorce that she senses they are contemplating.) From such a perspective, the family may be understood as "needing" the patient to be symptomatic if it is to maintain its balance.[1]

As Wachtel and Wachtel (1986) point out, the systems-oriented clinician might ask: What would happen to other family members if this person were to change (become symptom-free)? Is he or she expressing feelings through the symptoms that other members are denying or not permitting themselves to experience? Is the individual really being "helpful" to others by not functioning well? We might wonder, too, if other family members need one person to be emotionally disturbed in order to assure themselves of their own emotional well-being.

If the person's symptoms or problematic behaviors are not as clearly understood separated from the family interconnections out of which they emerge, then the counselor must examine the family relationship network. To understand a problem situation adequately, according to Karpel and Strauss (1983), a counselor should ideally hear it described by each family member from his or her unique, separate perspective; at the same time, the counselor needs to observe the family members interacting with each other in characteristic ways. We believe, further, that a family systems perspective is equally desirable when working therapeutically with a single client, with a combination of family members, or with an entire family.

Specifically, the counselor needs to appraise the family as a functioning unit to determine (1) if treatment for the entire family is called for; (2) who are the appropriate members with whom to work; (3) what underlying interactive patterns fuel the family disturbance and lead to the complex symptoms; (4) whether the counselor has the competence, interest, and motivation to take on the case; and (5) how to plan effective clinical intervention.

Reiss (1980) notes that accurate family assessment is important for precisely the same reasons that accurate individual assessment is important: (1) to determine whether family counseling is an appropriate treatment, and, if so, what specific modification the family in question may require; (2) to develop a short-term and long-term **prognosis**; (3) to know the strengths and resources the family has and is willing to commit in order

---

1   The notion of symptoms serving functions for the family, enabling them to cope, avoid disruption, and thus maintain the integrity of the family system, has the support of most family counselors, including Jay Haley, Mara Selvini-Palazzoli, and Salvador Minuchin. However, this "functionalist" view of symptoms has been challenged by Bogdan (1986), and especially by members of the Mental Research Institute Brief Therapy Center in Palo Alto, California (Segal, 1987). These critics contend that family interpersonal difficulties do not cause symptoms; rather, symptoms develop and persist because of the mishandling of normal life difficulties, including ordinary family life-cycle transitions (beginning school, children leaving home, divorce, death in the family). Segal (1987) argues that such an original difficulty ultimately produces a problem when mismanagement leads to the repeated use of the same flawed "solutions." A vicious cycle is set in motion, producing a problem whose eventual size and nature may then bear little resemblance to the original difficulty. Correspondingly, these counselors' efforts are directed at helping families change the way they go about solving problems, and not at searching for the role symptoms play in family homeostasis.

to improve the chances of a favorable therapeutic outcome; and (4) to establish a baseline so that whether treatment produces improvement or deterioration can be determined. In addition, assessment results provide an economical and effective way to communicate to clinical colleagues and interested agencies.

While the goals of appraisal are indeed worthy, they are not meant to imply that the family must undergo a full and comprehensive assessment before *any* clinical action is undertaken. Clearly, a certain amount is learned about the family by interacting with its members as a group. Counselors continuously make therapeutic moves on the basis of a partial assessment of the family, and learn more about the family by noting the outcome of their prior interventions.

THE APPRAISAL PROCESS

Gauging a family's functioning as an ongoing system is obviously a complex undertaking, when you consider the complicated tangle of experiences, temporary or semipermanent alliances, family histories extending over several generations, varying degrees of openness to inquiry, shifting roles played by the same individual over a number of years, and other factors that must be considered. Where do you begin to make some sense out of this labyrinth of potentially useful data? Just how do you distinguish essential from interesting but nonessential material?

Reiss (1980) makes the useful suggestion that a number of pathways are open to the counselor in carrying out the appraisal; as yet, no single most valuable approach has emerged. Among the available choices are the following:

Whether to adopt a cross-sectional or developmental view: The counselor may choose to attend to the family as it is currently functioning or to take a more long-term view of its development. Most family counselors choose the former, and attempt to characterize major family patterns and themes at the time of the appraisal. Others adopt a developmental perspective, reconstructing how the family has evolved over time as it has passed through various phases of its life cycle (marriage, birth of the first child, and so on).

Whether to conduct a family-based or an environmental-based inquiry: Both perspectives focus on the family's interactions with its social surroundings, differentiating families on the basis of the breadth and quality of their outside relationships (with extended family members, other families, community agencies such as schools). However, the family-based approach views interactive processes within the family as the primary shapers of these transactional patterns. On the other hand, the environmental-based approach emphasizes the examination of the family's external relationships and seeks to discover the impact of these outside dealings in which the family is embedded to better understand the family's internal patterns.

Whether to adopt a crisis or character orientation: Familiar to most clinicians, this distinction is one of emphasis and outlook. Immediate problems and family complaints are the focus of the crisis orientation. Some family counselors go so far as to type family crises according to the diagnosis of the most conspicuously disturbed member (schizophrenic families, depressed families, alcoholic families), although this is less frequently the case nowadays than in the past. More likely, counselors adopt a character orientation, searching for and defining the family's enduring interactive and adaptational patterns. Any attempt at typology of the family follows from how these patterns translate into family rules, role assignments, and so on.

Whether to focus on family pathology or family competence: While the search for family disorder or dysfunction is a familiar one to counselors trained in psychodiagnostic methods, a more current view is to seek family strengths and resources along with deficiencies (Karpel, 1986). Reiss (1980) particularly emphasizes those psychological and social resources that a family can call upon to meet crises as well as conduct their daily lives. From this perspective, differences between families— in role relationships, family rules, and interactive patterns—are not judged as to degree of psychopathology, but rather understood as shaped by differences in values, objectives, and long-term family goals.

Whether to emphasize underlying family themes or observable behavioral events: This choice is shaped by the counselor's theoretical view of how human behavior is to be analyzed and understood. The thematic position assumes that overt behavior is but a surface phenomenon and that underlying but largely inaccessible unconscious experiences determine the basis for actions. The task, then, is to determine those hidden events and especially unresolved conflicts, typically in the past, that influence the frequency and force of the current behavior. In marked contrast to this primarily **psychoanalytic** view is the **behavioral** position: that maladaptive or problematic family interactional patterns, like all behaviors, are learned, and therefore may become unlearned or extinguished if not reinforced or rewarded. The assessment task, then, is to focus on the frequencies of the undesired behaviors, as well as their antecedent events and consequences, as an initial step in identifying and ultimately eliminating them to reduce family distress.

Beyond these choices made by the counselor, we believe at least four interactive factors influence the appraisal process: (1) the counselor's theoretical framework; (2) his or her personal counseling style; (3) the unique structure and patterns of the family being appraised; and (4) what the appraiser wants to learn about the family. Although these cannot really be separated in practice, we intend in this book to emphasize these last two aspects: how different family configurations elicit different appraisal and therapeutic interventions, and how the purpose of the undertaking determines what assessment methods will be used.

We believe it to be most instructive to divide the appraisal process into two distinct parts. The first, the evaluation phase, consists of initial investigations directed at gaining a feel for what the family is all about, why they are seeking help, and whether family counseling is needed or appropriate. The assessment phase is one we consider to be an ongoing process, as the counselor continues to probe and gauge the family's functioning throughout treatment in order to evaluate the effectiveness of various therapeutic interventions.

THE EVALUATION PHASE

Three conditions must be met, according to Caille (1982), before a first meeting between a counselor and a family seeking help can occur. To begin with, family members at some level need to agree that they have a particular problem (what we have been referring to as a symptom). Second, the family or an influential outsider (a close friend, a trusted doctor) must decide that the problem exceeds the family's capacity to deal with it, so that the family ultimately is persuaded to present the symptom to a counselor to whom healing responsibility is delegated. Finally, the counselor needs to decide whether the symptom falls within his or her domain of competence or whether the family should be referred to others (other counselors specializing in the presenting problem, say of drug abuse; social or legal agencies; the police).

One particular family member, or a coalition of members, usually begins the process by seeking help outside the family. Perhaps their efforts to solve a personal or family problem have been ineffective and psychologically costly to one or more individuals. Note that this initial decision to step outside of the family for help with the problem is influenced by a number of nonpersonal considerations. Social class factors, ethnic considerations, familiarity with and belief in the psychotherapeutic process, all may play a role.

Thus, the appearance of a symptom in a family member as a sign that the family needs therapeutic help may have a varied outcome, to a large (and often arbitrary) extent dependent on the family's position in society. As Caille (1982) reminds us, it is not unusual to meet families who live with serious problems such as violence, psychosis, or drug addiction without seeking treatment. Even if they are put in contact with a counselor, a fragmented or truncated presentation of their problems may make the problems seem incomprehensible or unsolvable, and therapeutic action may be impeded. The counselor's or agency's point of view regarding the provision of services on an individual or family basis will also structure the evaluation, and ultimately the intervention process.

The Initial Telephone Contact

All human systems, including families, develop symptoms or find themselves in crisis at one time or another; most relieve the symptoms or resolve the crisis without therapeutic intervention. Even among those who do not, only a relatively small proportion of families call a counselor asking specifically for family counseling. More typically, according to Karpel and Strauss (1983), one adult member calls to arrange an appointment for himself or herself or for another member.[2] In actuality, this seemingly routine initial telephone contact may be crucial in determining the course of the subsequent evaluation and counseling.

This first telephone contact with a counselor is an opportunity for both the caller and the counselor to size each other up and sense something about each other's attitudes and personalities. The counselor gets some idea of how the caller perceives the problem and, perhaps more subtly, how he or she views the family as an interactive system. The caller, too, is making an evaluation, and forming an impression: Have I contacted a person who is friendly, understanding, helpful, warm, insightful, has a sense of humor, someone who is willing to listen beyond a moment or two, who is willing and able to find time for me, who gives me hope that finally I have reached the right person who can help with my (our) problem?

In addition to gathering some preliminary information about the caller and his or her reasons for seeking help, the counselor is forming some hypotheses about the family based on the caller's view or explanation of the problem. How much self-awareness does the caller seem to have? What sort of impression is he or she trying to make? What other family members are involved and will they willingly attend the initial session? Who should the counselor ask to see for this first meeting (the caller alone, both parents if a child is identified as the patient, the child alone, the parents and the child together, the parents and all the children)? How does the counselor best present his or her decision and make an effective opening move in scheduling an appointment?

Generally speaking, most counselors tend to opt for as many participants as possible during the first session, especially if relationship conflicts (between parents and one or more of the children, or between children) are involved. In some cases, divorced parents may need to attend together with a troubled youngster, or grandparents may be key players in the family system and should be present.

---

2 This phenomenon may be changing as the general public becomes more aware of the marital and family counseling fields.

The rule of thumb is to ask as many significant persons as are available to attend, whether or not they reside together as a family unit. While some may resist ("Why do I need to include my oldest child? He's no problem." "My husband can't take time away from work; besides, it's my child and not us who has a problem." "Does my divorced husband [or wife] have to attend? We always end up screaming at each other."), the majority will cooperate, if for no other reason than wanting to appear cooperative. The counselor's matter-of-fact statement that this is the procedure he or she usually follows, emphasizing that all members are necessary in order to fully understand the problem, usually proves to be sufficiently persuasive.

In general, then, how the counselor uses this telephone opportunity to make a mini-evaluation and take the first step in entering the family system, may be critical in determining if the family makes (and keeps) the appointment, who will attend the first session, and the family's (and each member's) degree of participation in the subsequent counseling process. Even if the counselor must acquiesce to a caller's insistence that the parents attend the first session alone, before others become involved, it may be worth engaging the otherwise resistant family and making later modifications in attendance. The counselor, however, must not allow the caller to determine the course of counseling, even if, having stated a desire for the entire family to attend, he or she settles for less for this first session. Allowing the caller to be in control takes power and control from the counselor, who may never again be in charge of the counseling with this family. Carl Whitaker (Napier & Whitaker, 1978) is particularly adamant about winning this "battle for structure." He believes that the counselor must insist on establishing the rules of the game, and will not begin the counseling until he is convinced that this has been accomplished.[3]

The Initial Session

Once the initial session begins, the counselor's first task is to establish a relationship with the family, called "joining" the family (Minuchin, 1974) or "building a working alliance" with them (Karpel & Strauss, 1983). At this point, the counselor needs to present, through both verbal and nonverbal means, a picture of being a competent, fair-minded, empathetic, and understanding individual with whom the family can feel sufficiently comfortable to entrust their problems. Framing comments at the family's vocabulary level, adapting to the family's emotional pace, not challenging or contradicting a member's stated views prematurely, perhaps even making small jokes or adding a personal anecdote relevant to the topic under discussion, all enhance the view of the counselor as easy to talk to and

---

3 Not all family counselors insist that the entire family attend. In some cases, one spouse may even be absent in doing marital counseling. For example, the Brief Therapy Center noted in a previous footnote will, with the client's permission, work with anyone motivated enough to help with the presenting problem (Segal, 1987).

Box 3.1   Step-by-Step Guide to the Initial Family Interview

Beginning the first family session properly, without drifting or getting muddled in irrelevant details, is an imposing challenge, especially for inexperienced counselors. To aid the process, Weber, McKeever, and McDaniel (1985) offer a concise, step-by-step generic guide for conducting a problem-focused first family interview. According to these authors, four primary goals shape the conduct of the interview: (1) to join the family, accommodate to its style of interacting, and create an environment in which all members will feel supported; (2) to organize the interview so that the members begin to gain confidence in the counselor's leadership; (3) to gather information about the problem in ways that make family transactions around the problem clearer; (4) to negotiate a counseling contract, emphasizing the family's initiative in defining goals and desired changes.

To accomplish these ends, they break the interview down into 12 separate phases. Both pre-interview and post-interview tasks are included.

1. *Telephoning:* To make contact; to contract for first interview (who will attend, when, where); to determine referral source (if not self-referred), reason for referral, and how follow-up information will be given to referring person.

2. *Forming hypotheses*: To develop tentative hypotheses (based on family life cycle stage, reason for referral, and so on) to be tested in the interview; to plan strategy for gathering data to help test initial hunches.

3. *The greeting* (approximately 5 minutes): To welcome, identify, and greet each member separately; to observe seating arrangement family selects; to orient to counseling format.

4. *The social phase* (approximately 5 minutes): To build nonthreatening setting for the family; to attempt to engage all members; to note each member's language and nonverbal behavior in order to facilitate contact in future sessions.

5. *Identifying the problem* (approximately 15 minutes): To explore each member's view of the problem in behavioral terms, as well as specific solutions that have been attempted.

6. *Observing family patterns* (approximately 15 minutes): To have family describe or reenact examples of the problem; to note repetitive behavioral sequences that occur around the problem.

7. *Defining goals* (approximately 5 minutes): To crystallize treatment goals as viewed by each family member in specific and realistic behavioral terms.

(continued)

- Appraising Family Functioning 65

Box 3.1 (continued)

8. *Contracting* (approximately 5 minutes): To reach agreement regarding continuation of counseling and its structure (who will attend, fees, insurance, signing of consent forms for gathering further information from schools, previous counselors, and so on); if family chooses not to continue, to offer referrals or indicate how they might return in the future.

9. *First interview checklist:* To review session to determine how well previous goals of each phase were reached.

10. *Revising hypotheses:* To revise and refine pre-interview hypotheses and plan the next session.

11. *Contacting the referring person:* To obtain referring person's perspective, and to share initial assessment of the family; to lay groundwork for collaboration in carrying out treatment strategy.

12. *Gathering records:* To obtain all relevant information from professionals or social agencies.

---

nonintimidating. In the process, the counselor is gaining access to the system, from within which he or she is better able to direct change.

With the family seated in a circle, arranged as they see fit, the counselor needs to be free to address all members equally. Deliberately not beginning with the identified patient in order to avoid going along with possible family stereotyping that he or she is "the problem," perhaps the counselor turns to the father, the noncaller, in order to break any previously established set that the mother is the family spokesperson. An opening gambit such as "I've heard from your wife over the phone about how she sees the problem, and now I'd like to hear your view" is likely to encourage him (and, later, others) to get involved in the process. If this scenario is adopted, the counselor needs to make explicit what he or she has been told, so that no hidden information and/or hidden alliance exists between the counselor and the initial caller.

Of course, no hard and fast counseling rules exist about whom should be addressed first. However, Whitaker (1977), for one, is likely to involve the father by this tactic early in the treatment. Without prior information, his reasoning is that the father is the most likely family member to resist seeking help; moreover, he usually also has the power to pull the family out of treatment if some rapport is not established with the counselor from the beginning. In other cases, the counselor may wait to see who will present himself or herself as the family spokesperson, who will be silent, how free family members feel to talk to each other, and so on. When the identified patient is a frightened child, the counselor may begin with him or her, to reassure the child that it will be safe to speak.

Certain identifying data need to be gathered at the outset from each family member. Names, ages, occupations, current living arrangements, and other such details are, of course, necessary; beyond such basic information, the counselor begins to obtain some face-to-face impressions of each member and to develop some hypotheses concerning his or her role in the overall family constellation. By addressing each member, the counselor establishes that each member's comments are valued, and that each member will be heard, thus starting to develop a connection with each person present. Every member should have an opportunity to talk before the close of the initial hour or hour-and-one-half session.

The reason for being here occupies the family, and early on in the initial session they will want the counselor to hear about the problem from which they are seeking relief. As one member, preferably not the caller, begins, others are encouraged to add individual comments, and silent members in particular are encouraged to participate. As the counselor directs the discussion, perhaps over several sessions, he or she seeks clues to the following (Caille, 1982; Doherty & Baird, 1983):

- Why is the family seeking help *now*?
- What are the sources of stress on this family?
- Who has the symptom? How severe? Chronic or acute? Why this person?
- When did the problem or symptom first begin, and who is most affected by it?
- What function does the symptom serve for family stability?
- How often, when, and under what circumstances does the symptom occur?
- Are interactive patterns discernible that may be related to the onset or termination of symptomatic behavior?
- Is an enmeshed or disengaged family system operating?
- What is the current level of family functioning?
- Are noticeable alliances or coalitions operating?
- How permeable are the boundaries between subsystems?
- In what manner, and with what degree of success, has the family dealt with this or other problems in the past?
- Has the family sought professional help before? With what degree of success?
- How adaptable or rigid is the family? How receptive to help?
- What apparent family interactive patterns are related to the perpetuation of the problem?

While these questions may seem overwhelming to the beginning family counselor trying to keep them all in mind, several words of reassurance may be in order. They need not be memorized; you will think of those relevant for your family as you attempt to learn more about them as an ongoing system. In addition, these questions need not all be addressed in one or even two or three sessions; the data will probably evolve slowly and in stages as the counseling proceeds. We merely offer these questions as a checklist or set of guidelines to help the counselor organize his or her thinking in systems terms when dealing with a new family. They should provide a framework for generating clinical hunches or hypotheses about the family's structure and interactive processes, and thus form the basis for planning more effective clinical interventions.

History Taking

How much background information does a family counselor need before deciding on and implementing a counseling plan? Histories for each family member? Histories for the family only? Going back how many generations? Does the counselor obtain a formal case history through a series of straightforward questions, as in some forms of individual counseling? How relevant to the present are the facts of the past?

Counselors vary considerably in the emphasis they place on historical information, dependent primarily on the theoretical viewpoint from which they operate. A secondary factor may be the purposes for which the evaluation is being carried out (for example, in a crisis situation following a suicide attempt, the counselor most certainly would deal with immediately precipitating factors and look for family resources to deal with the emergency; in a more long-lasting situation in which parent-child conflict is at issue, the counselor might conduct the counseling at a slower pace and make use of relevant historical data).

At one end of the spectrum, systems theorist Murray Bowen (1978) takes the position that multigenerational patterns and influences are crucial determinants of current family difficulties. Consequently, he investigates the genesis of a family's presenting problems or symptoms by detailing the backgrounds of husband and wife through at least three generations. To aid the process and to keep the record in pictorial form in front of him, he constructs a **genogram** in which each partner's family background is laid out.

In their simplest form, genograms are schematic diagrams, in family-tree fashion, depicting information about several generations of a family. Figure 3.1 illustrates some commonly agreed-upon genogram symbols. Beyond providing a concise and graphic picture of a family's current composition, a genogram reveals relevant data concerning families of origin and extended family networks. Ages, dates of birth and death of key family members, divorces and remarriages, birth order, and other such details may be included, all potentially useful in elucidating relationships and family transactional patterns.

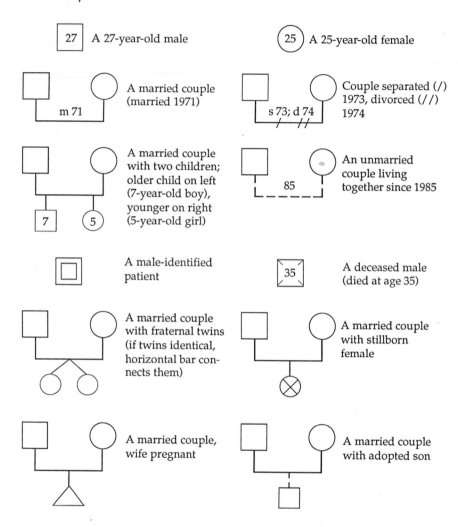

Figure 3.1 A partial set of commonly agreed-upon genogram symbols. (Based on McGoldrick & Gerson, 1985.)

Since the functioning of family members, from a systems view, is profoundly interdependent, with changes in one part reverberating throughout the system, a picture of the happenings over several generations may be very enlightening. McGoldrick and Gerson (1985), strongly influenced by Bowen, believe that families tend to repeat themselves; what happens in one generation will often occur in the next, as the same issues get replayed from generation to generation. Counselors who seek such multigenerational connections for assessment clues are thus more prone to use genograms in their quest.

Genograms are typically prepared with the aid of the family during the first session or two. For both the counselor and the family, they help provide a framework for understanding family relationship patterns, and also provide a well-defined structure for families to begin to think in inter-generational terms about themselves. For example, Figure 3.2 is a three-generational map of a family who has contacted a counselor because their son, Ivan, is having school difficulties, disrupting class activity and gener-ally being inattentive. The genogram reveals that his mother, Loretta, was adopted, after her adoptive parents tried unsuccessfully to have a daughter after three sons. She married early, at 20, soon after the death of her adoptive mother. Steve, a middle child whose parents divorced when he was a preteenager, lived in a single-parent household with his mother and two sisters until he married Loretta. Steve and Loretta started their own family before either was 25, perhaps in an effort to create some stability in contrast to what they had known growing up.

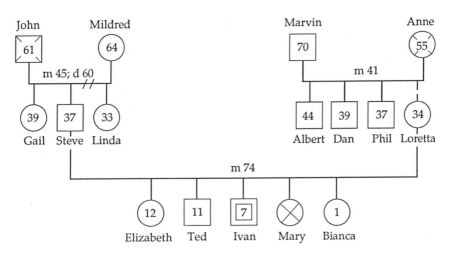

Figure 3.2 Genogram of a three-generation family.

The fact that they now have four children (one died at birth) suggests a strong involvement in family life, especially because the children's ages are spread over more than ten years. Are the parents being overprotective, perhaps to compensate for what they felt deprived of as youngsters? What has been the effect of Loretta's pregnancies over the last several years on the other children? To what extent does Ivan feel he is being displaced as the youngest child by the birth of Bianca? These are some of the issues a counselor might begin to explore on the basis of the genogram data, to be checked out as he or she learns more about the family. The counselor with a systems viewpoint is likely to see symptoms in the identified patient as reflecting the family system's adaptation at this given moment in time. Both historical and current family patterns may point to dysfunctional family structures.

A more moderate position regarding the importance of history taking is offered by **structural** theorist Salvador Minuchin (1974) and **strategic** theorist Jay Haley (1976). Both, stressing a systems outlook, attend primarily to more immediate presenting problems and ongoing family transactions, and only secondarily to intergenerational patterns. Both also attend to a family's hierarchical structures, especially possible coalitions that cross generational boundaries. While Minuchin concentrates on a family's organizational patterns and Haley its communication patterns, both focus on repetitive sequences in the current behavior between and among family members. Not adverse to dealing with family history as it relates to a here-and-now problem, they may elicit such information, for example, if it helps to better understand what may have precipitated a current crisis.

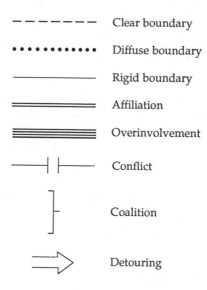

Figure 3.3. Minuchin's symbols for family mapping.
Source: Minuchin, 1974, p. 53.

Minuchin (1974) prefers the technique of **family mapping**, another type of family diagramming useful in depicting the structure and patterns of family systems. In particular, he views a family's structure as "an invisible set of functional demands that organizes the ways in which family members interact" (p. 51). Again using symbols (see Figure 3.3), Minuchin is interested in delineating the clarity of current family boundaries (clear, diffuse, or rigid), subsystem operations, and family transactional styles (enmeshment or disengagement). He uses the map as a guide to the family's transactional patterns, developing hypotheses in the process for how best to help change family structures; thus, evaluation and assessment are integrated into the therapeutic process. Figure 3.4 illustrates the use of family mapping to depict parental conflict detoured onto a child (upper figure) and intergenerational coalitions within a family (lower figure).

Father (F) and mother (M), both stressed at work, come home and criticize each other, but then detour their conflict by attacking a child (C). This results in less danger to the spouse subsystem, but stresses the child.

Father criticizes mother, who seeks a coalition with the child against the father. Note the inappropriately rigid cross-generational subsystem of mother and child as well as the diffuse boundary between mother and child; both have the effect of excluding the father. Minuchin refers to this result as a cross-generational dysfunctional pattern.

Figure 3.4. The effect of stress on the subsystem boundaries of a family, as depicted by family mapping.
Source: Minuchin, 1974.

A family evaluation and assessment model based on structural and strategic theory has been offered by Friesen (1985). (A case of family triangulation was described in terms of this model in Chapter 2; see especially Figure 2.2.) Emphasizing interpersonal interaction, Friesen has developed a schema for locating family patterns along a number of dimensions as a guide to the therapeutic process. Specifically, Friesen has developed the following eight scales for assessing aspects of the family system:

Scale 1: Family Developmental Issues—Each stage in a family's life cycle presents its own developmental tasks and creates a potential crisis event. The view here is that family dysfunction emerges from within the family system itself, and that developmental stages simply color the expression or define the nature of the symptom.

Scale 2: Family Life Context—The concern here is with the extent to which those environmental factors that sustain, enhance, or impair the family's operations are present. Seeing the family within its social context includes its relationships to schools, work, ethnic and religious groups it belongs to, societal expectations, and so on.

Scale 3: Family Structure—The family "code" regulating relationships, transmitted from generation to generation, is investigated here. The flexibility of boundaries, power and leadership, coalitions, and their impact on how well the system carries out its functions are studied.

Scale 4: Family Flexibility—Here the focus is on the degree to which the system's rules are open enough to allow for the adequate exchange of information between systems or within the family system itself.

Scale 5: Family Resonance—This scale measures the degree to which the family is sensitive to the needs of its individual members. Openness, fluidity, the expression of affect, the level of tolerance for differing beliefs are important here.

Scale 6: Family Communication Processes—This scale attempts to identify the communication patterns within the family. The assumption is that the manner of communicating will offer clues to the family's underlying interactional patterns.

Scale 7: Marital System—The degree of vitality in and commitment to the marriage by the parents provides clues to overall family functioning.

Scale 8: Individual Issues—Effort is made here to identify individual members' problems within the context of the family and social structure.

Behaviorists such as Stuart (1980) are least likely to turn to historical material. Instead, they concern themselves with the present interpersonal environments that maintain and help perpetuate or reinforce maladaptive or problematic family behavior patterns.

Returning to the general issue of history taking, for some families the problems that have brought them to counseling can be stated briefly and succinctly. Typically, their explanations are couched in current behavioral terms: an ongoing extramarital affair; a bad school experience for one of the children, leaving the single mother feeling frantic and in need of guidance and support; a breakdown in communication between a young child and his newly remarried mother. Other families view their current problems in longitudinal terms: a husband and wife grown more distant since the birth of their first child three years ago; a steady deterioration in a marriage since the wife decided to return to school; a recognition that a husband has distanced himself from his wife and children over the years, without knowing exactly why or when it began. Such families offer historical explanations, and insist the counselor know the background history in great detail. From a counselor's viewpoint, too much emphasis on history may signal an unwillingness to look at the present; such families must be brought back into dealing with why they are seeking help today. Conversely, families who insist on seeing all issues in current terms and suggest any history is irrelevant may be, wittingly or not, covering up crucial details that might play a key role in providing understanding of presenting difficulties. In the latter case, the counselor may need to probe selected areas of the family's past to gain better awareness of the problem's genesis.

History taking has the advantage of giving the family as well as the counselor something concrete and nonthreatening to do early in the evaluation, although there is the risk that the exchange may become stilted and tedious. It may make a family feel reassured that the counselor is learning some essential facts about their past; similarly, it may buy time for the counselor to get his or her bearings with this family. Nevertheless, the process of history taking must not obscure that the family is there to work together on a current problem. Even if the counselor has taken a formal history, he or she must at some point signal, through word or gesture, that it is time to shift from a question-and-answer mode to a more interactive one.

THE ASSESSMENT PHASE

Counselors probably get a better sense of how a family functions by interacting with its members over a period of time than from any initial interviewing in the evaluation phase. Observing the formation of coalitions and family triangles, scapegoating, how subsystems carry out necessary family functions, how differences are negotiated, what forms of communication exist and their degree of effectiveness in dealing with family issues, how the family as a group deals with stress, and other details provides vital information about family structures and ongoing family processes.

As we noted earlier, assessment goes on throughout family counseling, as the counselor broadens his or her understanding, develops, modifies, and discards hypotheses, and makes suitable interventions based upon progressively refined appraisals of the family (as well as continuing assessments of the effectiveness of previous interventions). In other words, gaining knowledge about the family occurs as a result of a continuous interactive process between family and counselor, based upon the family's perception of the problem, the counselor's analysis of that perception and subsequent interventions, the family's response to those interventions, and the counselor's response to the family response (deShazer, 1983).

FAMILY MEASUREMENT TECHNIQUES

Many clinical practitioners find that planned intervention, whether with an individual client or a family, is facilitated by the precounseling use of appropriate tests and measurements. By selecting instruments and procedures tailored to the situation, and using the results to form a multidimensional "family profile," these counselors feel better prepared to outline treatment goals, devise treatment strategies, and evaluate treatment outcomes (Bagarozzi, 1985). In the process, they attempt to derive the benefits of obtaining both an "insider" (family member's) and "outsider" (counselor's) perspective on family processes and functioning.

THE CIRCUMPLEX MODEL: IDENTIFYING TYPES OF FAMILIES

One useful "insider" view of two central properties of family life—adaptability and cohesion—can be gleaned from a research-based technique developed by David Olson and his colleagues (Olson, 1986; Olson, Russell, & Sprenkle, 1983; Olson, Sprenkle, & Russell, 1979). Grounded in family systems theory, sociological models of family functioning, and concepts concerning family life-cycle changes, these researchers' efforts have been directed at understanding how families cope with various situational stresses and demands throughout the life cycle. Over 1000 families participated in their study, at least 100 at each of seven family life-cycle stages.

These efforts have produced the Circumplex Model, a family typology based primarily on two dimensions, adaptability and cohesion, with a third dimension, communication, facilitating family movement on the primary two. Taken together, the researchers believe, these dimensions adequately describe family functioning. Adaptability refers to the family's ability to permit change—in its power structure, rules, and role relationships—in response to changes in members' life situations or life-cycle transitions. Cohesion is defined as family members' emotional bonding with one another. Steps along these two dimensions are divided into four levels each, resulting in a four-by-four matrix yielding 16 possible family types, as illustrated in Figure 3.5.

A family's placement on each of the intersecting scales is determined by their responses to a 20-item self-report test, the Family Adaptability and Cohesion Evaluation Scale (FACES III) (Olson, 1986). The scores provide an assessment of how individuals perceive their family system and also their ideal description. (The perceived-ideal discrepancy is an indirect measure of family satisfaction; the greater the discrepancy, the less the satisfaction derived from family life.) Plotted on the Circumplex Model, of the possible 16 family types, the 4 central ones are considered most balanced in our society (although other configurations may work best in other societies).

According to Olson (1986), balanced families function more adequately than extreme families, and they typically demonstrate more positive communication skills. Families with extremely high scores on both dimensions fall at the outer extremes; midrange families may have middle scores on one dimension but extreme scores on the other; balanced families are those whose scores place them in the middle range of each dimension. Thus, this model assumes a curvilinear relationship between cohesion and adaptability in problem families: too little or too much of either is viewed as dysfunctional in the family system.

Balanced family functioning, in this schema, may take the form of any of four types: flexibly separated, flexibly connected, structurally separated, and structurally connected. These types of families combine stability, the

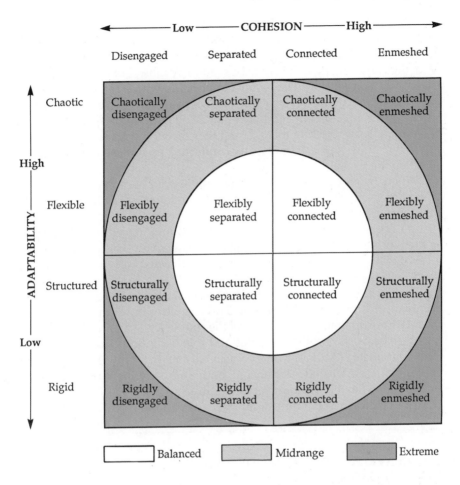

Figure 3.5. The Circumplex Model, representing 16 types of marital and family systems.
Source: Olson, 1986, p. 339.

ability to change, and sufficiently open boundaries to permit effective communication. They are more resourceful, make use of better coping strategies, and thus are less likely to succumb to stressful events than extreme families.

The model is dynamic in the sense that changes can occur in family types over time. Olson, Russell, and Sprenkle (1983) offer the following illustration:

◆◆◆

Steve and Sally were both raised in traditional homes. Three years after they were married, they became parents for the first time, and Sally resigned from her teaching job. Because of the dependency needs of their son and their own desire for mutual support in this transition period, they developed a moderately high but not extreme level of family cohesion. Also, their upbringing led them to be moderately low, but not rigid, on the adaptability dimension. They were comfortable with a rather traditional husband-dominant power structure and segregated role relationship, preferring the relative security of these established patterns to the ambiguities of continually negotiating them. Using the current model, we would classify their family type as **structurally connected**, an option that seemed to be satisfying to them at the time.

When their son became a teenager, Sally started pursuing a career, and both parents experienced a good deal of "consciousness raising" about sex roles through the media and through involvement in several growth groups. Because of their son's needs for more autonomy at this age, as well as the parents' separate career interests, they began operating at a lower level of cohesiveness, moving from being connected to being more separated.

Furthermore, the family power structure shifted from being husband-dominant to a more shared pattern. Sally exercises much more control in the relationship than previously, and the couple are struggling, almost on a weekly basis, to redefine the rules and role definitions that will govern their relationship. Although they occasionally yearn for the security of their earlier, more structured relationship, both find excitement and challenge in this more flexible relationship style. In short, **flexibly separated** best describes their current family organizational pattern. (pp. 75–77)

◆◆◆

THE BEAVERS SYSTEMS MODEL: RATING FAMILY COMPETENCE

Providing a similar but more "outsider" or counselor's view of family functioning, Robert Beavers and his associates at the Timberlawn Psychiatric Foundation in Dallas, Texas, developed another worthwhile instrument for assessing family functioning, the Beavers-Timberlawn Family Evaluation Scales. The studies began with an early research effort (Lewis, Beavers, Gossett, & Phillips, 1976) to understand how "healthy" family systems differed from those in which one or more members required psychiatric treatment or hospitalization. The experimental design involved assigning both groups an identical series of tasks, observing and videotaping the results, and then having trained judges rate the resulting interactions along five major dimensions—family structure, mythology, goal-directed negotiation, autonomy, and family affect—along with subtopics under each rubric. Results indicated that while differences in style and patterning existed, essentially no single quality or thread differentiated the two groups. Among the key differences were: (1) the family's capacity to communicate thoughts and feelings, and (2) the central role played by the parental coalition in providing family leadership as well as serving as a model for interpersonal relationships.

The Beavers-Timberlawn Model (more recently renamed the Beavers Systems Model) portrays family life as existing on an infinite linear continuum of competence, thereby underscoring the Beavers view of a limitless potential for growth (Green, Kolevzon, & Vosler, 1985). At one end are leaderless, invasive, chaotic families, with diffuse boundaries between members. Closer to the midpoint of competence, families show rigid interpersonal control, with frequent distancing, projection, and little consequent closeness. Families at the high end of the scale tend to be better structured; they are composed of autonomous individuals who share intimacy and closeness as well as respect separateness (Beavers, 1981; Beavers, 1982; Beavers & Voeller, 1983).

In the Beavers Systems Model, shown in Figure 3.6, families are classified on a five-point scale according to their degree of functioning. Optimal and adequate families are considered competent or healthy. Midrange, borderline, and severely disturbed families represent progressively poorer levels of functioning. The Beavers Systems Model is similar to the Circumplex Model in that it too represents a cross-section of current family functioning and makes use of two axes to conceptualize differences among families. In this case, however, the structure, flexibility, and competence of a family and its members are scored on one dimension and their style of interaction on the other.

As formulated by Beavers, the horizontal axis reflects the family's structure and its adaptive flexibility. In systems terms, we might think of it as a negentropy continuum, since the more negentropic (or more adaptive and flexible) the family, the better able the family is to deal effectively with stressful situations and events. In order to remain highly adaptive, the family must have a stable structure but at the same time be able to negotiate changes in its structure, as needed to meet the changing needs of its members, without the loss of that stability. In addition to adaptability, autonomy (the family system's capacity to allow or even encourage members to function competently in making choices, each member assuming responsibility for his or her own choices) is called for in competent families. According to Beavers & Voeller (1983, p. 89), "capable families intuitively have a systems approach to relationships, with an appreciation of the interchangeability of causes and effects."

The vertical axis, curvilinear rather than a continuum, reflects the family members' style of interaction. Members of **centripetal** families view most relationship satisfactions as coming from from within the family. By contrast, members of **centrifugal** families see far more promise in what the outside world has to offer than what their family can provide. The arrow shape of the diagram is intended to convey that extremes in style—whether profoundly centripetal or centrifugal—are associated with poor family functioning. Thus, as noted in the diagram, as families become more competent, or more adaptive, their excessive centripetal or centrifugal styles tend to diminish.

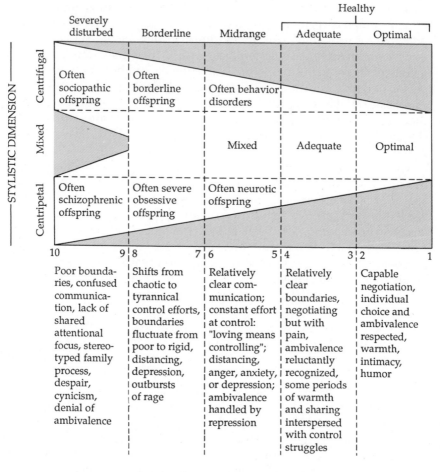

Figure 3.6. The Beavers Systems Model, in the form of a sideways A, with one leg representing centripetal families and the other leg representing centrifugal families.
Source: Beavers & Voeller, 1983, p. 90.

Families who are profoundly at one or the other extreme are most entropic, with the greatest risk of producing disturbed children. Beavers believes that in a severely dysfunctional family with a centripetal style, a good chance exists that one or more offspring will become schizophrenic—socially isolated, progressively withdrawn, and disorganized—as an adult. Children from severely dysfunctional families with a centrifugal style are more prone to sociopathic behavior—antisocial, irresponsible, egocentric.

As Beavers sees it, the sociopath's self-defeating behavior, redefined in family terms, may represent an expression of rage at an uncaring world. In midrange families, both groups are less discrepant, although one tends to behavior disorders and the other to neuroses. Within the healthy category, extremes are rare and the structure aids effective functioning for individuals as well as the family as a whole.

THE MCMASTER MODEL: ASSESSING FAMILY COPING SKILLS

The McMaster Model of Family Functioning is perhaps the most carefully crafted of the measurement techniques we have been considering. This model has evolved over a long period of time, first reported in the late 1950s at McGill University in Montreal, Canada (Westley & Epstein, 1969). The systems-based research shifted to McMaster University in Hamilton, Ontario, in the 1960s and 1970s, and now continues to be refined at Brown University in Providence, Rhode Island (Epstein, Bishop, & Baldwin, 1982). Throughout its history, the research has focused on the family's structure and transactional patterns, attending particularly to how the family develops and maintains itself by dealing with certain necessary tasks.

Families are assessed in this model with respect to their current functioning in three areas:

1. *Basic task area*: How they deal with problems of providing food, money, transportation, and shelter.
2. *Developmental task area*: How they deal with problems arising as a result of changes over time, such as first pregnancy or last child leaving home.
3. *Hazardous task area*: How they handle crises that arise as the result of illness, accident, loss of income, job change, and so forth.

Families unable to cope effectively with these three task areas have been found to be those most likely to develop clinically significant problems.

To evaluate how the family manages these tasks, six aspects of family functioning are investigated:

1. *Problem solving*: The family's ability to resolve issues that threaten its integrity and ability to function effectively.
2. *Communication*: How, and how well, the family exchanges information and affect.
3. *Roles:* How clearly and appropriately roles are defined; how responsibilities are allocated and accountability is monitored in order to sustain the family and support the personal development of its members.

4. *Affective responsiveness:* The family's ability to respond to a given situation with the appropriate quality and quantity of feeling.

5. *Affective involvement:* The extent to which the family shows interest in and values the particular activities and interests of its members.

6. *Behavior control:* The pattern the family adopts for handling dangerous situations; for handling social interaction within and outside the family; for meeting and expressing members' psychobiological needs (eating, sleeping, sex) and drives (aggression).

The counselor using the McMaster Model, is interested in determining how well the family carries out its primary mission of providing an environment in which social and biological development can flourish.

More recently, Epstein and his associates (Epstein, Baldwin, & Bishop, 1983) have turned their attention to constructing a 53 item self-report questionnaire to evaluate families according to the McMaster Model of Family Functioning. The Family Assessment Device (FAD) is made up of seven scales that measure each of the six aspects of family functioning just outlined, plus the family's collective health/pathology. Each family member responds to each set of items by indicating his or her opinion on a four-point rating scale, ranging from "strongly agree" to "strongly disagree." (For example, one item to measure problem solving: "We confront problems involving feeling"; an item to measure affective responsiveness: "We are reluctant to show our affection for each other.") Still in an early stage of development, the test at present is probably best used for screening purposes, to quickly identify a family's problem areas, rather than in any more diagnostic ways.

SUMMARY

Counselors need to appraise the family as a functioning unit to determine if treatment is in order, which members should be seen, and which underlying interactive patterns lead to symptomatology in one of its members. The appraisal process itself can be divided into two distinct stages: the evaluation and assessment phases. The former begins with the initial telephone call, an occasion for counselor and caller to gain some image of the other's attitudes and personality. For the counselor, it is also an opportunity to size up the situation and direct the caller to bring in as many significant family members as are available to attend the first session. The assessment phase of the appraisal continues throughout the subsequent counseling.

Counselors vary in their reliance on family history, primarily according to their theoretical orientation. Bowen views multigenerational patterns as highly influential in understanding current family difficulties, and constructs genograms to diagram such information. Minuchin, more concerned with learning about ongoing family patterns and structures, relies on family mapping techniques to depict current transactions.

Many family counselors make use of measurement techniques in carrying out their appraisals. The Circumplex Model stresses a family's adaptability and cohesion as indicative of their overall functioning; the resulting four-by-four matrix yields 16 family types. The Beavers Systems Model provides a five-point scale—optimal, adequate, midrange, borderline, and severely disturbed—for evaluating family functioning. In the McMaster Model, three major areas of current functioning (how the family handles basic tasks, developmental tasks, and hazardous tasks) and six aspects of family life (problem solving, communication, roles, affective responsiveness, affective involvement, and behavior control) are investigated.

Part III

◆◆◆

Counseling Families with Alternative Lifestyles

Chapter 4

♦♦♦

Counseling the Single-Parent-Led Family

While divorce has become a familiar and recognized fact of American life—approximately 1 million divorces occur annually in this country—it is never routine for the family members undergoing the often agonizing experience and its aftermath. Indeed, for many if not most families, the decision to split up is often a traumatic event filled with uncertainty and perhaps even dread about the future. Moreover, despite its common occurrence, divorce may still frequently be greeted with shock and embarrassment, if not hostility, by family and friends (who may find themselves in the uncomfortable position of having to reevaluate their own marriages). According to Ahrons and Rodgers (1987), who urge that divorce be viewed as an enduring societal institution (much as marriage is perceived in our culture), many people still cling to the long-held attitude that divorce is inherently pathological; if two people are unable or unwilling to maintain a lifelong commitment, goes this argument, one or both partners must have some psychological defect or deficit. Divorcing partners, then, especially if young children are involved, must often deal with a sense of failure, of guilt over breaking up a home, of anguish at being labeled by many as socially deviant—all at a time when significant life changes are taking place and important decisions about the future must be made.

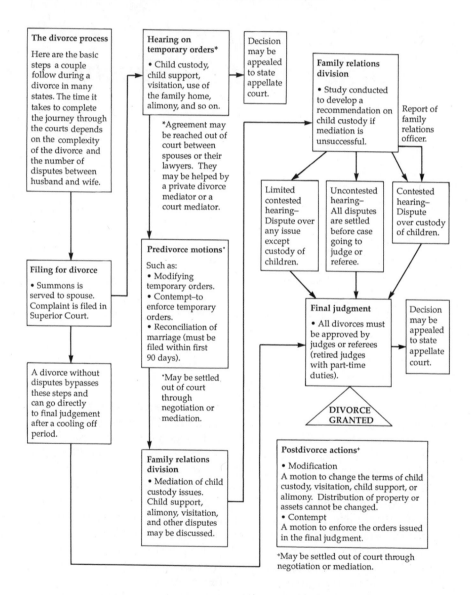

Figure 4.1. Steps in a typical legal divorce process.
Source: Gullotta, Adams, & Alexander, 1986, p. 240.

For a variety of reasons, many of which we discussed in Chapter 1, couples are less willing today to make emotional compromises or remain in an unhappy situation for economic security, for the sake of the children, or for social appearances. No-fault divorce laws make divorce more readily obtainable, with less stigma of blame attached. Despite a generally more accepting position regarding divorce on the part of most people, however, families led by a single parent continue to be viewed as flawed or imperfect versions of the "normal" two-parent family. In contrast with this commonly held view, recent studies by Morawetz and Walker (1984), Ahrons and Rodgers (1987), Mednick (1987), and others challenge the assumption that single-parent households represent some deviant family form; their findings indicate that good adjustment, well-being, and satisfaction with life are possible for single parents.

For our purposes, the term *single-parent household* is preferable to either *broken home* or simply *single-parent family*. *Broken home* is pejorative, implying that the family deserves second-class status due to the parental split, and that serious consequences are inevitable. *Single-parent family* is, in our opinion, misleading, in that it suggests that only one parent is involved after divorce. In point of fact, divorce does not necessarily mean that the family no longer exists, but only that the marital relationship has ended; particularly where children are involved, the family relationship continues even if the parents are physically separated. Counseling such families, the counselor must keep in focus the impact of the absent family members (parent, siblings, grandparents) as much as those who happen to live together under the same roof.

VARIETIES OF SINGLE-PARENT HOUSEHOLDS

Before considering some of the issues encountered in counseling single-parent-led families, we should define our population. Marital disharmony leading to separation and divorce is perhaps the most easily recognized but hardly the only avenue to single-parent status. While families led by a single parent as a result of divorce have emerged as a highly visible family form in the last decade, such a family structure actually represents a traditional form of family organization in the United States.

Seward (1978) notes that beginning in the mid-19th century and extending to 1970, perhaps one out of ten families was maintained by one parent, most likely the mother. Especially in the earlier period, death of a spouse or desertion were more likely than not to be the cause of the absent parent. Only since the early 1970s, as Thompson and Gongla (1983) report, has that pattern changed. The proportion of single-parent-led households in the population has doubled to more than a quarter of all families with dependent children at home; separation and divorce are now the most common causes of such families, and the number of unmarried women bearing children has risen sharply.

Nevertheless, single-parent-led families are not a homogeneous group. Hill (1986) identifies at least eight different types of female-headed[1] single-parent households (see Table 4.1). Note that, for one thing, it is important to distinguish between those women who will ultimately remarry and those who will not. These groups are likely to have different economic lives, different expectations concerning the future, different sets of problems brought to the counselor.

Table 4.1   Eight Possible Types of Single-Parent Families

	Degree of Permanence of Single-Parent Status	
Origin of Severance of Spouses	*Temporary*	*Permanent*
Separation or divorce	Type I Divorced, remarriage	Type II Divorced, no remarriage
Death of spouse	Type III Widowed, remarriage	Type IV Widowed, no remarriage
War-separated spouses	Type V War separated but reunited	Type VI Permanent separation– missing in action
Unmarried parent	Type VII Post pregnancy marriage	Type VIII No marriage, single parent of illegitimate child

Source: Hill, 1986, p. 24.

For example, Type 1 women (those who are temporarily single but who remarry) and their children must adapt to a stepfamily and to a possible return to childbearing (thus forcing the family to deal simultaneously with an infant/toddler and, say, an adolescent from the previous marriage). They are also vulnerable to a second divorce and a return to single-parent status. The Type 2 single parent (who does not remarry) has a shorter period of child rearing, but runs a far greater risk of financial impoverishment, to say nothing of increased feelings of loneliness and despair. She also is likely to find her single life ultimately unrewarding and to find herself relegated to a status that is without honor or respect (Weiss, 1979).

The family counselor needs to be aware of the following factors:

1 According to Hill (1986), the overwhelming proportion of single-parent-led families are headed by females. His data indicate that only a modest percentage of single-parent households are male-dominated (wife absent), despite their relatively high visibility as a result of films such as *Kramer vs. Kramer*.

- How the parent became single (for example, through divorce, desertion, never married)
- At what stage in the marriage that parent became single (for example, after 6 months of marriage or after 15 years)
- The apparent precipitating factors of a marital breakup (for example, infidelity, chronic quarreling and dissatisfaction, in-law intrusions, immaturity of one or both partners, sexual incompatibilities, financial problems)
- The number of children, the age of the children as well as the age of the parent at the time of becoming a single parent, the presence and degree of involvement of grandparents or other parts of an extended family
- The pile-up of stressor events preceding family dissolution (for example, constant fighting between parents about to separate, forcing the children to choose sides, threats and counterthreats between parents)
- The pile-up of stressor events following dissolution and family reorganization (for example, moving to a new location, job, or school; making new friends; establishing a self-identity as a single person or as a member of a single-parent-led family)
- The unfamiliar roles family members have been called upon to play (for example, as head of a one-parent household, or as a child called upon to take on more adult responsibilities in the absence of the same-sex parent)

In addition, the counselor needs to be aware that single-parent households led by fathers are likely to experience different sets of problems and different lifestyles, including different financial status (more likely to be considerably higher in father-led homes), from those led by mothers; and social class, as well as racial and ethnic group membership, often are telling factors in how effectively such families function.

The counselor needs to appreciate, too, that while families led by a single parent may or may not share a common lifestyle, the more relevant point is that they probably share certain experiences. For example, all families led by one parent, whether as a result of separation, divorce, or widowhood, have experienced some loss. Thus, feelings of loneliness, sadness, guilt, and anger are inevitably present in some degree and in some combination. Morawetz and Walker (1984) report that women in such situations recount the same sets of problems: feeling overburdened, unsupported, and guilty over not being up to the task of raising a family alone. The frequent case of a father severing contact with his ex-wife and his children, perhaps paying child support sporadically or not at all, only adds to the hardship and despair.

However, while the widowed person may dampen or even mute these wearisome feelings in time—indeed, may even comfort herself by exaggerating the positive memories of a previous spouse—the divorced person is far less likely to do so (Weiss, 1979). Part of the reason, of course, is that the divorced couple, especially if children are involved, may continue their conflict (for example, over child support payments or child visitation) long after the legal divorce is final. In addition, as Getty (1981) points out, if the divorce was initiated by one spouse against the wishes of the other, then the latter may in particular be filled with feelings of failure, unworthiness, and self-doubt.

Consider, for example, the differences between the situations of a middle-aged widow with adolescent children and a young divorced woman, briefly married and with a 2-year-old child.

◆◆◆

Margaret and Ted were married when they graduated from college. She worked for several years as an elementary school teacher while he continued into medical school and through an internship and residency program in ophthalmology. Once Ted established a practice as an ophthalmologist, however, family income was sufficient and they decided to start a family. Margaret had no hesitation in discontinuing her teaching job, since she had long looked forward to having and raising children. Together they had three children—two boys and a girl—and for 25 years Margaret and Ted lived a generally fulfilling and economically comfortable life. However, sudden disaster struck the family when Ted had a massive heart attack at work one day and died shortly thereafter, at age 50.

Unlike many single-parent-led families, Margaret and her children did not suffer any severe economic upheaval, since Ted had provided well for their financial future. On the other hand, Margaret's loneliness was at times almost unbearable, particularly after the initial period when friends rallied to her side and invited her to their social get-togethers. After six months, few such invitations were forthcoming, and Margaret found herself, at age 49, depressed, alone, not knowing where or to whom to turn. One thing she was sure about, however, was that she must allow her children to lead their own lives, and not make them feel obligated or burdened by taking care of their mother. She did, nevertheless, feel responsible for offering them guidance to the best of her ability, although she often bemoaned the fact that she had to be both mother and father to them, and the strain of solo decision making was taking its toll on her health.

As she slowly began, at the urging of her children, to socialize with old friends, she found herself being asked out on dates. Quickly she realized that she had had few experiences with men, having married Ted at such an early age, and that the changing sexual mores were beyond her ability to accept. After six months, she had not found anyone to match her husband, whom she now missed more than ever.

Lynne, at 24, was the mother of a 2-year-old child. Her marriage to Tom three years earlier had come after knowing one another for only several months, and had been filled with problems from the start. Ever since high school, Lynne had thought about settling down and being a housewife like her mother. She had just barely managed to graduate from high school, had few marketable skills, and had taken a number of jobs in fast food restaurants in order to have some way to occupy her time. She disliked having to support herself, and preferred living at home and spending any money she did earn on clothes and entertainment. Overall, she seemed to be biding her time until the right man came along. When he finally did, in the form of an auto mechanic, she moved in with him after knowing him one month, and shortly thereafter they were married. Despite their frequent quarrels, they were always able to "kiss and make up"—sex between them was very satisfying and frequently followed one of their prolonged arguments. After a year of marriage, they decided to have a baby. Lynne was sure that a child was exactly what the marriage needed to make it stronger.

Unfortunately, the arrival of Lisa, their daughter, only made matters worse. Tom complained that Lynne cared more for the baby than for him. Lynne, on the other hand, could not understand why her husband spent so little time with Lisa, and why he was so impatient when she cried or in some way interrupted his plans. The couple bickered more than ever, and their sex life, once a certain way to reduce conflict and drain off tension between them, became infrequent and mechanical. When Tom began staying away from home for hours and then days at a time, it was clear to Lynne that nothing was left in their marriage and she sued for divorce.

Although Lynne was awarded custody (uncontested by Tom) and a small amount of child support money monthly, she soon realized that she needed to make some immediate decisions—where to live, how to get a job that paid enough so she could become the primary breadwinner, where to find babysitters, how to get adequate child care on her meager income. Her fears concerning Tom's ultimate unwillingness to pay child support soon proved to be well founded: his payments were late for the most part and often nonexistent. His visits with Lisa became less and less frequent, and finally stopped after a year or so, leaving Lynne with all the child-rearing responsibilities. The strain on Lynne became unbearable, financially, emotionally, socially. Within eight months she had moved back home with her parents. Her nighttime job as a cocktail waitress allowed her to be with Lisa during the afternoons; mornings and evenings, Lisa was cared for by the grandparents. Her work schedule made dating all but impossible for Lynne, although she occasionally went out with a customer when the bar closed.

These cases illustrate some of the major themes a counselor will encounter in assessing a single-parent household:

• Single-parent households are far more apt to involve women than men.

- Single parenthood is not necessarily a transitional stage on the way to remarriage, but rather a probable end point for many of today's families.

- The life-cycle stage of the single parent at the time of separation determines to a significant extent the problems that are likely to be confronted (for example, an older woman might become widowed or divorced at a time when her children are themselves having family or marital difficulties; a younger woman is likely to be beset with many problems of child care as well as economic survival).

- The age of the dependent children strongly influences the family's subsequent response and adaptation to separation. Widows are more likely to be older than divorced women and therefore, in general, are more likely to have older and thus more self-sufficient children; on the other hand, two-thirds of all women who divorce do so before age 30, and consequently most children are under age 7 at the time of divorce (Beal, 1980).

- The duration and degree of intimacy of the marriage influences postseparation adjustment. Separation later in life reduces the options, especially for a woman, of developing another long-term, close relationship; at the other extreme, very young parents, especially teenage mothers, probably have poorer parenting skills, and are economically and socially burdened in future relationships.

- Since three-fifths of all children (more than half of all black children) born today will, according to best estimates (Morrison, 1986), spend at least part of their childhood living with one parent, issues of child custody and visitation rights must be addressed and resolved.

- One-parent families have differing resources and differing levels of organization; the single parent's coping skills and sense of mastery of her situation will influence her ability to maintain family integration while adapting to changing environmental stresses and changing developmental needs of family members.

COMMON PROBLEMS IN SINGLE-PARENT-LED FAMILIES

After a divorce, as nuclear family ties are disrupted, various adjustments and rearrangements are called for. Most children, especially those below the age of 12, will live with a custodial mother; they may see their father on a regular weekly (in rare cases, daily) basis, intermittently, or not at all. Inevitably, the divorce and its immediate aftermath is a critical experience that affects the entire family system. No one is immune. The functioning and interactions of all of the members are changed permanently.

Hetherington, Cox, and Cox (1982) point to two factors that must be attended to in appraising the impact of the divorce. To begin with, the outcome of divorce will affect each member differently, depending on that individual's personal stresses, support systems, and coping strategies. Parents and children differ in their coping styles and abilities; children of different ages call upon different resources. These authors note that needs and adaptive strategies of different family members are not always compatible. Indeed, "the pathway to well-being for one family member may lead to a disastrous outcome for another" (p. 234).

Second, Hetherington, Cox, and Cox (1982) remind us that it would be a mistake to view divorce as an event occurring at a single point in time. Rather, an extended transition is usually required for parents and children alike. Moreover, in some families, the sequelae of divorce (emotional distress, denial, depression, anger, loss of self-esteem) occur immediately following parental separation; for others, these effects may increase over the first year and then abate; for still other families, such signs may not emerge until a considerable period of time has passed. The counselor, then, must always be aware that the point at which he or she taps into the family following divorce will largely determine its effects on all the members.

For pedagogical purposes, we will consider the impact of divorce on each set of family members—the custodial parent, the noncustodial parent, and the children—separately. In point of fact, of course, they cannot be so easily separated, and as part of a system each impacts on the other.

THE CUSTODIAL PARENT

Box 4.1 offers the counselor an overview of some typical problem areas to explore with custodial single parents.

Particularly for women raising young children alone,[2] economic impoverishment is more likely than not to be a daily fact of life. As Thompson and Gongla (1983) report, considerable evidence exists that low incomes, high rates of poverty, and fewer employment opportunities are characteristic in such situations. They contend that the major problem faced by women in such cases is not the lack of a male's presence but the lack of a male income.

Pearce (1978) has coined the phrase "feminization of poverty" to characterize the typical problems of such women, many of whom are unemployed and on welfare. Even among those who are fortunate enough to

---

2   Research on custodial fathers has been meager, probably because this situation is relatively new and still infrequent. For the discussion to follow, then, we will assume that the mother has physical custody of the children. In those cases where fathers achieve custody, it is likely to be decided out of court and by mutual consent of both parents. It should be noted, however, that some fathers are starting to gain custody through court battles, especially if they have remarried and the ex-spouse has not. Greif (1985) found that the father's better financial situation, emotional stability, or personality fit with the child were determining factors in such decisions.

Box 4.1. A Problem Appraisal Checklist for Custodial Single Parents

Custodial single parents may experience problems in the following areas:

- Change in economic status (for most, especially women, this translates into economic hardship)
- Grief, self-blame, loss of self-esteem, and depression
- Role overload (attempting to play a multitude of roles—such as organizing a household, caring for children, producing income—previously divided between both parents)
- Social stigma and disapproval over being divorced
- Disruption of customary living arrangements (may include change in residence, community, school district for children, and return to work force)
- Loneliness, feeling of social isolation, loss of friends (especially married couples), need to develop new social circle
- Lack of adequate support system (formerly provided by mate, in-laws, friends in old community)
- Strain from solo decision making (taking major or perhaps full responsibility for family decisions, unlike past experiences in which such judgments were likely to have been shared or at least discussed)
- Child care arrangements (depending on the age of the child or children of the parent working or returning to school, this may require considerable planning, energy expenditure, and flexibility in schedule, particularly in the case of illness of the child or parent)
- Interpersonal conflict (with children, ex-spouse, parents and ex-in-laws, babysitters, lovers, roommates)
- Sex and dating (new person introduced into family circle, decisions regarding resumption of a sex life, concern over reactions of children)
- Custody and visitation (continued relations with ex-spouse, concern over child's loyalty, upset as children are introduced to new friends or lovers of ex-spouse)

---

have a full-time job, Mednick (1987) estimates that women heading their own families have a poverty rate that is two and one-half times that of the two-parent family. Part-time and unemployed women workers are, of course, even worse off. Moving back as an adult and custodial parent to one's own parents' home, as we saw in the case just presented, is sometimes a makeshift solution, although it in itself may add other sources of stress.

Taking in lodgers to share expenses or moving in with other women in similar straits are other possible solutions, again with potential problems.

Norton and Glick (1986) summarize the economic circumstances of most one-parent families in general and mother-child families in particular as follows:

> By most objective measurements, the vast majority of these families hold a disadvantageous position in society relative to other family groups. They are characterized by a high rate of poverty, a high percentage of minority representation, relatively low education, and a high rate of mobility. In short, as a group, they generally have little equity of status in American society and constitute a group with usually pressing social and economic needs. (p. 16)

Mothers with sole custody (particularly if the father is closed out of the reorganized family system) are frequently overburdened by responsibilities and become depressed (Brandwein, Brown, & Fox, 1974). Belle (1982) notes that one in three female-headed households lives in poverty; those women who live in financially strained circumstances and who have responsibilities for young children are particularly prone to feelings of hopelessness, loss of energy, and depression.

Makosky (1982), a participant in the Stress and Families Project funded by the National Institute of Mental Health, found that low-income mothers with young children represent a particularly high-risk group for mental health problems. This group is constantly confronted with having to adjust to stressful life events, as we have indicated in Box 4.1. The group of women at greatest risk, however, are those who have endured the most difficult ongoing life conditions during the previous two years. According to Makosky's data, the critical attribute in the majority of cases is low income.

It is hardly a surprise to learn that money problems pose a severe stress on people, or that one result is often depression. Of more significance, psychologically speaking, may be the *change* in economic standing and the subsequent fear of losing control over one's own life as well as the lives of children for whom one feels responsible. When Bould (1977) interviewed mothers with sole custody whose situation was long-standing, she found that those women who had developed a stable income, regardless of amount, were more likely to have achieved higher self-esteem than those who stayed at home. As Mednick (1987) notes, the sense of control over income, combined with the feeling of being effective as a self-supporter, represent significant predictors of life satisfaction and reduced stress. Together, they help diminish the inevitable sense of powerlessness to which custodial mothers are so vulnerable, particularly in the period immediately following the divorce.

Hetherington, Cox, and Cox (1982) have this to report as the result of their two-year investigation of the impact of divorce on families (the Virginia Longitudinal Study of Divorce):

The main areas (for the custodial parent) in which change and stress were experienced were, first, those related to practical problems of living such as economic and occupational problems and problems in running a household; second, those associated with emotional distress and changes in self-concept and identity; and third, interpersonal problems in maintaining a social life, in the development of intimate relationships, and in interactions with the ex-spouse and child. (p. 244)

THE NONCUSTODIAL PARENT

Noncustodial parent roles vary widely, from a cessation of contact with ex-spouse and children (a closed boundary) to remaining a vital part of the family despite living separately (as in the binuclear family). Where any one person fits depends largely on his or her previous role in the family system, interest and availability, and the freedom of access he or she is permitted by the custodial parent.

In some cases, as Morawetz and Walker (1984) report, the level of fury toward the noncustodial spouse, who is seen as abandoning or betraying the marriage, is so great that the counselor will meet strong resistance when attempting to help the family work through their feelings about the divorce. In such situations, the absent spouse may be kept from the children on one pretext or another, or he or she may be scapegoated or called names ("untrustworthy," "cruel," "crazy") by the custodial parent. The custodial parent may attempt to coerce the children into showing loyalty to him or her by sharing his or her rage. Not only does this place the children in conflict, but it also forces the noncustodial parent into becoming an outsider. That parent's reaction, in defense, is to distance himself or herself from the family, sometimes confirming for the others his or her indifference and irresponsibility.

Box 4.2 is intended to alert the counselor to the possible problem areas to consider with noncustodial parents. Beyond the divorce itself, which may be a prolonged and often embittering process, the result in a great many cases leaves the noncustodial parent feeling deprived of ongoing involvement with the children. (The negative consequences of the separation for the children will be discussed in the following section.)

When Hetherington, Cox, and Cox (1976) studied the effects of divorce on noncustodial fathers, they found that of all the necessary adjustments, the most compelling was the pervasive sense of loss of the children. Particularly for those who had been highly involved, affectionate parents while married, many reported that they could not tolerate seeing their children only intermittently. Two years after the divorce, these fathers had diminished the frequency of their contact with their children in an effort to lessen their own unhappiness. Nevertheless, they continued to feel depressed and to mourn the loss. Greif (1979) also found in his study of

---

Box 4.2.   A Problem Appraisal Checklist for Noncustodial Parents

Noncustodial parents may experience problems in the following areas:

- Change in economic status (lowered living standard due to contributing to the support of two homes)
- Diminished relationship with one's children (pain over loss of day-to-day sense of what's happening in their lives)
- Feeling of devaluation as a parent (no longer feeling important and necessary in the lives of one's children)
- Disruption of customary living arrangements (change of residence, feeling of starting over, loss of friends)
- Necessity of learning to cope with new tasks (especially for men, having to provide own care, feeding, cleaning, and other services formerly provided by mother or wife)
- Development of new connections with children (including visitation activities, providing a space for children to spend the night, making purchases unilaterally that may provoke the ex-mate)
- Social stigma and disapproval over being divorced
- Necessity of dealing with recurrent memories whenever returning to pick up children
- Grief, self-blame, loss of self-esteem, and depression
- Loneliness, feeling of being at loose ends, need to develop new social circle
- Interpersonal conflict (with children, ex-spouse, parents and ex-in-laws, lovers, roommates)
- Necessity of learning to deal with events to which parents in intact families go together (school open house, graduation, weddings, funerals), especially when former partner has new mate
- Sex and dating (decisions regarding resumption of a sex life, concern over child meeting new lover, especially if that person has children)
- Custody and visitation (planning activities may be an unfamiliar experience, being sole caretaker may be difficult if young child is involved)

---

middle-class divorced fathers that many dealt with the pain of separation by distancing themselves from the children. Many of these men developed physical symptoms (weight loss, hypertension, headaches) following separation from their wives, and those who especially experienced the loss of their children manifested signs of depression (sleeping, eating, working, and socializing problems).

What of fathers who had limited contact with their children while the family was intact? Wallerstein and Kelly (1980a) discovered that their predivorce father-child connection was a poor predictor of their postdivorce relationship. In many cases they became closer to their children and more involved in their children's activities than they had been before the family reorganization. For most children, especially the younger ones, these researchers found such an increase in closeness to be particularly beneficial.

As we noted for custodial parents, the divorced father is most at risk for psychological disturbance around the time of the marital separation. **Crisis intervention** by the counselor may be necessary at that time, perhaps followed by more exploratory forms of counseling after the crisis has abated. Jacobs (1982) urges the counselor to try to remain flexible, shifting back and forth between treatment of the individual, the couple, and the entire family as needed. As he advocates, the counselor must remain aware that in most cases it is in the best interests of all family members that both parents be as actively engaged as possible with the children.

THE CHILDREN

Every family experiences impaired functioning during and after a divorce. Box 4.3 outlines some of results of the ordeal for children. The emotional impact of the experience is perhaps most telling for younger children (elementary-school age and below), precisely because they are not able to comprehend the events unfolding around them, while at the same time they sense the emotional upheaval in their parents, on whom they depend for their security (Kurdek, 1981). Such distress is likely to continue for a year or perhaps longer as the parents go through a period of mourning for the lost marriage.

In a long-term, comprehensive research undertaking, the California Children of Divorce Project, Wallerstein and Kelly (1974, 1975, 1976) studied the reactions of 60 divorced families over a five-year period. In all, 131 children, ages 2 to 18, took part. Age turned out to offer important clues about eventual adaptation to the divorce. While preschool children tended to react with denial ("It's not happening to me"; "When is daddy coming home?") and on the surface appeared to be untroubled, many were found on closer inspection to be anxious and self-blaming for the breakup of the family. Fears of abandonment, regression in toilet training, clinging behavior, and temper tantrums were common.

Slightly older children (7 or 8 years of age) were more apt to become withdrawn and uncommunicative about their feelings and to become depressed. School problems and difficulties in making new friends were common reactions. Those youngsters aged 9 or 10 at the time of family dissolution were more likely to be angry and ashamed and to verbalize

---

Box 4.3.   A Problem Appraisal Checklist for Children of Divorced Parents

Children may experience problems in the following areas when their parents divorce:

- Shame, embarrassment, lowered self-esteem
- Diminished relationship with noncustodial parent
- Self-blame for parental split
- Depression, sadness, moodiness, emotional withdrawal
- Conflicting loyalties (upset and anger over being caught between feelings for both parents)
- Continuing fantasies of parental reconciliation
- Anger and rage at both parents (blame of custodial parent for the other parent's absence; blame of noncustodial parent for leaving)
- Anxiety over an uncertain or unfamiliar future
- Parentification (prematurely pressed to act as adult, overattached to custodial parent, and as a surrogate parent to younger children)
- Lowered economic status
- Disruption of customary living arrangements (new school, new home, new friends)
- Antisocial behavior, poor school performance
- Adaptation to visitation activities
- Response to parent dating (diversion of parental attention to person outside previous family; fear of being replaced by parent's new friend)
- Fear of loss and abandonment if custodial parent is absent

---

blame at the parents for what they felt they were being put through. Adolescents as a group were more successful at making sense out of what had happened and why the marriage had failed; in many cases they even saw the decision by their parents as a good one.

In a follow-up study several years later, Wallerstein and Kelly (1980b) discovered considerable differences in how well the children had resolved their earlier experiences. To a significant extent their adjustment depended on how well the parents had worked out their discord following the divorce. In those instances where bitterness and conflict between the divorced couple continued (or perhaps even escalated), and where a parent sought alliances with the children against the ex-spouse, postdivorce adaptation was seriously impaired. In such cases, children's disturbed behavior patterns were more a reaction to what was going on at present than what had transpired in the past when the family was intact. For the 37 percent of the sample who showed clinical signs of depression, the war between the parents had continued into the postdivorce period.

On the other hand, both Wallerstein and Kelly (1980b) and Hetherington, Cox, and Cox (1982), who conducted a two-year longitudinal study of 144 white, middle-class families with children (half from divorced families, half from intact families; half girls, half boys) reach the same conclusion: to the extent that conflict between ex-spouses can be reduced and the noncustodial parent can remain involved and offer support to the ex-spouse, the children can get on successfully with their lives.

Hetherington, Cox, and Cox (1982) found, based on a study of mother-custody families, that families in which a divorce has occurred tend to encounter many more stresses than do nondivorced families, and correspondingly contain members who show more personal signs of disturbance. However, if the divorce is not compounded by continued adversity, both parents and their children (average age: 6 years) are likely to adjust to the new family situation, usually within two years. Adaptation is facilitated by an adequate support system; single mothers with sole custody who are exposed to prolonged pressures without such help may continue to show deleterious effects from the breakup of the family for a long time.

Counselors need to help single parents identify and develop effective support systems in order to aid in the transitions associated with the divorce process. Data from both Wallerstein and Kelly (1980b) and Hetherington and her associates (1982) suggest that as part of the family system, a child is influenced in his or her adaption to the family reorganization in the recovery period following divorce probably more by the nature of the ongoing interaction between the parents than by the divorce action itself.

Counselors should note, however, that boys living with custodial mothers typically have a more difficult time adjusting to separation and divorce than do girls. Compared to boys from nondivorced families, boys living with divorced mothers have been found to show more antisocial, acting out, coercive, and noncompliant behavior both at home and in school. In addition, boys from divorced homes have been found to exhibit difficulties in peer relationships as well as in school achievement. Girls from divorced homes, on the other hand, have been found to function well after the two-year crisis period, and generally experience positive relations with their custodial mothers.[3]

In a recent follow-up study of family relations six years after divorce, Hetherington (1987) expanded her sample to 180 families, including 124 of

---

3   As Hetherington (1987) acknowledges, there is some indication from other studies that children adjust better in the custody of same-sex parents. Age may also be a factor in sex-differential responses: reports of more severe, long-lasting disruption of behavior in boys than in girls following parental divorce generally come from studies of preadolescent children. Wallerstein (1988) has recently suggested that boys, especially young boys, may have a more difficult time immediately following a divorce, but girls from divorced homes actually may have more stormy adolescence and conflict-ridden entry into young adulthood.

the families from the original longitudinal study. In general, she found that custodial mothers who had not remarried had more emotional problems and were less satisfied with their lives than those who had never divorced or had divorced and remarried. Once again, Hetherington (1987) found that even after six years, divorced mothers continued to struggle "in intense, ambivalent relationships and in coercive cycles with their sons" (p. 203), whereas their relationships with their daughters tended to be positive ones. Many boys, now an average of 10 years of age, also showed behavioral problems such as noncompliant, impulsive, aggressive behavior.

CHILD CUSTODY, VISITATION, AND CHILD SUPPORT

The dissolution of a marriage by no means needs to signal the dissolution of the child's relationship with the nonresident parent. Increasingly, for a variety of legal as well as psychological reasons, the courts have deemed it best for all concerned that a shared custody arrangement be worked out, if at all feasible, between divorcing parents. In this way, the child continues to have the benefit of frequent contact with both parents; bitter, drawn-out custody battles are avoided; the nonresidential parent is more apt to remain involved (and to continue child support) rather than drift away or be kept away from the children; the incidence of kidnapping by a disgruntled, embittered parent who acts out his or her anger at the court or former mate by running off with the child is substantially reduced. Pressures on an overburdened single parent, possibly leading to child abuse, frequently are lessened when the responsibilities for child care are shared. Changing custody arrangements also permit women choices beyond the traditional ones of custodial mothers, without the social stigma or personal guilt formerly attached to women who chose to give up or share custody of their children.

Historically, before the 19th century, women and children were considered part of a man's property. Since the time of early English common law, the father as household head had been awarded child custody after a marriage breakup unless it could be established that he was an unfit parent. Such reasoning was based on fathers being economically better able to provide for their children (Derdeyn, 1976). That standard began to change in the latter half of the 19th century when the criterion of "tender years" was introduced into custody decisions. Mothers were now considered to be in a better position to provide for their children's welfare, particularly in the case of minor children of "tender years." In the United States, the dramatic increase in divorce rates as well as the corresponding liberalizing of social attitudes regarding alternative family lifestyles led to the altered custody law that in general used the criterion of "the best interest of the child" as a yardstick for such decisions. By the 1970s, the gender-based bias favoring

Table 4.2. Summary of U.S. Child Custody Laws by State (1984)

State	Psychological investigation may be ordered by court	Neither parent preferred because of that parent's sex	Joint[a] custody specifically allowed (if parents are suitable)	Access to child's records by non-custodial parent allowed	Similar relevant factors are used in determining custody	Wishes of the child considered by court	Parental conduct not affecting relationship with the child will not be considered	Grandparent visitation rights allowed
Alabama[b]								X
Alaska		X	X					
Arizona	X	X			X	X		X
Arkansas		X						
California[c]		X	X	X		X		
Colorado[d]	X	X	X		X	X	X	
Connecticut			X			X	X	X[e]
Delaware	X	X			X	X	X	X
Florida	X	X	X	X	X	X		X
Georgia	X		X			X[f]		X
Hawaii	X		X			X		X[e]
Idaho	X	X	X	X	X			X
Illinois[g]	X		X		X	X	X	X
Indiana	X	X	X		X	X		
Iowa			X			X		X
Kansas	X	X	X		X	X		X
Kentucky[d]	X	X	X		X	X	X	

(continued)

State	Psychological investigation may be ordered by court	Neither parent preferred because of that parent's sex	Joint[a] custody specifically allowed (if parents are suitable)	Access to child's records by non-custodial parent allowed	Similar relevant factors are used in determining custody	Wishes of the child considered by court	Parental conduct not affecting relationship with the child will not be considered	Grandparent visitation rights allowed
Louisiana		X	X	X				X
Maine[d]	X		X			X		
Maryland								
Massachusetts		X		X				
Michigan			X			X		X
Minnesota	X	X	X		X	X	X	X
Mississippi						X[g]		
Missouri		X			X	X		X
Montana	X		X	X	X	X		
Nebraska		X				X		
Nevada		X	X			X		
New Hampshire		X	X			X		X
New Jersey		X				X		X
New Mexico		X			X	X[f]		
New York		X						X

(continued)

Summary of U.S. Child Custody Laws by State (1984) (continued)

State	Psychological investigation may be ordered by court	Neither parent preferred because of that parent's sex	Joint[a] custody specifically allowed (if parents are suitable)	Access to child's records by non-custodial parent allowed	Similar relevant factors are used in determining custody	Wishes of the child considered by court	Parental conduct not affecting relationship with the child will not be considered	Grand-parent visitation rights allowed
North Carolina		X						X
North Dakota	X					X		X
Ohio	X		X		X	X[g]		
Oklahoma								
Oregon		X					X	
Pennsylvania	X		X	X				X
Rhode Island								X
South Carolina								
South Dakota		X				X		X
Tennessee						X		X
Texas		X				X		
Utah	X					X		X[c]
Vermont	X	X			X	X		

(continued)

State	Psychological investigation may be ordered by court	Neither parent preferred because of that parent's sex	Joint[a] custody specifically allowed (if parents are suitable)	Access to child's records by non-custodial parent allowed	Similar relevant factors are used in determining custody	Wishes of the child considered by court	Parental conduct not affecting relationship with the child will not be considered	Grand-parent visitation rights allowed
Virginia		X						X[c]
Washington	X				X	X	X	
West Virginia	X	X						X
Wisconsin	X	X	X		X	X		
Wyoming		X						

[a] A number of other states may allow joint custody, but do not so specify in their law (for example, Utah).

[b] If the wife abandons the husband, he may receive custody of the children over age 7. Also, the court may order an injunction to protect the safety of the wife or children if needed.

[c] Stepparents, relatives, or other interested parties may petition for visitation rights.

[d] If a parent leaves home because of spouse abuse or threat of spouse abuse, the leaving will not be considered abandonment and will not be held against the absent parent.

[e] Any person interested in a child's welfare may petition for visitation priviliges.

[f] Children over the age of 14 may choose which parent with whom to live.

[g] Children over the age of 12 may choose which parent with whom to live.

Source: Howell & Toepke, 1984, pp. 58-59.

maternal custody had begun to change once again, as more men sought custody for their children. Despite these recent changes, Bray (1988) contends that many men still insist that a sex bias favoring women as custodial parents exists.

Today, there is no uniform child custody law for the entire United States, although the laws in all of the states are similar in that a child's welfare and best interests are the prime factors in determining custody (Howell & Toepke, 1984). As noted in Table 4.2, as of 1984 the majority of states (28) held that neither parent is to be preferred over the other in awarding custody; the child's wishes were considered, although not binding, in 33 states; 22 states specifically provided for joint custody.

Custody decisions, along with determinations of child support payments and visitation rights for the nonresidential parent, are made during the divorce process (see Figure 4.1). A number of alternate arrangements, established by parental agreement or judicial decision, are possible. According to Schwartz (1987), they include **sole custody** (one parent is awarded total physical and legal responsibility for the children), **split custody** (each parent is awarded the custody of one or more of the children, or the children alternate living with the nonresidential parent on weekends or during vacations) and **joint legal custody** (both parents participate in the major decisions, such as religious upbringing or choice of school, for their children).

Sole custody, in most cases by the mother, remains the most common pattern despite recent increases in some fathers' efforts to participate with their children following divorce (Clingempeel & Reppucci, 1982). Under such an arrangement, fathers have visitation rights, plus any additional rights or privileges agreed upon in the divorce settlement.

Joint custody is an increasingly popular arrangement in which both parents have equal authority in regard to their children's general welfare, education, and parenting. In practice, it may take a number of forms. Generally speaking, the most common plan of joint custody is for the children to reside in one home and for the other parent to have access to them (rather than live with one parent and be visited by the other).

In some states, such as California, joint legal custody is presumed in all divorces unless a ruling to the contrary is made. As noted previously, under this arrangement each parent retains legal rights, privileges, and responsibilities as a parent. However, joint legal custody does not necessarily mean shared parenting on a daily basis. The child's primary residence is likely to remain with one parent, but the child may also live with or have access to the other parent at specified times.

In a variation of joint custody called **joint physical custody** (sometimes confused with joint legal custody), both parents take part in the day-to-day care of and decision making for their children, although the parents may live separately. The family continues to function as when they were intact, at least as far as the children are concerned. For the children's part, they may move between households every week or every month, or perhaps spend weekdays with one parent and weekends with the other; in some cases, they may even alternate during each week, spending three days with one parent, four days with the other, who usually lives in the same vicinity to permit the children to attend the same school. In relatively rare cases, the children remain in the family home while the parents take turns moving in or staying at another residence.[4] Joint physical custody obviously works only to the extent that the parents are able to cooperate and there is not a high level of conflict between them.

Although legal and physical custody arrangements are jointly agreed upon, in practice they may not work quite as neatly or be as conflict-free as we have outlined. Not unexpectedly, in some cases the arrangements made for custody, visitation rights, and child support payments simply provide additional arenas for battle between combatants, particularly those who remain intensely angry and bitter over what they perceive to be past injustices. Wallerstein (1986), in a more recent follow-up of the women from her California Children of Divorce Project, reported that anger associated with divorce can persist 10 years after dissolution of the marriage, even into remarriage; such chronic bitterness can continue to infuse interactions with the ex-mate in regard to the children. According to her data, the ongoing anger, rooted in a sense of outrage and betrayal, was especially prevalent in those women who had been married to their ex-mate for an extended period of their adult years.

Such sustained antagonism is not inevitable, of course, depending on how well previous problems can be resolved once the couple is apart, or perhaps merely accepted and lived with in order for both people to continue to be effective parents. In a large number of cases, a "declined relationship" (Duck, 1982) exists, with a moderate amount of interaction and shared information about issues related to the children, and perhaps even an element of friendship.

Ahrons and Rodgers (1987), referring to the binuclear family (two households, one family), observe five distinct types of relationships between former marital partners:

Perfect Pals: Still friends; jointly decided to live separate lives but retain mutual respect; in earlier generations would probably not have gotten divorced; may have had some anger during separation but now each

4 The controversy among experts over the relative merits of joint custody compared to sole custody continues today. Those in favor of the former emphasize the importance of the father's contribution to the child's ultimate well-being, citing evidence by Wallerstein and Kelly (1980a) and others. Their influence has been felt particularly on the West Coast; according to Richards and Goldenberg (1985), in Los Angeles in 1983, 45 percent of all awards gave joint custody, while an additional 7 percent awarded joint physical custody. East Coast legal thinking is more apt to be influenced by the writings of Goldstein, Freud, and Solnit (1979), who argue that children need continuity of psychological care from one parent and that shared parental decision making promotes conflict. Data offered by Richards and Goldenberg (1985) indicate that in New Jersey in 1983, only three reported decisions affirmed joint custody.

considers the other a responsible and caring parent; still in some conflict at times, but overall accommodating to one another.

Cooperative Colleagues: No longer good friends but able to cooperate successfully as parents; may no longer like each other in many ways but recognize need to compromise for the sake of the children and to fulfill own desires to be active and responsible parents; some current disagreements but able to avoid escalating power struggles.

Angry Associates: Still bitter and resentful about the marriage and the divorce process; continuous fights over finances, visitation schedules, custody arrangements; each continues parenting but children often caught in ongoing loyalty conflicts.

Fiery Foes: No ability to coparent; intense anger, even years after divorce; perceive one another as enemies; each parent may have limited parenting ability; continuing legal battles; children caught in the middle and forced to take sides; noncustodial parent probably sees children with decreasing frequency over the years.

Dissolved Duos: Discontinued contact between former partners after divorce; one partner may leave geographic area; kidnapping by noncustodial parent may occur; truly single-parent family.

These authors offer the following illustration of the reactions of each of the relationship types to a child's high school graduation: (1) Perfect Pals plan dinner together, sit together during the ceremony, perhaps give one joint gift; (2) Cooperative Colleagues both attend the ceremony, and if sitting together do so under some strain; (3) Angry Associates celebrate separately with the child, sit separately at the ceremony, and avoid contact as much as possible; (4) Fiery Foes exclude one parent from the celebration and perhaps from the ceremony itself, leading the excluded parent to feel hurt and angry; (5) Dissolved Duos do not bother informing the noncustodial parent of the graduation, nor would he or she acknowledge the event if aware of it.

SOME COUNSELING GUIDELINES

Working therapeutically with a single-parent-led family, the counselor must remain aware of the psychological presence of the other parent, even if, as is likely, that person is physically absent from the consultation room. To ignore the "ghosts" of the earlier marriage by focusing on the parent-child dyad alone, is to ignore that the absent person (or the memories of that person) may continue to exert considerable influence on what transpires between those presently attending.

After a bitterly fought divorce, in which Linda would settle for nothing less than sole custody of Craig, their 12-year-old only child, she soon found that the boy was only adding to her unhappiness. He was a constant reminder, in appearance, mannerism, voice, and behavior, of his father. To make matters worse, the more she vilified her ex-husband, the more Craig defended him and complained about not having him near anymore. Whenever Craig was with his dad, his dad told him what a miserable person his mother had been to live with, attempting to justify his departure to his son. The pressures from both parents for his undivided loyalty began to take their toll on Craig, who became sullen, angry, and withdrawn. Soon a battle began to rage between mother and son; he became increasingly defiant and she continued issuing gloomy forecasts to him about how he would turn out to be just like his father. Counseling for the two focused on working through previously unexpressed feelings about the divorce on both of their parts, and creating a less bitter home environment. The father attended several sessions and, while his relationship with his ex-wife was no more loving, they were able to tolerate one another better and not use Craig to get back at one another.

On the other hand, the "ghost" may be the spouse who met an untimely death:

Hilda and Charles had had a solid and loving marriage for 14 years when he succumbed to cancer. Although the death was by no means sudden, his dying having stretched out over a year and one-half, Hilda felt devastated when it actually occurred. Beyond missing him terribly and trying to cope with life without him, she felt unprepared to manage by herself. Charles had made few demands on her, and seemed to take care of everything—the car, paying bills, banking, repairs around the house, vacation planning, and so on. Now all decisions were up to her. However, fearful of facing the world on her own, she began to rely more and more on her 12-year-old son, Paul, as a partner, often blurring generational boundaries and burdening him with decisions far beyond his capacity or experience to make. In one sense, she was keeping her husband's memory alive, behaving as though nothing had changed from before Charles's death. At the same time she was not allowing Paul to grow up and pursue a life of his own nor herself to learn to become self-sufficient. When both Paul and his mother sensed that something was wrong, they sought counseling. The counselor was understanding of the sudden burden thrust upon Hilda, and also of the fact that the father's death had somehow brought mother and son closer. However, he also helped them see some negative consequences from their enmeshed behavior patterns. Both needed to complete their mourning and get on with their lives; parent-child boundaries needed to be clarified; remaining intertwined hampered the process. Together they were able to let go of one another sufficiently so that they could remain available to offer support and encouragement to one another but at the same time begin to pursue separate lives.

The first case illustrates how some people may be legally and physically separated, but are hardly finished fighting with one another. As we can see, the children of these Angry Associates often feel caught in the middle—loyalty to one means disloyalty to the other—and are in a no-win situation until the parents resolve or at least diminish their conflicts. Otherwise, the children may remain the long-term recipients of any unfinished business between their parents.

In the second case, we are dealing with a **parentified child** forced to give up his chance to be a child and to take on parental executive responsibilities without the knowledge or ability to carry them off successfully. He may become overly serious and prematurely burdened, overworked and undervalued, the recipient of confidences inappropriate for his stage of development, alienated from peers at school, missing a childhood in which to learn to have fun and engage in age-appropriate activities.

These cases too point up the fact that the counselor is most likely to see a custodial mother and her child when the latter is in trouble (with the school, the police) or becomes symptomatic (sullen, withdrawn) or when parent-child conflicts become chronic and seemingly unresolvable. Otherwise, the woman's everyday life is probably too cluttered with work, child-care arrangements, and domestic as well as financial pressures to allow her the luxury of counseling.

In addition to the single mother's lacking the motivation or the money or simply the energy for counseling, a number of other roadblocks hinder easy entry by the counselor into the family system. With an intact, two-parent family, as Fulmer (1983) points out, the family counselor can rely on the inherent strength or excitement of a revived or reunited parental dyad to alter the rules of the family system. Here, however, no such relationship exists. Instead, a rebellious adolescent may be difficult to reach at first, while a younger child has fewer resources to call upon. Neither is helpful in facilitating a therapeutic atmosphere at the start of the experience. So, more often than not, according to Fulmer, the counselor must begin any clinical interventions with the mother, who has little inclination or wherewithal to take on new (counseling) projects outside the home. The mother's depression noted earlier in this chapter thus becomes a problem to be dealt with early in the counseling if progress with the family is to be made.

A number of counseling approaches have been proposed: brief strategic family counseling (Bray & Anderson, 1984); structural family counseling (Weltner, 1982); a combined psychodynamic-strategic approach (Morawetz & Walker, 1984); and a skills-building psychoeducational approach (Levant, 1988). Bray & Anderson contend that a brief technique is especially applicable to single-parent situations because their problems usually represent difficulty in making a transition from one family life-cycle stage and structure to another. Because finances are usually limited, short-term treatment is particularly cost-effective. They offer several examples (for example, overburdened families, families with unresolved divorce issues) of successfully reframing family problems in a more constructive and acceptable framework to change the family's perceptions of the presenting problem.

Weltner (1982) points out that the single mother faces numerous problems, as we have noted throughout this chapter, and that their combined weight may overburden her, undermining her competence and sense of self-esteem. Thus, he argues, the counselor's first concern must be to make sure that she adequately performs her executive function as family head. Recognizing that her countless tasks (providing family meals, maintaining family routines, protecting the children, managing the budget, disciplining and guiding her offspring, and so on) may collectively be beyond the energies of a single parent (particularly if, as is likely, she must work outside the home), Weltner urges that supportive help be directed at aiding her to expand the executive system.

In the following case, an ex-client of the counselor contacts him again several years after the previous counseling had terminated:

Rosemary and Jack met at church when each was 20 years old, and after going steady for a year they married. Both had few social experiences with others, and seemed to be drawn to one another primarily because each was unhappy at home. Jack lived with a widowed mother who drank and was physically abusive to him. Rosemary's parents were together, but were busy professionals who had little time for her. Whether by design or because of their demanding schedules, they neglected her and provided poor models for her regarding parenting. Jack and Rosemary had a brief and conflict-ridden marriage. Each had an insatiable need for attention, and neither knew how to give attention or much love back. By the time they contacted a counselor, their relationship had deteriorated to the point where little was left of the marriage, and after five sessions they agreed to separate and obtain a divorce.

The counselor did not hear from either of them for two years, at which time Rosemary called to say she had met someone at work (both were newspaper reporters) whom she wanted him to meet. James, 30, turned out to be an intelligent, hardworking, driven person who seemed to neglect his appearance and, for that matter, his health. While he seemed to care a great deal for Rosemary, he admitted to her and the counselor that he had a drinking problem, and while he had stopped drinking for the last six months, he could not guarantee that he would not start again. Rosemary claimed that it made no difference, that his love was all she cared about, and that because they would love one another the drinking would take care of itself. Despite efforts by the counselor to get them to explore some of these issues further, Rosemary insisted she had met the man she wanted to marry. The drinking issue, to plague their marriage later, thus never got resolved. The counselor, reluctant to terminate the sessions without dealing with the drinking, left them with an open invitation to keep in contact.

Rosemary sent the counselor Christmas cards and, over the years, announcements of the birth of her two children, Joey and Max. In one note she mentioned that James had tired of newspaper reporting, and in order to pursue his interest in fine wines, had bought a liquor store that he would run. Several years passed, and the yearly notes stopped. The counselor lost touch with them, although he continued from time to time to wonder what had happened to them, and especially if James could handle being around liquor all day.

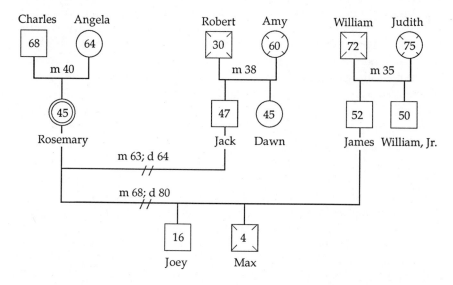

Figure 4.2. Genogram of Rosemary's case.

A full ten years passed before Rosemary once again called for help. She seemed to have aged considerably over that time, not surprisingly, considering the story she had to tell. She had endured a number of hardships, but two in particular were devastating. The first concerned the death of Max, at age 4, when a babysitter failed to stop him from running into the street after a ball and being hit by a car. While this had happened six years earlier, it was clear from her telling of the event that she had never fully recovered from the loss, and continued to grieve. James's periodic drinking became more serious after Max's death. Their marriage, already weakened by James's drinking and neglecting his business, could not survive the death of their child, and several months thereafter James moved out. By this time, he was unable to control the drinking, nor was he able to hold a job. He lived with various friends or family members for several days at a time and held odd jobs for short periods between bouts of drinking.

Rosemary's presumed reason for calling was to bring the counselor up to date, and to seek help for her loneliness. She was desperate for companionship, but at the same time fearful of involving herself with a man again. She blamed herself for her situation, and said she could understand if no man would ever want to be with her. She felt very much alone in raising Joey (now 16), and had few friends to turn to for support. Her parents, never very supportive, were now elderly and even less available than before. With the counselor's help, she did begin to socialize by attending Parents Without Partners meetings. While the depression seemed to lift, she began to tell of her problems with Joey, especially her feelings that she did not know how to raise him by herself, did not have sufficient parenting skills, and wished James or someone (the counselor?) would rescue her.

Joey evidently was a school truant, spending countless days looking for his father along Skid Row. He had also been in trouble with the police over numerous speeding tickets he had failed to pay. Rosemary insisted it all was beyond her ability to cope, and that Joey could drop out of high school and go off on his own if he wanted to, as long as she did not have to take care of him. The counselor wanted Joey to attend the sessions with his mother, but he refused. He stayed away from home some nights, took money from her purse, emptied his bank account to spend money on his friends. Rosemary felt incompetent to control the situation.

The counselor began by helping her explore her relationship with her parents, to help her gain some understanding of why there was a deficit in the parenting she received growing up. As counseling proceeded, it became clearer that the parents, like Rosemary herself, lacked nurturing skills but were not uncaring as she had believed. Caught up in the same situation, she was able to understand them better, and to begin to forgive them. On a more practical note, she was also able to call on them to help her in small ways with Joey, especially when she was away from home on a work assignment. Her newly enhanced relationship with them made her feel less alone.

The counselor thus focused his efforts on building family resources and helping Rosemary develop a support network, while also providing aid in reestablishing her as family head. He and she worked on improving her coping skills and gaining a sense of control or mastery over what was happening to her and Joey. As she began to reorganize the family, she began to monitor his activities more closely, to demand they do more things together, that they eat their meals together every night, that she go to school to determine just what was happening there. She no longer left her purse out for him to open and remove money, as she had done before. She talked to Joey about her new social life, and brought her new boyfriend for him to meet. She encouraged Joey to talk to her about his problems, to go with her to meetings for children of alcoholics, to bring his friends home if he so wished. For the first time she told him about her life with James, something she had deliberately kept from him before, and invited him to tell about his feelings about their divorce.

As Rosemary assumed an executive function as family head, she began to divide family responsibilities with her son. However, she was careful to maintain generational distinctions and not cross generational boundaries with him. Although there were only two of them, a hierarchical structure was established and maintained. Her newly developed sense of empowerment seemed to help Joey understand the new family organization and his place in it. Each learned to respect the other's privacy and not to intrude. After eight months of counseling, the workable alliance established between Rosemary and Joey was holding, and counseling terminated.

In this case as in others, the single mother may need therapeutic help in developing a support system. She might, like Rosemary, be encouraged to restructure the family by assigning her children certain supportive tasks or chores around the house, under her guidance, each according to age and appropriate skills. Other restructuring, as in this case, may involve extended family members, such as grandparents, who may also be pressed into service, once again under the mother's direction and periodic surveillance. In both cases it is essential that generational boundaries not be blurred. This may be especially difficult if working mother and children live in grandmother's house, where the mother may run the risk of losing her executive function to the more available person. Under these circumstances, it may be necessary for the counselor to include the grandparents in some family sessions, to help define roles and place the mother back in charge of her children.

The mother-led family also should be encouraged to seek the help of resources beyond the family. Friends, members of church congregations, co-op baby sitter groups, single-parent groups such as Parents Without Partners,[5] employer-sponsored child care groups, and various women's organizations may all offer exactly the kind of aid a beleaguered single mother needs. An even minimally involved ex-spouse who helps out in emergencies or on weekends or one weeknight can offer considerable comfort and support.

5 A number of organizations offer social as well as educational events for divorced parents and their children. The largest is probably Parents Without Partners, with over 1000 chapters in all 50 states and a number of foreign countries, and with a membership of 200,000 single parents.

In their work with single-parent-led families, Morawetz and Walker (1984) begin by attempting to involve all those present in the counseling process. One early task is to assess the family structure (who is the spokesperson, who is silent, who seems resistant, what coalitions appear to exist, and so on). As they carefully join the family, they begin the process of reorganizing family interaction patterns. The family, which comes to counseling with their own linear explanations of the problem (A happened, which caused B to occur), has to be taught to think in terms of circular causality, in which the problem stems from input from the family as an interacting unit. Helping the family to begin to think of themselves in systems terms may facilitate later interventions aimed at specific family structural changes necessary to alleviate the symptomatic behavior in a family member.

In the matter of conflict between custodial parents and children, Morawetz and Walker (1984) suggest a number of possible scenarios requiring therapeutic intervention:

- When a child is seen as the embodiment of the absent parent, either as a reminder of the denounced parent or as a permanent memory and symbol of the deceased parent (see the two cases earlier in this chapter that refer to "ghosts" from a previous marriage).
- When a parent "marries" his or her child. (In an effort to compensate for the loss following dissolution of a marriage, single parents frequently replace their marital partnership to some extent by developing a closer partnership with their children, sometimes leading to confusion over hierarchical boundaries. Children may be treated as intimate confidantes by a lonely mother one moment and as disobedient children the next.)
- When a child is seen as an overwhelming burden (particularly in the case of the custodial parent who is unable or unwilling to let go of the anger or grief or self-pity, and who perceives any effort by the child to gain attention or be comforted as an intrusion that is resented).
- When perspective is lost in the struggle for survival. (In this case, unreasonable and excessive demands may be made on the child to grow up faster than his or her peers and to understand just what the parent is experiencing. Under such circumstances, the child's appropriate feelings of sadness, anger, or divided loyalties may be hidden or disguised, and an unhappy and uncommunicative child may present problems, as in the case of Rosemary, earlier in the chapter.)
- When the burden of guilt (for having put the parent's desires for ending the marriage ahead of the needs of the children) impedes effective functioning. (Unresolved, difficulties in disciplining may lead to family turmoil.)

- When reentry into the social scene is experienced as a return to adolescence (particularly difficult if one's own teenager is at a similar developmental stage, causing an unstable parent-child hierarchy).
- When the single parent becomes dependent on the family of origin (reawakening old conflicts between dependency needs and wishes to be independent).

Under these or other circumstances, the counselor's role may go beyond traditionally defined counseling, sometimes extending into intervening on the parent's or entire family's behalf with a school, camp, or welfare counselor. Here the counselor must proceed cautiously, for two reasons: (1) to avoid permanently weakening and thus undermining the parent's executive activities; (2) to avoid being drawn into the family's neediness and willingness to listen by assuming the permanent role of the absent parent. The family needs to be helped to reorganize in order to reduce their stress, and for the counselor then to pull back, encouraging the mother to seek other adult relationships and the children to spend time with their peers.

Single-parent families pass through a number of predictable stages, according to Morawetz and Walker (1984): (1) the aftermath of the divorce; (2) the family regrouping or realignment; (3) the reestablishment of a social life; and (4) successful separation of parent and child. In their therapeutic work with single-parent-led families, these authors found that families who seek help in the wake of their divorce frequently experience rage, despair, overwhelming anxiety, and a sense that they will not be able to cope with the problems they must suddenly confront. The counselor can offer some first aid in stabilizing the family system at this point, by joining them temporarily as they regroup. (The risk of the counselor's stepping in as family rescuer is greatest at this phase of counseling.) Morawetz and Walker suggest that the counselor is most helpful here in assisting the family as they attempt to make sense out of some of the issues that led to the marital breakup and to help them begin the mourning process for the loss of the family.

The success with which the family can deal with its grief and bitterness in the aftermath of the divorce, and the speed with which it can be helped to develop self-esteem and overcome feelings of helplessness, sets the stage for phase 2, realignment. Now the counselor must facilitate the family's learning to adjust to the new reality brought about by the absent parent. The counselor can play a key role at this point, usually a stormy period, as the family is helped to accept as permanent the painful and unwelcome fact of the dissolution of the family as they have known it. Morawetz and Walker describe as common the surfacing of anger and violence, often on the part of the children, during this therapeutic phase, perhaps providing a symptom that serves to pull the custodial parent out of a depression or to signal to the noncustodial parent that the family needs his or her return.

By now, if counseling is successful, the children have learned to live with one parent or to accommodate to two households, and the custodial parent has abandoned any prior hope of reconciliation. In phase 3 of their counseling, the family begins to look toward the future, including seeking new social relationships. Dating by the single parent may prove disruptive to the children, who are apt to view this new development as a further loss of parental availability and possibly as behavior disloyal to the absent parent. By phase 4, the counselor is likely to be attempting to expedite the successful separation of parent and child from the bonding that followed the divorce, so that each may move on with their lives. This relinquishing of parent-child attachments may lead to an unbalancing of the family system, and the counselor may expect a period of intense feelings. Morawetz and Walker warn that truancy, delinquency, perhaps even teenage pregnancy may occur, all efforts to disrupt change, delay separation, and ensure a return to the earlier parent-child involvement.

In a somewhat different therapeutic approach, a number of counselors such as Levant (1988) have designed psychoeductional and skills-training programs to remediate specific family problems and in the process enhance aspects of family living. Generally brief or time-limited, didactic/experiential programs such as the Fatherhood Project at Boston University aim to promote family functioning by teaching fathers, often single custodial parents, how to improve their communication skills with their children. In particular, men wishing to develop a more nurturing role, but with few previous experiences or with poor role models from their own fathers, are offered an opportunity to enroll in courses where they learn various communication skills such as listening and responding to their children's feelings, and expressing their own feelings in a constructive manner. A basic understanding of child development and child management is also taught, from both the perspective of the child and of the father.

Levant (1988) employs a skills-training format, with participants role playing situations from their own family experiences, being videotaped for instant playback to them, and filling out workbook exercises at home with their children. The program is voluntary, offered as an educational experience for men who wish to improve their empathic sensitivity to what transpires in their interactions with their children. The Fatherhood Project thus provides a combined didactic/experiential series of group meetings in which, if successful, fathers undergo a cognitive restructuring regarding their views of ideal family life. The program is currently being expanded to include single parents of either sex, divorced parents with joint custody, stepparents and their spouses, and those couples about to become parents.

In our final example of counseling a single parent, an unwed working-class mother calls for help:

◆◆◆

Tammy contacted a counselor in the small university community in which she lived, ostensibly for guidance with her stepchild, Jolie. The counselor suggested that both Tammy and her husband come in together, and after some hesitation Tammy agreed. Although she and Brad gave different last names, it was not until ten minutes into the interview that the counselor realized that the couple was unmarried. The "stepchild" referred to over the telephone turned out to be Brad's daughter, Jolie, 7, from a previous marriage, who visited them during summer breaks from her school. In addition, Tammy and Brad had a child together, Rebecca, 4. Before the close of the first counseling session, it was clear to all three participants that Tammy had a more serious problem in mind than the one regarding Jolie; she was forcing a showdown with Brad regarding his degree of commitment to their relationship, especially whether he intended to marry her.

Subsequent sessions revealed that Tammy's and Brad's backgrounds could hardly have been more dissimilar. She was from a large working-class family from West Virginia, had dropped out of high school after one year, and had travelled to California on her own at age 17 to get away from an abusive father. After a series of odd jobs, she found work as a waitress at a restaurant near the university. Brad, on the other hand, came from an upper-middle-class northeastern WASP family, had been educated in private schools, and was now about to receive his doctorate in public health. Soon after they met at the restaurant, they began dating, and within three months were living together. Rebecca was born about one year later.

Although Tammy and Brad had now been together for five years, his parents knew nothing of Tammy's existence, nor of their grandchild. Brad had also taken great pains to hide her from all but his closest friends at school, telling himself that he was embarrassed by her poor grammar, her lack of sophistication, and what he considered to be her tendency to sound ignorant and uninformed. While Tammy did complain from time to time about such treatment, she was not someone who expected very much from life, and seemed more than willing to accept Brad's explanation that he was trying to work things out, and that it was only a matter of time before they married.

Tammy was able to get in touch with her anger and resentment early in the counseling sessions. She was furious and hurt that Brad denied her existence to his family and friends, and that he never publicly claimed Rebecca as his daughter. Although she loved Brad, she expressed her bitterness over feeling "tricked" into having a baby when he apparently had no intention of ever marrying her. Brad responded somewhat intellectually at first, trying to appear "modern" and thus not hampered by marriage certificates since "they were nothing more than useless scraps of paper." However, he did acknowledge his love for Tammy, but expressed his bewilderment over how to satisfy her as well as his family. After two months of joint counseling, Brad did finally agree to marry Tammy and to tell his parents that Rebecca was his child, despite his anticipation that they would never approve. Tammy, however, by now was sufficiently angry and disappointed by his behavior and past unkept promises, that she insisted they separate.

Tammy lived alone with Rebecca, and the counselor saw them together for two sessions. Rebecca, who carried her father's name, did not seem to feel too stigmatized, especially since they lived in a community where divorce was fairly common and she was not the only child in her class without a father at home. She did not know that her parents had never married. Brad did send money to support her, and visited her regularly before he graduated and took a job at a midwestern university. Within a year, however, he had met a woman with two children and married her, and his money to Tammy and Rebecca became sporadic and finally ceased.

Tammy continued to see the counselor from time to time, and eventually was encouraged to return to school. She obtained the equivalent of a high school diploma before registering at a local junior college to become a Licensed Vocational Nurse. She did expand her social life, and did manage to place Rebecca in a good child care facility after school, but life for Tammy continued to be hectic. She had periodic bouts of depression, and felt particularly alone and desperate at these times. Despite the counselor's support and encouragement, Tammy found herself with few options, little money, and no apparent prospects for the future's being brighter. She eventually moved to North Carolina where her cousins lived, and found a job at the local hospital. She never told anyone that she had never married, nor did anyone appear to assume this to be the case. Although her life was far from being fulfilled, she was managing, according to the periodic letters sent to the counselor, to support herself and her child and had regained some sense of self-esteem.

In this case, the counselor initially helped the clients determine the real problems they were having, necessary before they could begin to resolve their conflicts. By offering support and understanding, largely absent in Tammy's life, she joined the family system and provided some model for self-sufficiency. Such support seemed essential to the counselor if she was to help Tammy think out important life decisions. The counselor encouraged Tammy to develop marketable skills in order to help her build self-esteem. Finally, Tammy was helped to reconnect to another family system that would offer the support of an extended family. The overwhelming survival issues many single parents face are such that counseling may at times be primarily supportive while the parent gains the wherewithal to reunite with a more real and more permanent support system.

SUMMARY

Despite the fact that divorce has become a familiar phenomenon of American life, it is still viewed as representing a failure by many members of society, and single-parent-led families are often seen as flawed. Such families are not necessarily a homogeneous group; they are formed by death, desertion, as well as divorce, although in recent years separation and divorce have become the leading causes for the formation of these families. The counselor needs to understand the manner in which single parenthood occurred, the stage in the marriage in which it took place, as well as the number and age of the children involved.

Divorce is by definition disruptive to all family members. The custodial parent, still most likely to be the mother, faces a wide range of practical problems (finances, role overload, child care arrangements) as well as emotional distress connected with his or her loss of self-esteem, grief, and loneliness. The noncustodial parent must cope with many changes surrounding his or her customary living arrangements, although the most probable adjustment difficulty revolves around his or her sense of loss of the children, loneliness, and loss of previous social supports. Impaired functioning of children is common following divorce, with elementary-age or younger ones most vulnerable to distress. Boys living with custodial mothers tend to have a particularly difficult time adjusting after separation and divorce. The extent to which the parents remain involved with, and offer support to, one another, largely determines the extent to which the children make a successful adaptation to the divorce and get on with their lives.

Child custody decisions today increasingly favor shared arrangements between parents as being in the child's best interests. Joint custody, sometimes including the physical movement back and forth between parental households as in binuclear families, has become more common.

Counselors must be aware of the psychological presence of the absent parent in working with a single-parent family. Such families run the risk of creating a parentified child as an absent parent's substitute. The counselor, too, may have to deal with the single parent's depression and fear of reentering the world outside the home. Several counseling approaches (brief strategic family counseling, structural family counseling, a skills-building psychoeducational program) have been proposed for working with single-parent-led families. In general, they attempt to strengthen the executive function of the family head, to restructure the family by helping the children take on supportive tasks, to help develop an outside support group, and to teach custodial and noncustodial parents alike new skills aimed at remediating specific family problems.

Chapter 5

◆◆◆

Counseling the Remarried Family

Overall, as Ihinger-Tallman and Pasley (1987) observe, Americans seem to demonstrate an inherent "marriage bias." They enter first marriage at a greater rate than people in most other countries; they also appear to have higher expectations of the marital unit, so much so that they are prepared to abandon the relationship if it proves unfulfilling and to try again to find satisfaction, as evidenced by a higher remarriage rate than couples in other Western nations. In what Furstenberg (1987) refers to as American society's general acceptance of "conjugal succession," couples today are expected to stay together only as long as their marriage is emotionally gratifying. If one or both mates find that no longer the case, the partners are permitted, or sometimes even encouraged (particularly when the couple is childless), to break the marriage contract and search for someone who might provide greater emotional gratification. Most marriages (about three out of five) do involve children, however, and, according to Furstenberg's calculations, probably a third of all children growing up today will be part of a stepfamily before they reach adulthood. Glick (1984c), a demographer, goes so far as predicting that stepfamilies will be the predominant American family form by the turn of the century.

As for the experience of living as a single parent (see the previous chapter), it is temporary for many divorced people, especially in the middle class. Three out of five eventually remarry (three-quarters of divorced women and five-sixths of divorced men); about half do so within three years of their divorce (Glick, 1980). Remarriages after divorce are most likely to occur between the ages of 25 and 44, the median period being somewhere in one's early thirties. Not surprisingly, remarriage after widowhood occurs considerably later—between the ages of 45 and 64, more probably in one's early sixties. One of the interesting findings of Glick's research is that the odds of remarrying for both men and women in early middle age are greater if their earlier marriage ended in divorce rather than through death of a spouse.

According to Cherlin and McCarthy's (1985) analysis of census data, in 1980 there were between 9 and 10 million remarried households in the United States. In approximately a third, the wife had been married before; in a third, only the husband had been previously married; and in the remaining third, both spouses had previously been married and divorced. Glick (1980) discovered that better-educated and financially well-off men were most likely to remarry quickly; on the other hand, the higher a woman's educational level and income, the less likely she was to remarry. (Perhaps, as we noted in the previous chapter, in some cases the divorced woman trying to raise her children alone may feel the financial pinch without the support of her husband's income and may seek to remarry to regain that support; on the other hand, autonomous and economically self-sufficient women may not feel that need, and for that reason choose not to remarry.)

A successful remarriage has a great deal to offer adults and children alike. For adults, the experience can help rebuild self-esteem and a sense of being a worthwhile person capable of loving and being loved. Wiser as a result of the earlier failed experience, the adult has a second chance to form a more mature, more stable relationship, as well as "an opportunity to parent and to benefit from a supportive suprasystem.... Children can learn to appreciate and respect differences in people and ways of living, can receive affection and support from a new stepparent and the new suprasystem, and can observe the remarried parent in a good and loving relationship, using this as a model for their own future love relationships" (Crohn, Sager, Brown, Rodstein, & Walker, 1982, p. 162). After witnessing a destructive marital relationship, children may now observe positive and mutually enhancing interactions between adults.

On the other hand, a failed second try can lead adults to a renewed sense of defeat, self-blame, and frustration. Children may confirm for themselves that good and caring relationships are short-lived if they exist at all. Without a doubt, many adults enter a second marriage with fewer illusions or romantic expectations, and presumably experience some internal pressure to work harder to make the marriage work this time. Yet, despite a personal familiarity with the possible anguish and family upheaval brought about by the dissolution of a marriage, remarrieds divorce at a somewhat higher rate than for first marriages (Glick, 1980).

In an effort to convince others (and themselves) of their sexual desirability as well as their ability to be successfully married, divorced people may choose new partners who turn out to be all too similar to their ex-mates (for example, alcoholics), or more accurately, persons with whom they develop and maintain similar interactive patterns. Perhaps they have been psychologically fortified by their earlier experience to go through with what must be done to dissolve an unhappy union, or perhaps they are unwilling, having forged a sense of independence between marriages, to relinquish or compromise their position or accede to the demands of a new mate for too little in return. In many cases, the higher probability of divorce simply reflects the complexities involved in adjusting to a family structure that includes stepchildren and adults who must deal with two households (Jacobson, 1987). In other instances, financial burdens aggravated by the need to help support two households, including making alimony and/or child support payments, may prove the ultimate undoing of a remarried relationship. For whatever reasons, remarriers are about 10 percent more likely to get redivorced (56 out of 100) than are those who are divorcing for the first time (49 out of 100) (Weed, 1980).

VARIETIES OF REMARRIED FAMILY STRUCTURES

Remarriage following divorce has become a familiar marker event in the lives of many people in recent years. Although remarriage itself is hardly a new phenomenon, in the past its main purpose was to mend families fragmented by the premature death of a parent, restoring the domestic unit to its original nuclear or intact structure. Today, as Furstenberg (1980) contends, most remarriages follow divorce rather than death, and thus the surrogate parent augments rather than supplants the biological parent.

One consequence of this relatively new structural change, according to this family researcher, is that we have not as yet developed an adequate set of beliefs, or a language, or rules for this family form in which there are "more than two parents," despite the fact that more than 40 percent of all marriages today involve at least one partner who has been previously married. The blending together of two families is a complex and difficult process at best; the absence of clear-cut ground rules (for example, how to discipline stepchildren, whether loyalty to one parent means disloyalty to

Table 5.1. Twenty-four Possible Remarried Family Combinations

	Woman Previously Single	Woman Divorced or Widowed, No Children	Woman Divorced or Widowed, Custodial	Woman Divorced or Widowed, Non-custodial	Woman Divorced or Widowed, Both Custodial and Noncustodial
Man previously single	N.A.	1	2	3	4
Man previously divorced or widowed, no children	5	6	7	8	9
Man previously divorced or widowed, custodial children	10	11	12	13	14
Man divorced or widowed, non-custodial children	15	16	17	18	19
Man divorced or widowed, both custodial and non-custodial children	20	21	22	23	24

Source: Sager et al., 1983, p. 65.

the other, what to call an absent parent's new spouse) vastly complicates the merger.

Remarried families (variously referred to in the literature as Rem, blended, second, reconstituted, or step-families) come in a variety of forms (see Table 5.1), although for simplicity's sake we can divide them into three major types: ones in which the wife becomes a stepmother, ones in which the husband becomes a stepfather, and ones in which both occur. It is important for the counselor to understand that remarriage connotes far more than joining a simple dyadic relationship. On the contrary, as Sager, Brown, Crohn, Engel, Rodstein, & Walker (1983) point out, each adult entering such a developing dyadic system carries with him or her a plethora of attachments and obligations. That person's gender, previous marital status, and custodial and/or noncustodial children must be considered. For example, as noted in Table 5.1, the previously single woman who weds a formerly married man with children (combination #10), thus in one instance thrust into the unfamiliar role of stepmother, probably has considerably different expectations, experiences, and possible areas of conflict than does a previously married woman with children in the same circumstances (#12).

The following example illustrates the former (#10) set of circumstances:

Alan had been married for nine years to Joy and together they had had two children, Deidre, age 5, and Todd, age 2, by the time they consulted a marital counselor. Married in their senior year—they had both attended a large midwestern university—they had continued for several years to live relatively unburdened lives not unlike their student days. Alan, the more serious and scholarly of the two, had soon tired of his job as an accountant, however, and with Joy's encouragement had begun graduate studies leading to a Ph.D. in economics. Joy had worked at assorted jobs before signing on as an assistant to the head of an insurance agency, a position that took her away from home for long hours each day. After the birth of their children, Joy, advancing in her job, had continued her work, sometimes barely managing to come home for dinner before returning to see clients in the evening. More and more, Alan had taken over the care of the children, a task he found he did successfully and enjoyed. By the time they saw the counselor, they had grown apart sufficiently—emotionally, intellectually, socially—that little if anything was left of their marriage and they decided to get divorced. By mutual consent, reflecting their previously agreed-upon living arrangement, they shared custody of the children, but Alan retained physical custody. Over the following five years the children saw less and less of their mother, although she would occasionally call them and promise to see them as soon as her busy schedule allowed. As the children learned to predict, it was a promise that was rarely kept.

When Alan met Sara, a fellow doctoral student, they discovered that they shared many values in common. As their relationship blossomed, they found too that they were emotionally compatible, and soon they decided to marry. The children, now 10 and 7, liked Sara well enough at first, and Sara was enthusiastic about having a ready-made family. She was good with children, and since she was a bit younger than Alan and herself childless, she was anxious to prove to him that she could cope. However, she found it particularly hard to adapt to this "instant family" despite her efforts to be a good mother. She resented their demands, their intrusions, their possessiveness of their father. Without a honeymoon period in which to develop greater intimacy with her husband, Sara felt thrust into a series of child-rearing tasks for which she had no experience, and from which she received little reward. Her husband expected her to relieve him of some parental responsibilities, and could not understand her resistance to becoming an instant parent. The children, on the other hand, soon refused to listen to any rules she might impose, insisting she was not their parent and therefore did not have any rights to discipline. Sara felt that she was on the receiving end of all the abuse from children who resented her closeness to their father, without any of the pleasures, satisfactions, or displays of affection due a parent. Although Alan and Sara both had believed she would make a "wonderful" mother—she actually had very good success with caring for their needs early on—all four family members were soon involved in considerable turmoil.

Recognizing that the new family system was in trouble, Alan sought out family counseling, along with Sara, Deidre, and Todd. In the process, Alan learned to offer support to his wife and to help her out of the no-win situations in which she often found herself. By relinquishing some of his ideas about what constituted a good parent, he learned to reduce whatever rescue fantasies he had been experiencing of marrying someone who would be another "perfect" parent. Before the family counseling sessions, he had believed that only if she were perfect, according to his definition, could he relax and entrust the children to his new wife.

Through counseling, Sara was able to get in touch with her frustration and resulting bitterness, often directed toward Alan, at his insistence that she be the mother he would have liked Joy to have been. As this unreasonable expectation became clear to them—they both had bought into it—Alan relaxed his demands in this regard and Sara made an effort to stop competing with the children's natural mother to win their love. She slowly began to recognize that affection and acceptance from the children would come out of their daily living patterns, and that the verbal expression of such feelings from children the ages of Deidre and Todd is commonly limited, even in intact families. Particularly if the boundary around her and her husband became stronger, the children would respond to their father's feelings for her, and would start to treat her as their parent.

The children were helped to deal with their loyalty conflicts regarding their own mother, and to accept that while Sara was not their biological mother, she was in fact the person who was willing to carry out the day-to-day tasks of mothering. As the children became aware that loving Sara did not mean abandoning the tenuous hold they had on their natural mother, the relationship with their stepmother became closer and the family overall became a more cohesive unit.

A remarried family into which both partners bring children from previous marriages (#12) presents a different set of problems:

Both Marlene and Dan had been married briefly before ending their first marriages. Each had ended that marriage with a joint custody arrangement in which they were awarded physical custody—Marlene of her 2-year-old son Robert, Dan of his 3-year-old daughter Christine. Each adult had remained a single parent for several years, until they met at a church social, fell in love, and decided to marry. In their haste to connect with another adult in a loving relationship, however, they neglected to talk through any differences in child-rearing values, expected household rules, remaining financial and emotional ties to a former spouse, and a host of related issues involving the transition into the new family structure. As one indication of their lack of planning, the children did not meet each other until two weeks before the wedding ceremony.

The early period in a remarried family's life is usually a period of considerable reorganization and inevitable disequilibrium. In this case, chaos would be a more accurate assessment. The children in particular fought over space in the new house, which previous family routine (dinnertime, bedtime) was to be followed, who could be disciplined by whom. Each child aligned with his or her own parent to the point of seeming at times to represent two warring camps. Robert was vigilant in measuring how much attention Christine was getting, and Christine was equally on the lookout for any special benefits that might come her stepbrother's way. Needless to say, little bonding took place between the children, nor between each child and his or her stepparent. Marlene and Dan were dumbfounded, each having wanted to believe that because they loved their new spouse, they would automatically love (and be loved by) their spouse's children. For the first hectic year, nothing seemed further from the truth.

Nor was the conflict restricted to the children. The parents often found themselves defending the action of their own child against the other, and exchanged open criticism about the child-rearing practices of the other. On occasion, usually after a visit by a child with his or her noncustodial parent, that parent would call to criticize or complain about the child's alleged mistreatment; this typically had the effect of stirring up old conflicts between the ex-spouses. By the end of the second year of marriage, both Marlene and Dan had many doubts about the possibilities of the ultimate success of their marital union. Their earlier plan to have a child together was put on hold, and, as a last resort, they sought the help of a family counselor.

The counselor saw all four family members together, and helped them to redefine their conflicts in interactional terms as a systems problem to which each participant contributed. Instead of factions, based on earlier experiences living as single-parent households, he emphasized their wholeness as an expanded system in which each person's needs as well as responsibilities needed to be addressed. Rather than clinging to earlier parent-child patterns, the counselor suggested, here was an opportunity for creating new family guidelines and traditions. For example, both children could now give up being partners to their respective parents and return to being children again, something each seemed to desire. Family boundaries were slowly redrawn, and the children began to refer to one another with their friends as brother and sister, this despite some awkwardness over different surnames.

After two months, the counselor began working with Marlene and Dan alone, strengthening their bond and helping them work as a parental unit. At several sessions, the ex-spouses were brought in to help reduce friction as well as better coordinate activities with the children. After six months, Marlene announced that she was pregnant and that she and Dan were ready to terminate treatment.

Both cases illustrate that the basic integrative tasks for stepfamilies, as Visher and Visher (1988) point out, are twofold: (1) redefining and maintaining existing parent-child and ex-spouse relationships, but in a new context; and, (2) developing new relationship patterns to build trust within the household as a means of achieving a solid identity as a new family unit. Figure 5.1 depicts an intact, functional nuclear family (top), a new stepfamily (middle), and a mature stepfamily (bottom). If successful, the new stepfamily progresses from its early formation in which little connectedness exists between members, to the mature stepfamily where links between all members are strong and binding. As these authors note, the process of establishing themselves as a viable and integrated unit is often a lengthy one for most stepfamilies, since they usually have to overcome a combination of built-in parent-child alliances, problematic generational boundaries, influences outside the household, and a lack of family history or loyalty.

In a study of 88 remarried couples, Duberman (1975) found that stepfamily integration was facilitated if: (1) the previous spouse had died rather than divorced; (2) the new spouse had divorced rather than never

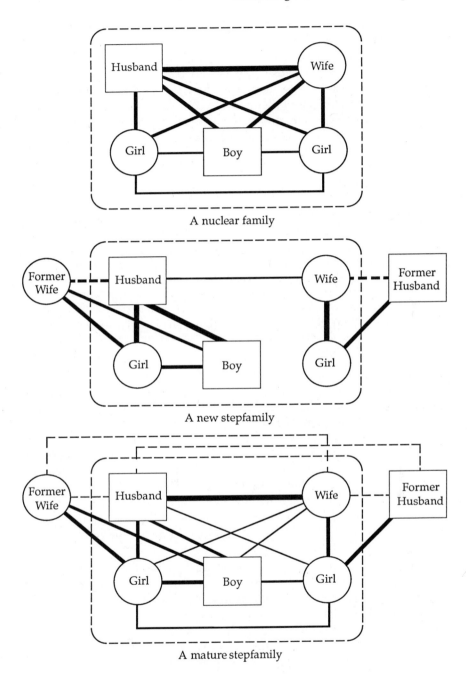

Figure 5.1.   *Interactive networks in three family configurations.*
Source: Visher & Visher, 1988, p. 13.

having been previously married; and (3) the remarried couple had children of their own together. She found further that parent-child relationships were helped when the wife's children from her previous marriage lived with her and her new spouse. On the other hand, men who left their children with their ex-wife tended to deal less well with their live-in stepchildren. Acceptance by the in-laws and other extended family members helped strengthen the remarriage. One noteworthy finding was that stepmother-stepdaughter relationships tended to be the most problematic of all stepfamily interactions.

STEPFAMILY LIVING PATTERNS

A remarried family has been defined by Sager and associates (1981) as

> one that is created by the marriage (or living together in one domicile) of two partners, one or both of whom has been married previously and was divorced or widowed with or without children who visit or reside with them. The couple and the children (custodial or visiting) comprise the Remarried family system. The "metafamily" system is composed of the Remarried family plus former spouses, grandparents, step-grandparents, aunts, uncles, and others who may have significant input into the Remarried system. (p. 3)

Jacobson (1987), in an effort to break away from an approach tied to conventional terms such as *nuclear, intact,* or *broken* families, prefers to conceptualize stepfamilies as "linked family systems." She believes the term *linked* more accurately reflects the web of interrelationships and the dynamic complexities occurring in such families. Her formulation goes beyond the common phenomenon of a child living with a custodial remarried parent and his or her spouse (usually the biological mother and stepfather). Instead, Jacobson views the child as likely to be related to two households— the custodial or lived in, and the noncustodial or visited—each of which represents a subsystem of the dual household or binuclear family system. In such a setup, the child is a "link" influencing and being influenced by those in both households.

Of particular relevance to counselors is the clinical observation made by Visher and Visher (1979) that in such linked families virtually all members have sustained a recent primary relationship loss with which they must cope. One implication we might draw, then, is that there is likely to be fear and apprehension regarding making a new commitment for adults and children alike. Adults may hesitate out of a feeling of vulnerability due to pain from past intimate experiences. Children, too, may pull back from trusting new adults in their lives. Not unexpectedly, they are likely to use the rules and roles of the earlier family life as guidelines for current behavior. Satisfactory stepfamily integration, then, is likely to take years to achieve.

McGoldrick and Carter (1988) adopt the additionally useful premise that interactions in the restructured remarried family are likely to be complex, with conflicting and ambiguous roles to be played by all members. As we illustrated in the case of Sara, rather than following any ordinary step-by-step progression, a previously single young adult is often expected to plunge into instant multiple roles as wife and stepmother, for which she has had little if any preparation and in which she cannot expect to be welcomed wholeheartedly.

Unstable and poorly defined boundaries may cause dissension and struggle; and intense conflictual feelings on the part of all participants in stepfamilies must be expected, particularly during the early period in the life cycle of any blended family. As McGoldrick and Carter (1988) note, such boundary difficulties often involve issues of membership (Who are the "real" members of the family?), space (Where do I belong? What space is mine?), authority (Who is in charge of discipline? Of money? Of decisions?), and time (Who gets how much of my time and how much do I get of theirs?).

Disequilibrium is inevitable, despite the wishes or even the good intentions of all of the members of the new family. Ultimately, at least two tasks must be accomplished before the participants can be anchored in a truly blended family: (1) the new partners must accept each other as executives in the new family hierarchy, and (2) the children must accept the new partner, having worked out the problems of territory or turf that arise from unclear or dysfunctional boundaries (Isaacs, 1982). The renegotiation of boundaries has two aspects that require attention. One involves restructuring within the subsystem of the new unit, among parent, new parent, and child; the other calls for renegotiation (relinkage) within the larger family unit that includes the former spouse (the child's other parent). The way the process unfolds—it should be started as early in the relationship as possible, even before marriage—can facilitate or impede successful blending.

What problems should the counselor especially screen for? Box 5.1 outlines some of the typical interpersonal difficulties likely to restrict, obstruct, or foil efforts of a remarried family to develop into a functioning unit. As noted, one area of frequent intergenerational conflict involves developing and maintaining rules, particularly as these rules affect the effectiveness with which the stepparent can assume a parenting role. Rules regarding discipline, manners, the delegation of tasks and responsibilities, eating and sleeping habits, the form and intensity with which feelings (both positive and negative) are expressed, all need to be established as ongoing family patterns (Ganong & Coleman, 1987). In most cases, such rules can be established only after any underlying fear, anger, and resentment has been cleared up.

Since roles and boundaries are almost certain to be unclear, especially during the new family's formative stages, confusion and disorganization seem inevitable as the family seeks to establish some equilibrium. Einstein

(1982) points out the importance of delineating physical boundaries (shared space, property, activities), psychological boundaries (the degree of intimacy, authority, and affection the family members share), and roles (the rights and duties that determine family behavior patterns). A new stepmother of an adolescent, for example, learns soon enough that such efforts may require considerable tact, thick skin, and the ability to tolerate frustration and rejection. (The same virtues may be expected in a biological parent when dealing with one's own adolescent.) Her desire to please her new spouse by rushing to be a much-loved substitute mother is almost certainly doomed to failure, and will likely be accompanied by a sense of personal defeat, rejection and, often, despair.

Box 5.1. A Problem Appraisal Checklist for Remarried Families

Remarried families may experience problems in the following areas:

- Difficulties of stepparent in assuming parental role
- Rivalry and jealousy between stepsiblings
- Boundary ambiguity
- Unfinished conflict between ex-spouses
- Competition between biological mother and stepmother (or biological father and stepfather)
- Idealization of absent parent
- Lack of intimacy between parent and nonbiological child
- Loyalty conflicts in children between absent parent and stepparent
- Loyalty conflicts in parent between absent children and stepchildren
- Children's surname differences
- Effects of birth of child from new marriage
- Financial obligations (alimony payment to ex-spouse, child support payments)
- Adolescent issues–change in custody requests

Under ordinary circumstances in an intact family, sibling attachments play a key role in helping children form a sense of identity, a self-concept. Ihinger-Tallman (1987) points out further that "siblings also serve as defenders/protectors of one another; they interpret the outside world to each other, and they teach each other about equity, coalition formation, and the processes of bargaining and negotiation" (p. 164). They may at times serve as buffers against their parents. As contributors to the family "culture," they share common experiences, help establish a family history, and play an essential role in intergenerational continuity. Despite occasional disputes and rivalries, they generally feel positively bonded to one another.

In stepfamilies, such a history is missing, making attachments and eventual bonding all the more tentative and difficult to achieve. Thus, integrating stepsiblings into the new family is a major task in most cases, especially (as in the case of Marlene and Dan cited earlier) when they have been part of established single-parent homes for any length of time. In these circumstances, where a special bond with the solo parent has been allowed to develop, particularly when the child's role becomes that of substitute spouse, it is understandable that the child feels betrayed at the very suggestion of remarriage. Data from Wallerstein and Kelly (1980b) on the children of divorce indicate that older children are especially resistant to accepting stepfathers, often requiring several years before coming to terms with the realities of the remarried situation. In a number of their cases, it seemed unlikely that such acceptance of the stepfather as a family member would ever occur.

Generally speaking, according to Visher and Visher (1979), children do not welcome remarriage,[1] for at least two reasons: (1) they may feel split in their loyalties to two sets of parents, and (2) they may continue to harbor the wish that their divorced parents will reunite, a fantasy that is undermined by the remarriage to someone else. As Keshet (1980) contends, a stepfamily by its very structure inevitably has strongly bounded subsystems to which members remain loyal. Unless such conflicting loyalties can be worked out, however, stepfamily integration will remain incomplete.

The initial assessment children make of their potential gains and losses connected with the formation of the new family (and the acquisition of new siblings) helps determine future stepsibling relationships (Ihinger-Tallman, 1987). Whether required to share attention and affection from one's own parent, or friends and possessions (rooms, toys, pets) with a stepsibling, one or both children may feel shortchanged, as though the loss exceeds the benefits of living in a new family. Conversely, in some cases, the children may perceive a mutual set of benefits without excessive personal costs, and strong emotional bonds may develop between them. The correlation between the ease with which the new parents form a close union and the stepsiblings form a close union is certainly a highly positive one, as one impacts on the other.

Residues from the former marriage of either or both newly united persons may afflict a remarriage, especially in its early stages of greatest vulnerability. As we have noted a number of times, divorce may represent the end of a marital affiliation, but it does not necessarily terminate the parenting relationship between ex-spouses. Thus, remarriage may cause custody arrangements or visitation schedules or financial support pay-

---

1 There are exceptions to this statement that should be noted by counselors. Some children are delighted when a single parent remarries, feeling relieved of the burden of offering adult-style companionship. In some cases, the parent's depression may lift with remarriage, there may be more money available, and so on. Such children, however, may be particularly distressed when they sense a new divorce on the horizon.

ments to be renegotiated, thereby reopening old wounds between ex-combatants. Or conflict may develop between the stepfather and the biological father, for example, over discipline; sometimes the child's mother joins in; the child usually adds fuel to the resulting conflagration.

As Westoff (1977) notes, "living ghosts"—photographs, furniture, laundry marks, monograms, habits—are a part of every remarriage, and thus a constant reminder of the time one's partner has spent with another in an intimate relationship. It is not surprising, then, that some divorced couples return to court, sometimes repeatedly, over issues ostensibly involving the children, when in reality they are continuing the battles that led to the divorce in the first place. Particularly when the single ex-spouse did not want the divorce to take place and is now jealous over being displaced by the new marital partner, bitterness may linger and attach itself to any cause justifying litigation and a chance at revenge.

The counselor should be alert to various other potentially conflictual relationships in stepfamilies. Bernard (1956), a sociologist, in an early work outlined six such relationship areas: (1) between the child's biological parents, (2) between the new parent and the biological parent of the same sex, (3) between the old in-laws and the new spouse, (4) between the new father and the children, (5) between the new mother and the children, and (6) between the children. Einstein (1982) points out that all of these conflict areas involve competition for the affection of the children.

Finally, all remarried families must come to terms with a number of persistent myths regarding stepfamily living. For example, the sterotype of the "wicked stepmother" plagues many women married to men with children. The term *stepchild* is a metaphor for neglect and abuse in many societies, and the stuff of endless fairy tales (Snow White, Hansel and Gretel, Cinderella) usually involving an uncaring or abusive stepmother and an uninformed or deceived or busy father. The myth no doubt originated at a time when stepfamilies were the result of death of a parent rather than divorce, and a stepmother was expected to raise her husband's child without much attention from her mate. In most cases, women were married by widowed fathers for the express purpose of raising the children, something men were not thought to be equipped for or expected to know how to do.

One consequence of these negative sexist stereotypes is the greater stress found in families with stepmothers than in corresponding stepfather families (Clingempeel, Brand, & Ievoli, 1984). Increased tension in such families is at least in part a function of increased social pressures on stepmothers and the general societal failure to fully accept this family form. For a variety of reasons, society expects more from a woman in her relationship with children than it does from a man with children. This seems to hold true whether the children are hers by birth, adoption, or remarriage. A man is expected to provide support or money (less so if his stepchildren are receiving child support from their father); whatever else he provides, and it may be significant, is all to the good, but in the eyes of many people in society not essential. Visher and Visher (1988) suggest that many women still derive much of their self-esteem from their role as good parent, and this in turn may help account for more tension between mother and stepmother than between father and stepfather, contributing to increased stress in stepmother families.

Pasley and Ihinger-Tallman (1987) indicate that compared to stepfathers, stepmothers tend to be less satisfied in their relationship with stepchildren, to feel more often that their marriage is negatively affected by their spouse's children, to be more dissatisfied with their role, and to feel more often that the relationship between them and the biological parent of the same sex is difficult. These researchers also found that compared to stepfathers, stepmothers tend to be less involved with their stepchildren and have more conflict with them; and children in stepmother families are at greater risk than their counterparts in stepfather families.[2] As we indicated earlier in reporting Duberman's (1975) findings, relationships between stepmothers and stepdaughters seem especially conflictual.

THE DEVELOPMENTAL STAGES OF REMARRIAGE

Remarriage is more than an event; it is a process, extending over time, in which a group of individuals without a common history or established rituals or behavior patterns attempts to unite and to develop a sense of family identity. Such a conversion or redefinition, which must be viewed as going back at least to the disintegration of the first marriage (McGoldrick & Carter, 1988), typically proceeds through certain predictable developmental phases, from the decision to separate, through the legal divorce and custody arrangements, to the remarriage and possible shifts in custody of one or more children, ultimately to forging an integrated stepfamily unit.

Bradt and Bradt (1986) provide the following colorful description of the stages of remarriage, beginning with the remarriage ceremony and proceeding, optimally, to the emergence of the new, integrated family structure. Progression from one stage to the next is made easier by the successful completion of the prior stage.

1. *Go back!* "What have I gotten myself into?" "Is this a mistake?" "I never thought it would be like this." The couple may be filled with doubt and apprehension; the children may protest in various ways and

2 Many family counselors believe that the quality of the relationship between stepparent and stepchild may actually be a better predictor of the family's ultimate adaptation to the remarriage than the quality of the marital dyad. It is entirely possible for a remarried couple to experience marital satisfaction while encountering dissatisfactions within the family regarding stepchildren. In many cases, such chronic problems may ultimately erode the marital bond. In other cases, however, the stepparent-stepchild interactive pattern may simply reflect the degree of connection and dedication of the marital couple to the remarriage.

attempt to undermine the remarriage; friends and relatives may withhold support.

2. *Making room:* The family members learn to share physical territory and emotional space with others, delineate work/home allocations, and avoid a sense of being an intruder.

3. *Struggles of realignment:* Loyalty conflicts, power struggles, protests, and negotiation occur as former relationship alliances break down and are restructured.

4. *(Re)commitment:* A family identity is established as a budding of family feeling occurs, family mythology and ceremony evolve, shared experiences are created and defined, rituals regarding celebrations or vacations or family meetings are developed.

5. *Rebalancing relationships:* Once recommitment is achieved, the family members can freely move back and forth between the old and new households, defining different membership in each and maintaining loyalty to each based on the present rather than the past.

6. *Relinquishing feelings of deprivation and burden:* Previously held feelings of being isolated, untrusting, overresponsible, unwilling to collaborate, and so on, are given up as each member better defines obligations to self and others.

7. *Growth toward integration:* Having accepted differences, addressed challenges, acknowledged complexity, established commitments, and relinquished feelings of deprivation and burden, the family emerges with an identity and cohesiveness much like any other functioning family.

8. *Moving on:* Members are free to move into complex networks of relationships focused on problem solving, growth, and interaction with broader systems outside the family.

In each of the stages just outlined, major dislocations must be attended to and major adaptations made. Each stage evokes stress; each provides an opportunity for further growth and family consolidation, but also the risk of relapse and family disruption. Carter and McGoldrick (1980) consider remarriage as one of the most difficult transitions a family is ever called upon to make. Because most members have experienced recent loss, pain, and a sense of ambiguity, they may wish prematurely for a feeling of closure without understanding that they must confront the built-in complexities of the remarriage process. In most cases, what lies ahead before stepfamily integration can occur, according to Visher and Visher (1982), is mourning the losses of past family relationships, developing new family traditions, forming new interpersonal relationships within the new family, renegotiating ties with the absent biological parent, and, for children, learning to move satisfactorily between two households. It seems hardly surprising that the remarried family, especially when children are present, may be a fragile entity for a considerable period of time, highly vulnerable to a wide variety of interpersonal, generational, and emotional stresses.

Carter and McGoldrick (1988), adopting a developmental point of view, contend that separation, divorce, and remarriage each represent significant dislocations in a family's life cycle, calling for additional restabilizing steps before the family can resume their ongoing development. Tables 5.2 and 5.3 represent their step-by-step outline of the process. In their view, the attitudes listed in column 2 of both tables are prerequisites for families to work out the developmental issues regarding divorce and postdivorce adjustment (column 3). The counselor who presses families to resolve the developmental issues without first helping them adopt the appropriate attitudes is, in the opinion of McGoldrick and Carter, wasting effort. These authors note further that restabilization calls for an additional ingredient, namely the passage of sufficient time.

If the future spouses come from different life-cycle phases (for example, an older man with adult children marrying a young woman with no children or with preteenage children), their differences in experiences and approaches to current responsibilities may delay stepfamily integration still further. The joining of partners at discrepant life-cycle phases calls for a process in which both learn to function in different phases simultaneously. Becoming a stepmother to a teenager before becoming an experienced wife or mother is disconcertingly contrary to normal life sequences. In the same way, the husband who is called upon to return to a life phase passed through years earlier—from beginning a marriage to raising young children—may find the experience unappealing, especially if his previous marriage had difficulties during this phase. (He may, of course, find it rejuvenating, just as the out-of-sequence experience for the younger wife may prove enlightening and enriching.)

Sager et al. (1983) argue that the precursor of remarriage has been the simultaneous disruption in three aspects of the life cycle—the individual, the marital, and the family—and that all three must be considered in order to obtain a comprehensive picture of what transpires in the transition to remarriage. By the time a man or woman contemplates remarriage, he or she has gone through a number of powerful structural life changes in all three areas. These researchers offer as illustration the case of "Amy Greenson" (Table 5.4) as she separates from her family of origin, marries, has children, separates, divorces, lives as a single parent, and then remarries, beginning a new family life cycle.

According to the formulation of Sager et al., the conflicts in remarried families are generated by each spouse's having to operate along "multiple tracks," dealing simultaneously with possibly incongruent individual, marital, and family life cycles. In remarried families, individual life cycles are lived out over the course of two or more marriages. As these authors observe, husbands and wives may be simultaneously biological parents and stepparents; conflicts may exist in a father, for example, between

Table 5.2.   Dislocations of the Family Life Cycle, Requiring Additional Steps to Restabilize and Proceed Developmentally

Phase	Emotional Process of Transition Prerequisite Attitude	Developmental Issues
DIVORCE		
1. The decision to divorce	Acceptance of inability to resolve marital tensions sufficiently to continue relationship	Acceptance of one's own part in failure of the marriage
2. Planning the break-up of the system	Supporting viable arrangements for all parts of the system	Working cooperatively on problems of custody, visitation, finances Dealing with extended family about the divorce
3. Separation	Willingness to continue cooperative coparental relationship Work on resolution of attachment to spouse	Mourning loss of intact family Restructuring marital and parent-child relationships; adaptation to living apart Realignment of relationships with extended family; staying connected with spouse's extended family
4. The divorce	More work on emotional divorce: overcoming hurt, anger, guilt, and so on	Mourning loss of intact family: giving up fantasies of reunion Retrieval of hopes, dreams, expectations from the marriage Staying connected with extended families
POSTDIVORCE FAMILY		
A. Single-parent family	Willingness to maintain parental contact with ex-spouse and support contact of children and his family	Making flexible visitation arrangements with ex-spouse and his family Rebuilding own social network
B. Single-parent (noncustodial)	Willingness to maintain parental contact with ex-spouse and support custodial parent's relationship with children	Finding ways to continue effective parenting relationship with children Rebuilding own social network

Source: Carter & McGoldrick, 1988, p. 22.

Table 5.3.   Remarried Family Formation: A Developmental Outline

Steps	Prerequisite Attitude	Developmental Issues
1. Entering the new relationship	Recovery from loss of first marriage (adequate "emotional divorce")	Recommitment to marriage and to forming a family with readiness to deal with the complexity and ambiguity
2. Conceptualizing and planning new marriage and family	Accepting one's own fears and those of new spouse and children about remarriage and forming a stepfamily Accepting need for time and patience for adjustment to complexity and ambiguity of: - Multiple new roles - Boundaries: space, time, membership, and authority - Affective issues: guilt, loyalty conflicts, desire for mutuality, unresolvable past hurts	Work on openess in the new relationships to avoid pseudomutuality Plan for maintenance of cooperative co-parental relationships with ex-spouses Plan to help children deal with fears, loyalty conflicts, and membership in two systems Realignment of relationships with extended family to include new spouse and children Plan for maintenance of children's connections with extended family of ex-spouse(s)
3. Remarriage and reconstitution of family	Final resolution of attachment to previous spouse and ideal of "intact" family Acceptance of a different model of family with permeable boundaries	Restructuring family boundaries to allow for inclusion of new spouse-stepparent Realignment of relationships throughout subsystems to permit interweaving of several systems Making room for relationships of all children with biological (noncustodial) parents, grandparents, and other extended family Sharing memories and histories to enhance stepfamily integration

Source: Carter & McGoldrick, 1988, p. 24.

loyalty to his natural children and to his stepchildren with whom he resides on a daily basis. With remarriage, the man is thus part of an old family life cycle, perhaps still involved with an ex-wife in an old marital cycle, beginning a new marital cycle and at the same time a remarried life cycle.

In the case of "Amy Greenson," as revealed in Table 5.4, we see at ages 45–50, for example, that previous and new marital and family cycles are current and overlap, and that she has added additional life-cycle tracks to her existence, rather than merely replacing one set with another. Here she must deal at one and the same time with difficulties allowing herself to love again, coparenting her daughters from her first marriage through adolescence, entering a new marriage, restructuring her family to now include a stepson as well as her new husband, and caring about her aging parents. As Sager et al. (1983) see it, conflict and stress for many dysfunctional remarried couples arise from attempting to deal with the "multiple tracks" that are by definition part of the remarried family suprasystem.

SOME COUNSELING GUIDELINES

Remarried family life is unique, stepfamily dynamics complex, and the counselor who insists on dealing with such families as though they resembled intact biological families has undoubtedly started with a false set of assumptions that require correction. Counselors working with stepfamilies need to be aware of numerous and important structural differences between this family form and intact biological families, bearing in mind that each of these differences may be accompanied by specific stresses and tasks.

Among the distinctive problems confronted by the majority of stepfamilies are the following (Isaacs, 1982; Pasley, 1985; Visher & Visher, 1988):

1. A stepfamily is born of relationship losses, and the relinquishing of marital hopes and dreams in the previous family. Special childhood positions in one family (for example, only child) may be lost with remarriage, and special household roles (for example, parent confidant to a single mother) surrendered. Thus, counselors must help stepfamilies address these losses, as well as fear of further losses, before new adaptations can be made.

2. The stepfamily is made up of members with separate family histories and traditions. In addition, each family may come together at differing points in their lifecycles (for example, late adolescent children and preschoolers) and with ways of doing things that seem incompatible. Thus, they are likely to have experiences and expectations significantly different from one another, and the counselor may need to help them negotiate differences that lead to interpersonal conflicts.

3. Parent-child relationships precede the new couple bond, and children frequently move back and forth between housholds of custodial and noncustodial parents. Children in stepfamilies thus often experience loyalty pulls between their natural parents, while at the same time feeling little loyalty to the stepfamily, especially in its early stages. The counselor may need to direct attention to helping all members learn to trust the new group and develop an identity as a remarried family member. For many children, this may mean giving up the fantasy that their biological parents will reunite. Helping the remarried parents strengthen their marital bond (without feeling they are somehow betraying an earlier parent-child bond) may go a long way toward helping the child relinquish the fantasy.

4. An absent biological parent exists, and if the previous struggle between the biological parents remains unresolved, the children will likely be torn between the parents. The counselor must further help the family to avoid fostering an adversarial relationship between the new parent and the biological parent of the same sex. Continuing contact with the absent biological parent may actually aid the child's ability to form a relationship with the stepparent.

5. Children often are members of two households, frequently with different rules and expectations and different parenting styles. Thus, transitions between the two may be stressful for all concerned, and stability may take time to achieve. Counselors may need to help children understand that a relationship with the noncustodial parent continues to exist despite periodic separations. In general, children should be encouraged to remain in contact with both parents, especially if the ex-mates can work out the details in an amicable fashion. Encouraging each set of parents to allow for tension on "reentry" into their household is often therapeutic for all concerned.

6. There is no legal relationship between stepparents and stepchildren (although later adoption is possible), and adults may therefore have reservations about getting involved emotionally with someone who may disappear from their lives at some future date. The counselor needs to be aware that stepfamily integration, and especially stepparent-stepchild bonding, takes time, perhaps years. To attempt to fit them into a biological family mold is doomed to failure, with the possible rare exception of stepfamilies forming when all the children are very young.

McGoldrick and Carter (1988) urge further that the counselor encourage the maintenance of an open system with permeable boundaries between current and former spouses and their families. An open coparental relationship is extremely desirable, especially if the former mates have worked out their emotional divorce and any lingering bitterness between them. The authors argue that children should never have the power to decide on remarriage, custody, or visitation, since that would violate the

Table 5.4. The Individual, Marital, and Family Life Cycle in Rem

Age	Individual Life Cycle	Marital Life Cycle	Family Life Cycle
18–21	Pulls up roots. Develops autonomy. (Amy M. moves out of family's home and attends college in another city.)	Shift from family of origin to new emotional commitment. (Amy meets George G. and they begin to date exclusively.)	During college, Amy still financially dependent on her family of origin; her old room is kept for her at home.
22–28	Provisional adulthood. Develops occupational identification. (Amy graduates and works as a teacher; shares apartment and then lives alone.)	Provisional marital commitment; stress over parenthood. (Amy and George engaged when Amy is 23; marry at 24.)	Self-sufficient vis-a-vis family of origin; her room at home is converted to study.
29–31	Transition at age 30; decides about commitment to work and marriage.	Commitment crisis. (Married six years, George is questioning the relationship. They receive marital counseling.)	Pressure from her family to stay together and have children; her father retires.
32–39	Settling down, deepening commitments. (Amy feels committed to George and desires children; she stops working with first child.)	Productivity: children, friends, work for George. (Their daughters are born when Amy is 32 and 34.)	Family with young children: need to accept new members, take on parenting roles.
40–42	Midlife transition; searching for fit between aspirations and environment. (Amy questions homemaker role, is restless and dissatisfied. After an impetuous sexual misadventure she avoids dating.)	Couple is summing up; success and failure evaluated. (Amy and George again receive counseling; George has affair; decision to separate is made when children are six and eight years old.)	Postseparation family: two households are set up. Amy returns to live with her parents; there is a resurgence of dependence on her family of origin as she returns to the job market. She has custody of children, who visit father. Grandparents very involved with children while Amy works and begins to date.

(continued)

Table 5.4 The Individual, Marital, and Family Life Cycle in Rem

Age	Individual Life Cycle	Marital Life Cycle	Family Life Cycle
43–45	Middle adulthood: restabilizing and reordering priorities; struggle to reestablish autonomy from her family of origin; dealing with work advancement. (Now begins to desire a loving relationship with a man.)	Continuing coparenting relationship although marriage is dissolved. Beginning to date. Testing out new ways of relating to men.	Double single-parent stage: girls are now 11 and 9 and are part of both parents' households.
46–50	Tasks of middle adulthood continue. Emotional divorce from George sufficiently complete for her to contemplate idea of marriage again. (Difficulty allowing herself to trust again as love relationship develops.) Remarries to fulfill coupling needs. Simultaneously continues coparenting of her children with first husband while taking on coparenting role with second husband.	MARRIAGE #1 Need to coparent the girls through their adolescence. Dealing with ex-husband on issues around the girls such as dating and their desire to visit father less often. MARRIAGE #2 (1) Entering new relationship with Steve. (2) Planning and conceptualizing new marriage. (3) Remarriage. (4) Making new commitment. (5) Commitment crisis: questioning choice. (6) Resolving conflicts and stabilizing remarriage.	OLD FAMILY Allowing adolescent children to individuate. Launching children and moving on. Dealing with aging and illness of her parents. REM FAMILY Restructuring family to include new spouse and stepson (age 10) who lives with Rem couple. Providing a nurturing environment to prepubescent child. Dealing with Steve's ex-wife. Family with adolescent child. (Cycle repeats what Amy experienced with her girls.) Launching child and moving on.

(continued)

Table 5.4 (continued)

Age	Individual Life Cycle	Marital Life Cycle		Family Life Cycle
51–59		Coparenting relationship is less important. Establish a workable relationship with George around their adult children.	(7) Supporting and enjoying friends and activities as children begin to leave home.	
59+	Looking ahead to enjoy the later years. Dealing with her own aging process.	Little contact with George except for milestone events of children and grandchildren.	(8) Continuing support; retirement, pursuit of interests, individually and together with Steve.	Relating to her c h i l d r e n ' s spouses and children. Relating to stepson's spouse and children.

Source: Sager et al., 1983, pp. 51-53.

parental boundaries and responsibilities; however, as children get older, their input into such parental decisions does deserve attention.

As a rule of thumb, McGoldrick and Carter (1988) as well as Visher and Visher (1988) strongly recommend the use of three-generational genograms in counseling remarried families. Carried out with the family at the beginning of counseling, the schematic drawing provides information about previous marriages, the length of any single-parent-household periods, and possible shifts in children's living arrangements. A clearer picture of the complexity of the suprafamily system is likely to emerge, offering some basis for understanding why the members are experiencing current stress and confusion.

STAGES OF STEPFAMILY DEVELOPMENT

Counselors also need to appreciate that stepfamily development occurs in stages. Each stage in the process of solidifying a remarried family calls for the renegotiating and reorganizing of a complex and dynamic network of relationships. Thus, there is risk at each juncture of unresolved issues from the previous stages reemerging and old feelings flaring up, especially if these have been covered over in the rush to form a united remarried family. Counseling efforts, in addition to persistently supporting the process of growth and integration of the new family, must address the relationship problems specific to the stage of the family's development. Early on, this may mean directing therapeutic attention to helping members successfully mourn lost dreams and relationships before stepfamily integration can begin. Stepfamily members may also require help in learning new roles, or perhaps beginning to examine boundary realignments now that a new family entity has been formed. Perhaps new conflict-resolving mechanisms can be encouraged by the counselor and new decision-making structures set in place.

Later in the history of the remarried family, relationship rules may need revision, or a child born to the remarried couple may need to be incorporated into the boundaries of the family. Whatever brings the family to the counselor, problems related to the phase of the family's development and integration must be scrutinized. McGoldrick and Carter (1988) draw special attention to the impact of remarriage in the cases of the two possible family life-cycle combinations:

> *When spouses are at different life-cycle stages:* Family members may experience greater difficulties in making the necessary transitions, and thus are likely to take longer to integrate into a working family.

> *When spouses are at the same life-cycle stage:* Stepfamily integration is generally easier in that family members are dealing with similar life-stage tasks. On the other hand, problems may arise from feeling over-

loaded by such tasks as coping with stepchildren, ex-spouses, in-laws, and others.

Whiteside (1983) contends that the early stages of remarriage require interventions that help the new family gradually develop a new version of family rules and values that feel right to all the members. Strengths carried over from the previous family need to be acknowledged, and feelings of tension, confusion, and frustration accepted as normal and to be expected. Later in the remarriage, unhappy coalitions within the stepfamily may challenge family stability and equilibrium, or perhaps normal life-cycle events (the birth of more children, shifts in custody arrangements at adolescence, children growing up and leaving home) may cause disruption in family functioning. At each transition, Whiteside urges that the counselor help the family reach back into its history, review its past solutions, and clarify and construct relationship patterns to meet the current challenge.

In the following case, a newly formed family was in trouble almost from the beginning:

Joyce and David Oliver had been married only eight months when they contacted a family counselor as a last resort. Both in their late 20s, Joyce had never been married, preferring a career in business, while David, previously married, had been divorced for about a year when they met at a ski resort. They had a great time together, and after seeing each other daily for several months when they returned to the city, they decided to marry. David had spoken briefly of Kiri, his 4-year-old daughter who lived with his ex-wife in another state, but Joyce did not see the child as having much to do with her since Kiri lived with her mother. She had met her future stepdaughter only once before the wedding ceremony.

The family problems began shortly after the wedding, when Rhonda, David's former spouse, announced that she was having some personal problems, including some with Kiri, and was sending her to live with David and Joyce. For David, who took his parental responsibilities very seriously, this was a welcome opportunity to see Kiri on a regular basis and take an active part in her upbringing. At last he would have the perfect family he had always dreamed of, and which he had failed to achieve in his previous marriage. Joyce wasn't sure what to expect, never having had experiences with children, but was willing to share parental responsibilities if it would make her new husband happy.

Unfortunately, David's dreams failed to materialize, in no small part due to his own behavior as well as Kiri's. She was not an easy child to live with, quickly becoming overattached to her father, excluding her stepmother. David, in turn, became very attached to Kiri, so much so that at times it felt to Joyce that he preferred the child's company to hers. Instead of learning to live with her new husband, Joyce soon felt she was saddled with an instant family in which she felt like an outsider in her own home. David would call Kiri daily before coming home from work, to see if she needed anything for him to bring home. When his wife objected and complained of feeling "frozen out," he defended himself as merely acting like any concerned parent would, adding that Joyce's jealousy forced him to do even more for Kiri than he might have, had Joyce done more.

Evenings, David would put Kiri to bed, and if he stayed more than the 10 minutes he had promised Joyce, she would get depressed, withdraw and not talk to him the rest of that evening. According to David, Joyce was a spoiled child herself, competitive with a 4-year-old, and he was losing respect for her. During the joint sessions with a family counselor, he spoke of being raised by a widowed mother as an only child, and how central to his life was the feeling of family closeness. Joyce, on the other hand, insisted that David did not allow her to develop a relationship with Kiri, expecting her to instantly love someone because he did, but doing nothing to instill in Kiri that they had to reorganize the family to include all three of them. She herself had been raised by a divorced mother in a relatively disengaged family where all three children lived relatively separate lives.

The conflict between them had reached the boiling point by the time they contacted the counselor. David labeled his wife a "wicked stepmother" whom he threatened to leave unless she "corrected her behavior." She, in turn, accused her husband of having a "romance" with his daughter, strongly implying that there might be more to the father-daughter relationship than was evident. Neither was willing to listen to what the counselor was saying, each apparently eager to win his favor and favorable judgment regarding who was right. Joyce would hear of nothing short of sending Kiri back to her mother; David insisted he would not be given an ultimatum regarding how to deal with his own child. While the counseling was in its early stages, Rhonda announced that she had gotten remarried, to Mel, and that she was pregnant.

The counselor began by indicating he was not there to judge who was right, but to help them gain some tools for understanding what was happening to them. It was clear both were miserable, as Kiri undoubtedly was also. If they continued this way, they would almost certainly get divorced, an unfortunate circumstance for both of them since their marriage had not had a chance.

In order to reduce the white heat between them so that counseling might proceed, the counselor attempted two early interventions. One was to reduce the tension by asking them to describe their own histories of child rearing. The information would be useful later, and for the moment would help each begin to grasp that they had come into parenting with different experiences and expectations. As another initial intervention ploy, he asked whether they would be willing to listen to what the other had to say, without condemning it or getting defensive or resorting to name calling.

The counselor thus appealed to their rational selves, and since each was anxious not to be labeled the difficult or unreasonable one, they agreed.

Each proceeded to discuss his or her view of child rearing. They had clear disagreements based on different experiences of their own, and the counselor helped each to listen and try to understand. Joyce's rejecting behavior toward Kiri was relabeled by the counselor as inexperience rather than wickedness; David's overinvolvement was relabeled as eagerness to be a good father. Joyce acknowledged she could learn from David, since she had known little parental attention and affection growing up; however, she insisted he would have to try to be less critical of her efforts if he really wanted her to make the effort. David allowed as how he might be overdoing the parenting, since he had not had a father of his own as a model. The counselor helped him understand that fathers who obtain custody often have unrealistic expectations of how a stepmother should behave. In this case, he was willing to relinquish some parenting chores as he became convinced that she was willing to try. He was encouraged to avoid any coalitions with Kiri against Joyce.

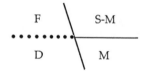

The diffuse boundary between father and daughter indicates they have formed an overinvolved or enmeshed relationship; the stepmother is isolated and excluded, as is the absent biological mother.

Precounseling

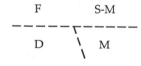

A restructuring has occurred, and a clear boundary now exists between the united parents and the daughter, as well as between the daughter and her biological mother.

Postcounseling

Figure 5.2. Pre- and postcounseling structural mapping of the Oliver remarried family.

The next phase of the counseling dealt with reestablishing boundaries. The counselor explained that blending does not come automatically or instantly, but only through a gradual rearrangement of the new family's structure. It was agreed that David would allow Joyce to do more of the parenting in the best way she saw fit—even if it differed from his way—and that he would explain to Kiri that while Rhonda was still her mother, while she lived with them Joyce would be taking over the day-to-day job, with his approval. That is, Kiri was told that Joyce was not replacing her biological mother, only supplementing her while Kiri remained with them. Kiri could visit her mother whenever it could be arranged, something she expressed an interest in doing, especially after her stepsister was born. Kiri was told by David and Joyce together that she was a member of two households; she could feel free to move between the two without loyalty conflicts.

David and Joyce had their own loyalty issues to resolve. As he came to understand that he had given his daughter his first loyalty, primarily out of guilt over the impact of his failed marriage on Kiri, he recognized that he was contributing to the diminution of his marital relationship. Joyce too recognized that as she felt in a secondary position, she struggled against the child excessively, forcing David to defend Kiri; thus, she too contributed to the deteriorating marriage. The counselor helped them untangle these difficulties, focusing them on working to strengthen their separate identity as a couple and their primary loyalty to each other. They were encouraged to spend more time alone as a couple, sharing activities that did not include Kiri. As this occurred, their bond grew; differences between the couple, while still present, began to be negotiated in a more open fashion rather than through a coalition of father-daughter vs. stepmother. New rules and happier solutions followed, as David, Joyce, and Kiri began to develop their own traditions and to define themselves as a family.

Note the counselor's goals in this case:

1. Reduce the accusations and blame-fixing between the adults

2. Relabel the behavior each finds objectionable in the other as well intentioned, thereby diffusing some of the self-righteous rage and indignation

3. Appeal to each adult's wish to be seen as reasonable and fair in hearing out the spouse's contentions

4. Define the problem as a systems one in which each member, including the child, is contributing

5. Strengthen the spousal subsystem, encouraging their loyalty to each other and their common purpose

6. Consolidate parental authority and unity in regard to the child

7. Help reduce loyalty conflicts in the child and adults alike

8. Keep the remarried system an open system with permeable boundaries, so that the child has a sense of security from the home where she lives, but also retains membership in her other household

9. Help the family to tolerate differences among themselves or from some ideal intact family model

10. Encourage the development of new rules, behavior patterns, and
    family traditions

With the Oliver family, as with all stepfamilies, the counselor's overall
task is to help the fragmented family become more cohesive and better
integrated. In addition to helping them develop a sense of identity as a
family unit and strengthening the new marital bond, the counselor needs
to pay attention to fortifying the sibling bond where stepsiblings exist.
Pasley (1985) advises that helping stepfamilies build generational boundaries within the new stepfamily system rather than supporting original
family boundaries will facilitate stepfamily integration. She recommends
further that counselors invite both households to participate in the counseling process in order to provide greater clarity regarding roles and
responsibilities of the various members in the enlarged stepfamily suprasystem.

In the following case, the counselor meets with all four main adults in
the suprasystem—the custodial parent, the noncustodial parent, the spouse
of the custodial parent, and the spouse of the noncustodial parent—despite
the fact that the identified patient is one of the preadolescent children:

Kevin, aged 11, was doing extremely poorly in school. The teacher
complained that he was hyperactive in class, and seemed unable to sit still
or attend to class activity for more than three or four minutes at a time. The
older of two children, Kevin, along with Mark, 8, lived in a joint physical
custody arrangement, generally staying at his remarried father's home
three days a week and at his remarried mother's four days. When the
teacher contacted both parents, each angrily blamed the other for the
problems Kevin was having, but ultimately their physician persuaded
them to take him to a university-affiliated pediatric clinic for an evaluation.

It was clear almost immediately to the pediatrician who worked on
Kevin's case that more was involved than simply what was going on inside
the boy. He was aware that the continuous fighting between both sets of
parents was having a damaging impact on Kevin, so before he prescribed
medication (in this case, Ritalin) for the hyperactivity, he recommended
that the four adults seek family counseling. Although they initially resisted
the idea, he finally insisted that he could not go ahead with treating Kevin
until the family conflict had been reduced. After two weeks of further
bickering between the couples, they agreed to see a family counselor the
pediatrician had recommended. However, each couple expressed doubts
about the wisdom of working together, since their prior efforts in conciliation court (over issues regarding finances, visitation schedules, and custody
changes) had proved pointless and unsuccessful.

The counselor made it clear from the start that she would only see them
as a foursome. When she greeted them in the waiting room, she could see

that they were poised to fight, an impression that was confirmed as soon as they entered the consultation room. They immediately attempted to set the counseling agenda along the lines of their previous conciliation court experience, each couple pulling out divorce settlements to back up their claims. The first session was spent identifying the players—Suzy had recently married Clark, Kevin's father; Stanley and Jane (Kevin's mother) had been married for four years and had a newborn child—and filling out a genogram.

Subsequent sessions revealed that while each former spouse believed that the other's new spouse had initiated the trouble between them, the truth seemed to be that the new spouses had simply empowered their mates to stand up and fight—Clark to limit his financial contribution to the support of the two children, previously given generously and seemingly without regard to limit, now that he had remarried; Jane to demand more time and help in picking the boys up from school and taking them more often on holidays, now that she had the additional responsibility of caring for her newborn, Lizzie.

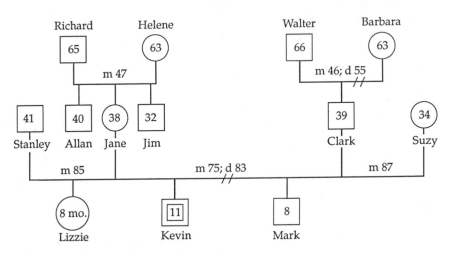

Figure 5.3. Genogram of Kevin's suprafamily.

Rather than deal with these seemingly intractable issues for the time being, the counselor refocused their attention on the presenting problem of Kevin's school performance, asking each couple how they understood what was happening to him at school. As each spoke, they began to be aware that Kevin showed similar behavior at home, and that what was more, each experienced him in the same way. He was obstreperous, irresponsible, fidgety, forgetful about doing his assigned chores, and he frequently fought with Mark. Whereas each had assumed previously that they were burdened with his problematic behavior and that their counterpart was spared, they now began to recognize that both sets of parents were having identical experiences, and neither was being handed a problem created by the visit for several days to the other, as each had assumed.

The counselor's strategy of getting them to work together on solving their common problem seemed to pay off. Each ex-spouse started to view the other's new spouse as a real person—someone who did indeed create some difficulties, but also not others, as previously assumed. With greater insight came greater sympathy and less scapegoating. Rather than remaining angry with one another, they started tentatively to work together on helping Kevin. As they spoke together in the counselor's office weekly, they recognized that each set of parents was alternately too rigid in their demands on Kevin, asking for more than he could give and thus creating an inevitable failure situation, and then giving up in defeat and frustration and becoming too lax and undemanding. The counselor helped them work at being consistent, offering specific suggestions ("You are asking him to perform too long a chore"; "Make sure he is expected to do the same thing in both homes") that, coming from a neutral authority, all four seemed to accept.

The consistency was not lost on Kevin either. Instead of getting a weekly bombardment in each home about the shortcomings (or evil intent, or "craziness") of the other set of parents, Kevin now heard the parents talk in more supportive terms about one another's efforts. His relationship with Mark improved, as he became less competitive with him for parental approval. Both sets of parents seemed less tense with one another and better organized, he believed, and that was comforting to Kevin. He became less confused at school and less agitated, although his short attention span continued to be a problem.

By strengthening the coparental coalition, the counselor had helped create a more secure set of home environments. Kevin was sent back to the pediatric clinic, where he was put on a trial run of Ritalin. Although it was dramatically effective at school, all four parents were frightened of keeping him on drugs, and began to compete at home over which set of parents was able to keep him off the medication longer while he resided with them during the week. After consulting with the pediatrician, the counselor persuaded the parents to accept the drug use, since it helped greatly in focusing Kevin's attention first at school and later at home.

All four parents were thrilled by Kevin's progress, as well as their ability to discuss issues about the children with one another without quarreling. Slowly they ironed out their scheduling, and ultimately their financial, differences. The counselor asked them to come a half hour early for their next appointment and to meet in the waiting room to work out solutions to practical issues between them. They did so successfully, and when the counselor was away on vacation, they continued to meet at the neutral territory of a local recreation center to continue talking.

The counseling dealt with such powerful issues as competitiveness and jealousy between the biological mother and stepmother, as well as economic and social conflict between the father and stepfather. The system in which both sets of parents participated remained open and the boundaries permeable. The parents felt an increased sense of self-esteem, considerably different from their earlier feeling of anger and helplessness regarding child rearing. Together they learned negotiating skills, vital in remarried family situations.

Some issues continued to be unsettled. Anger remained on both sides over money, and both of Kevin's parents continued to feel some injustices left over from the original marriage. However, they did agree to put aside their differences in the service of their newly developed family stability. Kevin became increasingly attached to his stepsister, Lizzie, and helped out with her when he could. Suzy and Clark, having survived a crisis over a stepchild that nearly wrecked their marriage, were feeling more optimistic about the future, and were planning to adopt a baby.

PSYCHOEDUCATIONAL PROGRAMS

Beyond family counseling, stepfamilies can often profit from reading about the experiences of other stepparents and stepchildren (for example, Einstein, 1982). Another important information resource is the stepfamily awareness movement, led by the Stepfamily Association of America. This national nonprofit organization founded by Emily and John Visher has state and local chapters that offer a variety of educational programs (training for professionals; referral to counselors who work with stepfamilies) and provide a network of mutual help services (survival courses in stepfamily living). Its quarterly publication, *Stepfamily Bulletin*, is intended to act as an advocate of stepfamily life, while keeping the readers, many of whom are themselves stepfamily members, informed on the latest studies and events that affect the stepfamily. Visher and Visher (1986) have developed a stepfamily workshop manual (an excerpt from which is shown in Box 5.2) to aid in discussion groups aimed at structuring new suprafamily systems.

Finally, a word about the positive benefits of remarriage and stepfamilies. Clearly, the heavy burden of single parenting is reduced. Not only are economic pressures lightened on the single parent, but the presence of another adult provides essential feedback information on child-rearing procedures. Further, the potential danger to the child of being pressured into assuming a spousal role with a single parent is lessened. The participation of grandparents and other extended family members in a remarried situation typically is a plus for the children. A stepfamily also provides an opportunity for parents to have a larger family, especially a benefit if one spouse is childless or has fewer children than he or she desires. An only child is certain to benefit from mingling with stepsiblings. A functioning remarried family elicits all the respect and social acceptance that an intact

---

Box 5.2.   Tasks That Must Be Completed to Develop a Stepfamily Identity.

1. Dealing with losses and changes
2. Negotiating different developmental needs
3 Establishing new traditions
4. Developing a solid couple bond
5. Forming new relationships
6. Creating a "parenting coalition"
7. Accepting continual shifts in household composition
8. Risking involvement despite little societal support

1. Dealing with losses and changes
   * Identify/recognize losses for all individuals
   * Support expressions of sadness
   * Help children talk and not act out feelings
   * Read stepfamily books
   * Make changes gradually
   * See that everyone gets a turn
   * Inform children of plans involving them
   * Accept the insecurity of change

2. Negotiating different developmental needs
   * Take a child development and/or parenting class
   * Accept validity of the different life-cycle phases
   * Communicate individual needs clearly
   * Negotiate incompatible needs
   * Develop tolerance and flexibility

3. Establishing new traditions
   * Recognize ways are *different*, not right or wrong
   * Concentrate on important situations only
   * Stepparents take on discipline enforcement slowly
   * Use "family meetings" for problem solving and giving appreciation
   * Shift "givens" slowly whenever possible
   * Retain/combine appropriate rituals
   * Enrich with new creative traditions

4. Developing a solid couple bond
   * Accept couple as primary long-term relationship

Box 5.2.   (continued)

- Nourish couple relationship
- Plan for couple "alone time"
- Decide general household rules as a couple
- Support one another with the children
- Expect and accept different parent-child stepparent-stepchild feelings
- Work out money matters together

5. Forming new relationships
   - Fill in past histories
   - Make stepparent-stepchild 1:1 time
   - Make parent-child 1:1 time
   - Parent make space for stepparent-stepchild relationship
   - Do not expect "instant love" and adjustment
   - Be fair to stepchildren even when caring not developed
   - Follow children's lead in what to call stepparent
   - Do fun things together

6. Creating a "parenting coalition"
   - Deal directly with parenting adults in other household
   - Keep children out of the middle of parental disagreements
   - Do not talk negatively about adults in other household
   - Control what you can and accept limitations
   - Avoid power struggles between households
   - Respect parenting skills of former spouse
   - Contribute own "specialness" to children
   - Communicate between households in most effective manner

7. Accepting continual shifts in household composition
   - Allow children to enjoy their households
   - Give children time to adjust to household transitions
   - Avoid asking children to be "messengers" or "spies"
   - Consider teenager's serious desire to change residence
   - Respect privacy (boundaries) of all households
   - Set consequences that affect own household only
   - Provide personal place for nonresident children
   - Plan special times for various household constellations

8. Risking involvement despite little societal support

(continued)

**Box 5.2.   Tasks That Must Be Completed to Develop
a Stepfamily Identity**

- Include stepparents in school, religious, sports activities
- Give legal permission for stepparent to act when necessary
- Continue stepparent-stepchild relationships after death or divorce of parent when caring has developed
- Stepparent include self in stepchild's activities
- Find groups supportive of stepfamilies
- Remember that all relationships involve risk

Source: Visher & Visher, 1986, p. 235-236.

---

family does. Last, doing something helpful and beneficial for someone you love, such as helping raise their children, is rewarding in and of itself.

SUMMARY

Remarriage is an increasingly common phenomenon; three out of five previously divorced persons remarry, usually within three years of their divorce. Perhaps 40 percent of all marriages in the United States today involve at least one partner who was married before. Such remarried families come in a variety of structural forms, depending on whether one or both spouses were previously single, divorced, or widowed, and whether children (who may or may not live with them) are involved. Each pattern brings with it a separate set of problems for the counselor to consider.

In general, all members of a remarried family have sustained a recent primary relationship loss. New interactive patterns are likely to be complex and prone to stress, as unfamiliar roles and rules are worked out and boundaries stabilized. Disequilibrium and conflict are the norm, especially in the early stages of a remarried family, and particularly so when children are present. Unfinished conflict between ex-mates adds to the overall turmoil, as does the presence of stepsiblings living under one roof. Loyalty conflicts in both children and adults are frequent. Early in a remarriage is also often the time for rearranging custody, visitation, or financial affairs between ex-spouses, sometimes reopening old wounds, a special problem because the newly married couple is at its earliest and thus most vulnerable point.

Remarriage is a process that proceeds through a number of distinct phases. Each has its potential for dislocation; each provides an opportunity for family consolidation. Counselors need to remain aware that disruptions may be occurring at three levels—individual, marital, and family—simultaneously for each member of the remarried family. Thus, members may need help in completing mourning for their earlier losses, in working out new relationship problems, and in forging boundary realignments as they attempt to form a stable, integrated family structure.

Counselors need to remain aware that remarried or stepfamilies are structurally different from intact biological families. They are likely to be far more complex as two distinct families, with different experiences and traditions, attempt to blend into a stable relationship with an identity of its own. Counseling efforts must address the numerous relationship problems specific to the suprafamily's stage of development. Psychoeducational programs directed at stepfamily life may provide useful help in achieving stepfamily integration.

Chapter 6

◆◆◆

Counseling Cohabiting Heterosexual Couples

One of the alternative or unconventional lifestyles to have emerged to a considerable and lasting extent in the 1970s is the living together of two adults of the opposite sex in a sexual relationship without the formality or sanction of being legally married. According to U.S. Bureau of the Census (1980) population data, close to 2 million unmarried couples shared such a living pattern by the end of the 1970s, some perhaps having lived through several such arrangements over varying periods of time. More recent census data indicate that the overall number continues to rise, although at a somewhat slower rate. The latest available count (U.S. Bureau of the Census, 1986) estimates that 2.2 million unmarried couples shared households in 1986. Although still representing little more than 4 percent of all American couples living together (Macklin, 1988; Spanier, 1983), the phenomenon nevertheless illustrates a dramatic increase in both practice and public acceptance of a heretofore little-noticed and infrequently practiced type of heterosexual union, particularly among young middle-class adults.

Cohabitation itself is not exactly a new occurrence—common law and other nonlegal unions have long been accepted in many societies, particularly among low-income persons—but what *is* new is its increased prevalence in a broader segment of American society, the fact that the participants do not consider themselves to be married or necessarily in a permanent relationship, and the increasing acceptance of this dyadic structure by the majority culture (Macklin, 1983).

Because cohabitation is still considered unconventional by the majority of society, few guidelines are available, and thus roles, interactive patterns, and styles of conflict management are often forged between partners on an individual trial-and-error basis, often at the cost of considerable interpersonal distress. Whether one or both partners have been married previously, whether children are included in the living arrangement, whether financial pressures are experienced, whether families of origin know of and support the arrangement—all these factors influence the kinds of stressors and levels of satisfaction each partner realizes from the cohabiting relationship. Without question, counselors can expect to see some couples living in a cohabital arrangement seeking help for resolving relationship problems, others attempting to settle conflicts over differences in commitment to the future together, some perhaps desiring premarital counseling, and others reaching out for therapeutic aid in the emotional upheaval accompanying the pair's breakup.

CHANGING MORES, CHANGING LIFESTYLES

Public media awareness of the phenomenon of two young people, more often than not college students, living together without being married, began in the latter half of the 1960s, a time of social ferment, changing sexual values, and a willingness to experiment with unorthodox lifestyles. As Macklin (1983) observes, prior to that time "only the most avant garde or the most impoverished, or those otherwise considered to be on the social periphery of society, were to be found openly cohabiting outside of marriage, and unmarried persons known to be living together could be expected to be referred to derogatorily as 'shacking up' " (p. 52).

Since that time, growth in the prevalence of cohabitation in all age groups has spurted; as Glick and Spanier (1980) note, rarely does social change relating to marriage and family life occur with such rapidity. College students and college-aged young adults in particular have gravitated toward this living arrangement in large numbers. According to one leading researcher (Macklin, 1978) reporting on her analysis of surveys of all regions of the United States taken more than a decade ago, one-quarter of all U.S. college undergraduates had had a cohabiting experience. Furthermore, an additional 25 percent said they would cohabit if the right partner came along (Peterman, Ridley, & Anderson, 1974).

Studies by Newcomb (1987) and others indicate that an increasing number of marriages today, perhaps as many as half or more, are preceded by cohabitation. As Gwartney-Gibbs (1986) observes, cohabitation has come increasingly to be looked at as a normative step leading to marriage for many of today's young people, who wish to "try out" a relationship before making a more permanent commitment. In addition, older people, widowed or divorced, including some senior citizens, have begun to live together without being married; in the latter case, companionship and the opportunity to informally merge financial resources without risking the loss of retirement or Social Security benefits or jeopardizing inheritance for their children as a result of remarriage are often the primary motivations. Later in this chapter we present clinical examples of various cohabiting relationships, together with a discussion of their interpersonal dynamics as well as the problems confronting the counselor and recommended solutions.

Counselors should certainly concern themselves with what sorts of individuals choose this living pattern, what motivates them, and why they choose cohabiting rather than dating or marrying. Are specific attitudes— for example, regarding male-female roles or delaying commitment or retaining a sense of independence while relating to another—likely to be typical of people in this lifestyle? Are cohabiters more unconventional, more defiant of traditional values? Do they as a group have more liberal attitudes toward sexual behavior? Clearly, the counselor needs to look at the specific dyadic relationship of the presenting couple, but we mention certain common patterns as guidelines to organize an appraisal.

Why the sudden change in social values and behavior, not only on the part of young people, which might be more expected, but also on the part of their elders? Several factors, some of which we have touched upon in previous chapters, seem to be operating here. More openness regarding sexual behavior, increased availability of effective contraception, and a growing acceptance of sexual involvement before marriage all seem to be pertinent. Moreover, a growing demand on the part of women for equal rights and the abandonment of the "double standard" vis 'a vis men is clearly a factor. An emphasis on a meaningful relationship and on the continued growth of both partners probably has played a part, as people of all ages explore new ways to achieve fulfillment and escape the many "games" involved in dating. Perhaps, in some cases, the fear of sexually-transmitted diseases has resulted in seeking a single partner. Delaying marriage in order to establish professional and economic identities has become of paramount interest to many women as well as men, and cohabiting may well be an important interim solution. The high divorce rate that we have noted has probably led many to proceed cautiously, to try out an intimate relationship before making a more permanent commitment. Cohabiting, for whatever reason—and the counselor would be wise to explore the exact reasons in detail—has by now been incorporated into the broader institutions of our society.

Are personal, social, and attitudinal differences likely to be identifiable between those who choose to cohabit and those who do not? Unfortunately, the little research data available are not sufficiently clear, perhaps because people in these relationships do not represent a unitary entity. Rather, as a number of authorities (Macklin, 1978; Newcomb, 1983; Peterman, Ridley, & Anderson, 1974) point out, *cohabitation* is really a general term for a cluster of heterogeneous relationship types (discussed in the following section)— some temporary or simply convenient and others more committed and permanent, some casual and others a "trial marriage," some preparatory to and others a substitute for marriage—whose only commonality is their living situation.

As for discovering a single path to cohabitation, once again none is likely to fit all participants. Although some couples may carefully plan the move only after considerable deliberation about the pros and cons, others seem to drift into living together without a great deal of forethought or formal joint decision making, as a natural next step after a period of steady and exclusive dating. In the latter case, staying over at the other's apartment on an increasingly regular basis gradually leads to accumulating clothes and other personal possessions there as a practical matter. Perhaps a lease that expires, a job offer in a new location, or acceptance in a graduate program in another city may then become the precipitating factor leading to the decision to move in together.

THE MYTHOLOGY OF COHABITATION

A variety of myths exist around cohabitation, depending on the viewer's outlook. For many younger people, learning that an unmarried couple shares living quarters conjures up an image of two loving and caring individuals, both independent and fearless, indifferent to convention, liberal at least in their attitudes regarding sexual behavior, opting for a monogamous relationship but rejecting the more traditional ideas concerning marriage. Not hampered by the bonds of matrimony, goes this romantic notion, they are free to explore an intimate relationship while maintaining a sense of independence. They stay together because they choose to, not because they are bound by some legal marriage document.

From another perspective, cohabiters are viewed as rebellious, defiant, and immoral people, without legal responsibilities to one another, unwilling to make a lasting commitment, but instead choosing a temporary alliance that is doomed to failure and that will leave both parties feeling heartbroken and guilty when the inevitable breakup occurs. If they really loved each other as much as they claim, goes this argument, they would get married and raise a family, something they are afraid to do.

Neither of these views is entirely accurate—or entirely inaccurate. Like most human relationships, living together outside of marriage involves a complex arrangement that is entered into for a variety of reasons, some of which may not be fully understood by the participants or their critics. In any specific cohabiting dyad (or triad, where a roommate or perhaps a child shares in the living arrangement), multiple motivations no doubt are operating, including a combination of factors described in the two previous chapters.

The counselor needs to be aware that despite the statements of the couple regarding their attitudes and values, other hidden agendas may be at work, and the clients may need help in uncovering them. With even minimum probing, it is common to find clear but unstated disagreements just below the surface. For example, one partner (most likely the woman) may want to get married but be afraid to say so, believing that such a view reneges on their no-strings-attached agreement. In another case, one participant may no longer wish to abide by a previously agreed-upon monogamous sexual relationship but be reluctant or fearful of broaching that subject. Or, conversely, he or she may wish for a rule change to make a previously open relationship into a monogamous one, but not know how to go about implementing that desire. The counselor has to guide the couple in unmasking and attending to these underlying but unexpressed conflicts.

The counselor, too, must be careful not to take statements at face value or assume that because the couple live in a cohabiting relationship they fit some preconceived stereotype. For instance, couples who may appear unconventional because they live in an atypical marital structure may actually live fairly conventional lives, dividing their responsibilities (for example, who does which household tasks) and priorities (whose career development takes precedence) along rather traditional sex role lines.

It is important, too, that the counselor be in touch with his or her own values regarding what is still an unorthodox living arrangement between unmarried adults. If that viewpoint is antithetical to this lifestyle, it may bias the therapeutic process, and in such cases the clients deserve a forthright and explicit statement of the counselor's views on cohabitation. For example, it is only fair for a religious counselor who believes the couple is "living in sin" to impart that outlook at the start. If the couple, having this knowledge, nevertheless chooses to continue counseling, then they do so bearing that counselor's view in mind. Thus, it is essential that the counselor have an explicit, articulated understanding of his or her own values, and how they might differ from the clients'. Effective counseling requires not imposing counselor values on other people's lives.

TYPES OF STUDENT COHABITATION

As we have noted, cohabitation is not a unitary entity, but rather an unmarried heterosexual living arrangement that may take a variety of forms, serve different functions, and come about for a multitude of reasons. Among college students, for example, at least four patterns have been differentiated: the Linus Blanket, Emancipation, Convenience, and Testing types of cohabiting patterns (Ridley, Peterman, & Avery, 1978).

In the Linus Blanket type of cohabital setup, named after the Peanuts comic strip character who is never too far from his security blanket, the counselor can expect at least one of the partners to need a relationship so badly that it hardly matters what kind or with whom.

The following cases, abstracted from our files, illustrate some of the transactional forces at play:

Josh and Nicole met one day at the Student Union of the college both attended. Nicole, 18, was a freshman with an undeclared major, living in the college dorm, away from home for the first time, 1000 miles from her family. Josh, 20, a junior business major, also lived several hundred miles from home, but in his own apartment. Nicole was immediately attracted to Josh's good looks, his intelligence, and especially his seemingly high sense of self-assurance. Josh, on the other hand, in addition to finding her physically attractive, was immediately taken by Nicole's sweetness, vulnerability, and apparent need to be taken care of. They dated for several months, developed a sexual relationship—Nicole's first, it turned out—and soon Nicole was spending more and more time at Josh's apartment. Midway through the spring semester, Josh's roommate moved out, and Nicole moved in. However, she retained her dorm address, because the school required dorm living for freshmen and because she tried to hide the living arrangement from her parents.

Problems began soon after they became roommates. Nicole, very dependent on Josh for her emotional security, was jealous of his friends and of any time he spent in activities where she was not invited. She worried about whether he was sexually faithful, despite his repeated reassurances. Also, she lived in constant fear that her parents would discover the living arrangement, would certainly disapprove, and might insist she not return to the school the following year. Josh was bothered by her overdependency, her immaturity, her seemingly few coping skills, and her poor self-esteem. Although he agreed to see a counselor together with Nicole, it was clear from the first session that he was simply going through the motions and wanted an excuse to end the relationship. They separated after three sessions, but Nicole continued on an individual basis with the counselor to work on her personal insecurities.

The Emancipation type of cohabiting relationship presents the counselor with a different configuration:

✦✦✦

Denise, 18, raised as a devout Catholic, had had few close relationships outside her family before going away to a college with a strong religious orientation. Growing up in a well-to-do large family and attending the best parochial schools in her community, she had been sheltered from most everyday problems of living. Her parents were protective and doting, and despite her being the oldest child, expected little of her except that she earn good grades, not smoke, and stay away from bad company. Denise did not disappoint them, since she was a top student, always had her assignments in on time, and never caused anybody any trouble. When she was ready for college, she consulted her parents as well as her school counselor, and together they decided on a nearby school with a reputation for a religious student body and serious dedication to scholarship.

Denise was driven to the campus by her parents, who expressed pleasure at the dormitory accommodations. They were pleased, too, by her roommate, Alice, also 18, who seemingly had a social class and religious background similar to their daughter's. By the time they left to return home, some 75 miles away, they felt Denise was in a safe, protected environment conducive to personal development.

Trouble began when Denise, now on her own, soon found herself caught in a conflict between internalized pressures from her religious upbringing, her own emerging need to develop an identity, and peer pressures from her classmates, especially Alice. Although raised as a Catholic, Alice had secretly rebelled against the teachings of the church, and in high school had had considerable experiences with drugs and sexual experimentation with several boys. At first, Denise was horrified—and somewhat intrigued—by Alice's accounts of her past exploits. As Alice began to bring some of the college men to the room, Denise became increasingly involved, and soon found herself particularly interested in Randy, a young black student from another part of the country.

Randy, 19, a bright, serious, hardworking student, also Catholic, came from a middle-class background. He was interested in going on to law school, and had spent the year following graduation working in order to save up enough money to supplement the support from his parents. In Denise he found a quiet, unassuming, but caring person with whom he felt comfortable. He and Denise recognized they both lacked sophistication or a great deal of previous dating experience, and that was a plus to their way of thinking. Both were shy and modest, and since neither was the kind to use a friend's apartment for a sexual liaison, Randy and Denise soon found an apartment near campus to which they retreated several nights each week and on the weekend. However, when Denise's parents decided to surprise her with a visit one Sunday, they were able to track her down, and soon, dumbfounded, discovered the situation their daughter had kept from them. Although they protested that racial issues were not involved, but that Denise was too young for such a living arrangement, it was clear that there was nothing about the situation to their liking. They refused to recognize the new relationship, insisted their daughter return home immediately, and that she not bring Randy or ever see him again. Denise refused, told them she loved Randy, and if they persisted that they would never see her again.

It was the parents who consulted a family counselor. Their dislike of the situation was accepted, but they were directed to examine what issues most incensed them. The racial issue called for special scrutiny, suggested the counselor, because it was essential that they be clear in their own minds just how they truly felt. They also were urged to deal with what was involved for them in letting go of Denise and allowing her to make her own judgments about her life. True, they disapproved of the situation, and yes, they had every right to let their daughter know in no uncertain terms how they really felt. But beyond that, how much risk were they willing to take of alienating her to the point that she might marry him out of spite? Perhaps by accepting the situation and getting to know the couple, they might remove the heated, rebellious motive that might exist in Denise's behavior. In such a case, they might influence the outcome in the direction they desired, instead of forcing the opposite resolution. Denise might or might not continue with Randy, but at least they would not lose contact with their daughter, and Denise and Randy could decide on a more rational basis what to do.

When these issues had been successfully dealt with in the opinion of the counselor, he suggested all four players come together for a joint family session. Denise spoke of her anger at her parents; she accused them of dishonesty regarding their racial attitudes, and of unwillingness to let her grow up out of their control. Because the parents had worked through the issues with the counselor previously regarding their feelings about Randy's color, they were not defensive. Instead they did discuss some of the complications of an interracial marriage, but insisted that was not the basis for their opposition. Rather, they were more concerned by her inexperience in other relationships, as well as Randy's. Denise made it clear that she and Randy were far from making any permanent commitments, and that actually they had decided to live separately next year precisely because they too recognized that each needed opportunities to explore new relationships.

The counselor had helped the parents to see Denise's behavior as transient and a necessary part of her development. By not making the conflict one over power, with one side forced to back down, any need to be rebellious or punitive was reduced and the young people were allowed to get on with their lives. By keeping down the uproar and emphasizing the need for clear and honest communication, the counselor had allowed Denise to confront her parents with normal late-adolescent issues, and for all four persons to benefit from the encounter.

◆◆◆

Turning now to an example of a cohabiting arrangement based on convenience, much like a "marriage of convenience," we find the following as typical:

——————————————— ◆◆◆ ———————————————

Terri, a college sophomore, answered an ad for a roommate in the college newspaper soon after the new school year began. She had decided during the summer break that she would live with a girlfriend from high school, but when that plan failed to materialize—the friend transferred to another school at the last minute—Terri sought other living arrangements. In responding to the ad, she found one to her liking, living in a three-bedroom apartment near campus with Nancy and Eric, two people she did not know before but seemed to like at first glance.

Nancy and Eric, old friends but not lovers, had a lot of friends who visited them frequently, and Terri enjoyed living with them very much. She and Nancy would talk at great length with each other, but Eric tended to be more reserved and aloof. He definitely was not her type, she thought; he was three years older, too serious for her tastes, and the fact that he was Jewish made any long-term involvement with him too complicated. Nevertheless, to some extent because of their proximity on a daily basis, within six months they had drifted into a sexual relationship. Nancy was aware of what was happening and did not object, since she was not romantically interested in Eric and was glad two people she liked liked each other. When Nancy decided to move to her own apartment, Eric and Terri remained without getting a new roommate.

Together they were sexually compatible, and enjoyed the luxury of domestic living without the responsibilities of a deeper or more permanent commitment. However, after two months, Eric began to find fault with Terri—she was too immature, and she was not serious enough about her studies. She, too, found fault with him—he was too involved with term papers, had little time for her, and when they were together he would find fault with her "childish" behavior in front of his friends. Both expressed resentment over feeling "tied down" and not able to pursue interests in other people to whom they might feel attracted.

When they went together to the school counselor, she pointed out that they had drifted into their living together at least in part because of convenience, and that they had not really made a commitment to one another. Each indicated a lasting fondness for the other that each was afraid to jeopardize, but the counselor observed that they could remain friends while living separately. Reassured that they had profited from the domestic experience together without too much pain, they acknowledged that there were no hard feelings and that each was now ready to go on alone.

——————————————— ◆◆◆ ———————————————

As indicated by these examples, neither the Linus Blanket, Emancipation, nor Convenience types of live-in formats are conducive to fostering a long-term nonmarital relationship. They are, however, characteristic of cohabiting arrangements among college students, in that they tend to be short-lived, typically terminating after several months or at the end of the school year. In that sense they can be thought of as more a courtship phenomenon (perhaps the next step following steady dating for many couples) than an alternative to marriage.

In a smaller number of cases, cohabitation is a temporary alternative to marriage. Both partners tend to be older, more mature, and more ready to make a permanent commitment to marriage. They may have decided to live together because it is more convenient until some roadblocks have been overcome (graduation, better income, parental disapproval). However, they are prepared to enter an intimate relationship with someone they love with an eye toward eventual marriage. Testing whether a conjugal experience will confirm their shared beliefs regarding their future together, this living arrangement has the best potential for both personal development and the achievement of interpersonal fulfillment.

Patti and Michael met during their last year at college, and immediately started dating each other exclusively. Both had had a number of earlier dating experiences, and Michael had lived with a female student during his sophomore year. Despite Michael's urging, Patti resisted the suggestion that they move in together, since they had only known each other for four months and she feared it would cost her some sense of independence, which she cherished. They discussed the matter at great length and agreed that they would see each other every night for dinner at his apartment or hers, and one would often end up staying the night, but it would be best if they retained their own separate lifestyles for the time being. In that way they could build the relationship slowly and determine whether a long-term living arrangement, perhaps ultimately marriage, made sense.

When Michael graduated, he went on to medical school in another part of the country. Although he wanted Patti to accompany him, he was aware that she had her own career plans, so he did not pursue the matter strenuously. Besides, he said to himself, medical school was demanding, and it would not be fair to Patti or himself if she lived with him during the first year or two. Patti too went on to graduate school in rehabilitation counseling, a two-year program that required a great deal of time and dedication. They did agree to speak together by telephone at least once each week, and to fly to each other's cities to see one another about every three months. Although each was lonely, and also somewhat apprehensive of losing the other because they no longer were in daily contact, the relationship continued to grow and be strengthened.

Upon graduation, and by mutual agreement, Patti found a job in the city where Michael was attending medical school, and they moved in together. Both worked hard at building the relationship, since the time apart had convinced them both that they wanted to spend their lives together. Cautious to the end, they contacted a counselor for some premarital counseling, more a kind of "checkup" to make certain that no hidden feelings would mar their future together. Satisfied that they could each retain a sense of independence while gaining much from relating to one another, they made plans to get married the following June.

◆◆◆

ADULT COHABITATION: TRIAL MARRIAGE OR SUBSTITUTE FOR MARRIAGE?

In considering unmarried students living together and sharing a bedroom, we were dealing with only one portion of the adult cohabiting population. What of the other portion? Some have opted for a permanent or semipermanent alternative to marriage, which may even include having children together, sharing a joint bank account, buying a house, and so on. For a variety of philosophical or practical reasons, these couples commit themselves to a long-term relationship very much like a marriage, but without the legal or religious sanctions.

Others in such an arrangement may be receiving alimony and child support payments from an ex-spouse, and thus may not be in a hurry to marry and relinquish such payments, especially if they do not intend to have additional children. As we noted earlier, middle-aged or even elderly persons may choose to live in a conjugal relationship, sharing expenses, providing companionship and a social partner to one another, but not willing to marry again, nor particularly interested in doing so. Young people busy forging careers and not ready for children, may look at cohabitation as less demanding than formal marriage (although breaking up after many years together can be just as painful as a divorce). Finally, as Newcomb (1987), Eidelson (1983), and others have pointed out, for many people, traditional marriage simply does not represent the ideal way to achieve an amalgam of independence and relatedness. Particularly for this last group, long-term cohabitation offers a structure for achieving the often-conflicting goals of autonomy and affiliation with another person.

The dramatic increase in cohabitation in recent years, then, can be explained in a number of ways, and the counselor needs to zero in on which set of factors is at work with the specific couple seeking counseling services. Does this couple live together instead of marrying because they lack the readiness to make a complete commitment? Because they are immature and fearful of the responsibility of making a marriage work? Because one or both fear being alone, but do not have the wish or sense of security to form a strong partnership or achieve real intimacy? Because unless children are involved, they both believe marriage is irrelevant or unnecessary? Because they feel unable to predict how they will feel in the future and thus want to keep open all options? Because they know few if any really happily married people, and want to avoid the legal entanglements and expense of a divorce? Because they can combine all the benefits of both an unencumbered single life (autonomy, independence) and married life (intimacy, sexuality, companionship) by living together?

Do they plan to marry? Does one partner want marriage and the other not, or not now? Is their present living arrangement temporary? Are they in a "trial marriage" because they seriously contemplate a permanent commitment and first want to check out their compatibility and the quality of their relationship? An increasing number of marriages today are preceded by cohabitation, perhaps indicating a wish to test out the strength and durability of the union before making the final commitment.

Cohabiting couples marry for different reasons. Some may be trying desperately to repair a failing union, probably hoping that the added commitment of a marriage contract will rescue their troubled relationship. (Couples in such a situation typically get divorced soon after their marriage, discovering that the identical conflicts they experienced as cohabiters are likely to remain unresolved despite the marriage vows.) Others are ready to settle down and have children. Some want to make it legal to please a dying parent. Perhaps a landlord or employer insists, or the Army requires a soldier to be married if he wants to live on the base. Tax deductions for married couples offer an inducement to some couples. Some are possessive or fear the consequences of an open relationship. Others are finally ready to make the commitment to someone they cannot live without.

ASSESSING AND COUNSELING COHABITING COUPLES

Cohabiting couples rarely consult a counselor about whether or not they should live together. They are far more likely to present problems common to all troubled couples (for example, poor communication, sexual difficulties, erosion of their previous love and compatibility). Cole (1988) refers to these areas of potential conflict as "relationship maintenance struggles"; they may be interpersonally induced (as in the examples in the previous sentence) or situationally evoked by outside forces (for example, emotional cutoff from parents). Therapeutically, the counselor needs to treat them as similar to problems occurring between marriage partners.

However, living together unmarried does present a unique set of challenges. Box 6.1 alerts the counselor to common problems most cohabiting couples must address as they enter into and attempt to advance an evolving relationship. While the social stigma, for example, may be minimal in one's own subgroup (such as among college students), that often is hardly the case in the larger social structure, public media to the contrary. Parents, other family members, fellow employees or employer, even friends may be kept in the dark about the live-in arrangement, all pointing to the couple's self-consciousness. Frequently the couple maintains two telephones in their apartment, each prepared only to answer his or hers, to keep up the illusion that they are living alone. In more extreme cases, the pretense goes as far as retaining two apartments while living together in one, in a further effort to avoid detection. Visiting parents may cause a temporary move by one partner to evade parental disapproval. If the arrangement is discovered, parents may urge a breakup, or in some cases may press for an early marriage. The counselor assessing the strengths and weaknesses or perhaps the durability of the relationship must certainly attempt to help the partners evaluate the degree of discomfort they feel in what is still an unconventional lifestyle.

Box 6.1. A Problem Appraisal Checklist for Cohabiting Heterosexual Adult Couples

Cohabiting heterosexual adults may experience problems in the following areas:

- Social stigma
- Term for cohabiting partner
- Unequal commitment between partners
- Lack of legal safeguards
- Dealing with families of origin
- Differing views of roles and lifestyle patterns
- Monogamous vs. nonmonogamous sexual relationship
- Division of labor, money, resources
- Parenting of other's children
- Differing views of autonomy connectedness
- Differing expectations regarding future
- Terminating the relationship

Another likely area of difficulty is what to call the cohabiting partner. Meet my live-in boyfriend (girlfriend)? The person with whom I share an apartment (bed)? My fiance? My housemate? My lover? My significant other? My domestic partner? According to U.S. census jargon, the man and woman are POSSLQ (People of the opposite sex sharing living quarters)! Meet my POSSLQ? The confusion, embarrassment, and discomfort at not knowing precisely how to describe the relationship reflect society's lack of clarity about how best to conceptualize what is occurring between and within these individuals who have committed themselves to one another, but in a nontraditional way.

Legal complexities and potentially damaging legal consequences may arise from an unmarried union. A bitter noncustodial father, for example, may demand that the court overturn an earlier custody ruling because the child is living with a mother who is cohabiting, arguing that such a living arrangement is detrimental to the child's moral and emotional well-being. Thus, the counselor may need to alert a divorced client with a live-in lover to the possible threat to custody, and may need to urge the client to evaluate his or her situation regarding conceivable legal action by an avenging or otherwise outraged ex-spouse.

In a similar way, a divorced custodial mother, particularly one who has been left by her husband in favor of another woman, may retaliate by restricting the father's visitation rights, claiming she wants to shield her child from visiting him because he is living with a woman to whom he is not married. Unfinished fighting between divorced parents often erupts over this emotional issue, as they repeatedly drag one another into court (or the counselor's office, where the former mates need to be seen jointly).

As we have noted, the emotional trauma of separation after a live-in arrangement, particularly one of long duration, may be every bit as painful as after a long-standing marriage. Terminating a relationship that has been intimate and binding is never done casually, as any marital/family counselor can attest. Losing the emotional closeness, the mutual sharing, the daily involvement in one another's lives is always accompanied by considerable anguish and a sense of failure, no matter how far the relationship has deteriorated. Cohabiters may reject traditional ideas regarding marriage, but that is not to say they survive the breakup with any greater equanimity than do divorcing spouses.

In addition to their lives having become entwined, the unmarried couple may have accumulated property together, and promises of marriage may have been made. In the widely publicized 1976 case of *Marvin* v. *Marvin*, involving the cohabiting couple actor Lee Marvin and Michelle Marvin, she sought court action to divide the considerable property accumulated by the couple during their unmarried years together. The California Supreme Court finally ruled that a cohabiting couple can make a contract—a *prenuptial agreement*—affecting their property rights, as the Marvins had done, as long as sex is not part of the consideration for signing the agreement. That is, a couple can sign a contract before moving in together regarding their earnings and property rights, as long as the contract does not involve pay for the performance of sexual services, which would in essence be an unlawful contract for prostitution. Not all states have followed the California ruling, although all recognize that legal remedies are often needed to divide property obtained by unmarried cohabiting couples. As Huber and Baruth (1987) suggest, some counselors working with cohabiting adults recommend that relationship interests be formalized, if not by marriage then by binding contract, in the best legal interest of both parties.

Additional legal entanglements, often the source of considerable distress, occur if the cohabiting partners have children together. Beyond that, cohabiting men and women continuously face social discrimination in matters such as buying a house together, obtaining a bank loan, and becoming eligible for the partner's health insurance benefits. Despite increasing judicial recognition of the cohabiting lifestyle, society does not yet grant full recognition of such unconventionality.

PREMARITAL COUNSELING

Cohabiting couples frequently consult a counselor when they are at the point of contemplating marriage, often as a kind of checkup on the health of their relationship. At other times, however, their motivation is different: one or both fear that some underlying conflict remains unresolved and may lead to a future deterioration of their relationship. Where one or the other (or perhaps both) has been divorced, such caution is especially apparent, in vigilance to spot flaws that may impair their future happiness together.

In the former case, the couple seeking a professional's help in assessing their relationship, one counseling tactic is for the counselor to devote four to six conjoint sessions, each an hour to two hours in length, to guiding the couple in examining their interactions in some depth. Here the aim is to provide an experience that will enhance and enrich their future married lives together. In the process, the counselor may occasionally ferret out some previously undiscovered but potentially insidious transactional patterns, make the couple aware of them, and try to repair them.

How long have the partners known each other? How long have they lived together? Why have they decided to marry now? Does one of the partners want to marry more than the other? How do they think marriage will be different from living together? How well do they communicate? Do they experience any discomfort when they attempt to be intimate or emotionally close to one another? How do they manage areas of disagreement? How deep is each partner's commitment to the marriage? Do they agree about having children, the division of labor around the house, handling money, friends of each, vacations, further schooling and/or career moves, where they want to live, and so on? Are they sexually compatible? How temperamentally suited to one another are they? Do they have any strong religious or political conflicts?

How similar are their socioeconomic backgrounds? Their educational levels? Their ages? Their value systems? Their racial and ethnic backgrounds and religious affiliations? Their life experiences? Does either have any previous history of medical or emotional problems? From what kinds of families do they come? Were their parents divorced?

Time is needed to explore these and other factors influencing the likelihood of a stable and satisfying marriage. That is not to say, of course, that conflict over any one of these issues by itself necessarily rules out the possibility of a happy and long-lasting union. An early identification of potential problems may actually head off future disharmony if addressed and resolved. On the other hand, significant and irreconcilable differences may be uncovered, and the couple may decide to postpone the marriage while they work out these problems, or even to cancel their marriage plans for an indefinite period.

As Stahmann and Hiebert (1987) point out, the purpose of premarital counseling is not to resolve all conflict, but rather to help the couple become aware of significant issues between them, to give them a new way of understanding those issues, and to teach them some skills in dealing with them. One of the counselor's major functions may be to raise questions the two have not raised between themselves, to open up areas they have neglected or avoided, and especially to expand their thinking about the nature of their relationship. Lewis and Spanier (1979) advise that "the greater the likelihood that the motivation to marry is independent of problematic circumstantial factors, including internal or external pressures, the higher the marital quality" (p. 278).

While some degree of conflict is an inevitable part of any ongoing interaction, certain seriously conflicted unmarried couples deserve the counselor's special attention. Stahmann and Hiebert (1987) identify the following transactional patterns that should alert the counselor to potential trouble:

The Uncommitted Partner: One or both partners may present an underlying inability or hesitation to make a firm commitment to marriage at this time, despite appearing verbally agreeable to doing so.

The Passive-Inactive Partner: In this profile, one partner appears socially inactive, repressed in expressing feelings, passive and dependent in the couple's interactions.

The Unresponsive and Insensitive Partner: Here one person is inhibited and overly restrained, typically insensitive, unfeeling, and often hostile and critical in dealing with the partner.

The Apprehensive and Pessimistic Partner: One partner is excessively tense, hyperemotional, and periodically discouraged about the future of the relationship.

The Angry and Aggressive Partner: In this transactional pattern, one or both are intense, argumentative, and frequently verbally or physically abusive.

All the patterns we have just identified should be looked at as part of a transaction with another person, rather than as a personality trait or characteristic in one or both individuals. The counselor is trying to determine if certain potential trouble spots or destructive interactive patterns exist, the extent to which they intrude on the stability of the relationship, and if uncorrected, whether they contain the seeds of eventual marital unhappiness and breakup.

Counselors doing premarital counseling often use one or more assessment devices or instruments to appraise the couple's compatibility as well as look for areas where the potential for interpersonal dysfunction exists. David Olson, who was instrumental in developing the Circumplex Model for identifying types of family functioning (see Chapter 3) also has produced a useful and reliable inventory for evaluating a couple's preparation for marriage (Olson, Fournier, & Druckman, 1986). Aptly entitled PRE-PARE (PREmarital Personal And Relationship Evaluation), this computer-scored 125-item inventory is intended to identify and measure relationship strengths as well as necessary work areas in 11 interactive categories:

Realistic Expectations	Personality Issues
Communication	Conflict Resolution
Financial Management	Leisure Activities
Sexual Relationship	Children and Marriage
Family and Friends	Equalitarian Roles
Religious Orientation	

Respondents rate each item on a five-point scale, from Strongly Agree to Strongly Disagree. Typical items in the Realistic Expectations category are "After marriage it will be easier to change those things about my partner I don't like"; "Some of my needs for security, support, and companionship will be met by persons other than my partner." In the Personality Issues category: "Sometimes I am bothered by my partner's temper"; "At times I think my partner is too domineering." In the Communication category: "It is very easy for me to express all my true feelings to my partner"; "When we are having a problem, my partner often gives me the silent treatment."

In addition, the instrument contains an Idealistic Distortion Scale, an effort to correct for any tendency on the part of either potential spouse to respond to items in an idealistic rather than realistic manner.

For each scale, an individual score is obtained (revised as necessary by the Idealistic Distortion score), as is a Positive Couple Agreement score measuring their degree of consensus on the issues raised in that category. Olson, Fournier, and Druckman (1986) contend that the scales are designed to promote couple dialogue and relationship enhancement. Fowers and Olson (1986) emphasize the inventory's ability to identify high-risk couples, as well as its preventive value, guiding the couple to potential problems that require attention, perhaps through more intense premarital counseling. The PREPARE scale is often used in conjunction with the Circumplex Model, assessing information from each partner about his or her family of origin, as in the following case:

◆◆◆

Marian, 38, had a successful career in publishing and had not really wanted to marry until now. She had lived briefly with men on two occasions in her late 20s, but those relationships, while they had had a sexual aspect that was satisfying to her, had not really provided much in the way of emotional closeness. Each had lasted for approximately 8 to 10 months, and then had split up at her insistence. In both cases, Marian, an intensely emotional person, had periodically expressed doubts about continuing the relationship, each time finding fault with her partner that led her to conclude that they had no future together and should separate. Only after the man pleaded that they continue would she relent, but it had taken little time before her dissatisfactions resumed.

For the last two years, Marian had lived with Paul, a 46-year-old, previously married, land developer. In background as well as temperament, Marian and Paul could not be more different. She was from a lower-middle-class family with a Jewish father and a Protestant mother converted to Judaism, and grew up in a large city in the West. He, on the other hand, was from a small Tennessee town, raised as a Baptist (but no longer a practicing one) in a well-to-do family, and had never left his home state until he was inducted into the Army during the Korean War in the early 1950s. Paul had married his high school sweetheart when he returned from the service, and that marriage, an unhappy one almost from the beginning, had produced two children, now aged 23 and 20 and living on their own on the East Coast. Unable to express his dissatisfactions directly, Paul had slowly withdrawn from his wife, having less and less contact with her over the years. However, they had stayed married for 24 years, at which time Paul, at the urging of his children, had initiated divorce proceedings and soon thereafter moved to the West Coast. He met Marian at a party, they dated for several months, and after knowing one another a year they moved in together.

Marian called a pastoral counselor, in this case a rabbi, in what seemed to him an urgent voice one day, and after she had explained her situation, the counselor set up a joint appointment for her and Paul the next day. (Note: Pastoral counselors provide more premarital counseling in the U.S. than do physicians or mental health professionals.) Marian was in tears soon after sitting down, explaining that they needed to work out right away whether they should continue together. Paul was quiet, seemed to be listening, and when Marian became upset reached for her hand to comfort her. He indicated that he loved Marian and wanted to marry her, but that she was unsure and was continuously changing her mind in what he called a "she loves me, she loves me not" fashion. She stated that two issues were urgent: she wanted children and believed he did not; she worried too that marrying a non-Jew would be unacceptable to her family and friends.

The counselor noted Paul's passivity and Marian's apprehensive style. After hearing each tell of previous relationships, he suspected that there surely were reasons why Paul had stayed in an increasingly unhappy marriage for so long, and also why Marian had found fault with all previous relationships and seemed to be doing so again. The counselor's working hypothesis at the end of the first session, possibly to be modified or corrected later as he came to know them better, was that Marian had a fear of commitment and possibly of trusting a man in an intimate, sustained relationship; however, she did seem to have access to her feelings and that would be helpful as the couple probed more deeply into their interactions in later sessions. The counselor speculated too that Paul was far less aware of his feelings and motives, probably because he felt they were often hostile and therefore unacceptable to others. Paul was someone who wanted very much to be liked, and it probably would be difficult for him to own up to feelings or motives he thought Marian would find objectionable. Sensing discomfort with one another but not knowing why, perhaps they had seized upon their differences in background or the issue of children because these seemed tangible and thus reasonable explanations for their growing uneasiness as they approached marriage. In order to check out some of these hunches, the counselor had each take home and independently fill out a PREPARE inventory, to be returned the following session.

During the next meeting the following week, the counselor observed that the couple seemed closer. They spoke of wedding plans, and, at the conclusion of the session, the counselor pointed out to Marian that the two issues that had seemed so urgent to her the previous week were not even mentioned today. Were they merely a smokescreen on her part to cover up her discomfort at getting close to marriage? She acknowledged that their previous session had made her realize that their difference in religious background was a minor factor, especially since neither was particularly religiously oriented. As for children, she said she had been thinking that perhaps her earlier statement represented more a response to reaching the end of her fertility period than any strong wish to have a baby. Paul, on the other hand, had also been thinking about that first session, and had concluded that although he thought his parenting days with young children were over, he would agree to have a child if that was what it would take to make the relationship work. The counselor urged Paul to fully examine how he really felt, and not simply to tell people what he thought they wanted to hear, as he had done in the past. As for their transactions with one another, the counselor pointed out that Marian's intensity frightened Paul away, keeping him from expressing what he was feeling. Thus, it had the opposite effect from what she claimed she wanted to achieve. Paul, on the other hand, by withholding feelings, especially when he was annoyed or irritated, forced Marian to pursue him in the only way she knew, by expressing her feelings in no uncertain terms. He too, through his passive behavior, was drawing out of Marian the opposite of what he wanted. The counselor's efforts were thus directed at forcing them to look at their interaction, rather than individual personality traits in one or the other. If they could modify their ways of dealing with one another, and if each took responsibility for his or her own reactions as well as some responsibility for what he or she drew out of the other, then future interactions between them would proceed more smoothly.

The following week, the couple and the counselor discussed each of their families of origin. Filling out the brief Family Adaptability and Cohesion Evaluation Scale (FACES III) (see Chapter 3) separately, each saw his or her family as reasonably well balanced (see Figure 6.1); Marian viewed hers as structurally connected and with good communication, Paul saw his as flexibly separated but with less-effective communication patterns. She believed hers were strongly bonded—highly cohesive—but not entirely able to accept change. In Paul's view, his family's rules and relationships were more flexible and adaptable to change. It was easier for him to separate from them than it was for her to separate from her family. Exploring their families of origin helped each understand that while some differences existed in their backgrounds, the differences were more apparent than real, and thus not likely to be the source of conflict they, especially Marian, had feared.

During the following session, after the PREPARE profile had been returned from computer analysis, its printout confirmed that no serious differences existed. Both had realistic expectations regarding marriage; they agreed on the personality issues that required attention; they were congruent in their views regarding handling finances and their preferences for dealing with leisure time. Marian wanted family to play a larger role in their lives than did Paul, but the differences were not irreconcilable.

Major areas requiring further work involved communicating thoughts and sharing feelings more easily. Paul especially had to work on this, but Marian could help by listening more patiently and by gaining more control over the intense expression of her feelings. Paul needed to be less idealistic and more prepared to deal with differences between them as they arose, instead of tending to deny or minimize problems. Trust was still an issue for Marian, but the counselor believed that problem would be reduced as she came to have faith that Paul was being honest with her and saying what he felt. They still were somewhat apart in their attitudes regarding the place of religious activity and values in their marriage but once again the differences were negotiable.

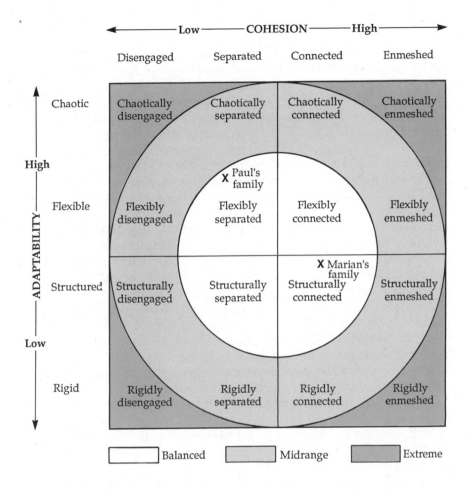

Figure 6.1. Marian and Paul's Circumplex Model scores.

The final session reviewed their outlooks regarding the future together, emphasizing that while some understanding of the issues between them had been gained, considerably more needed to be accomplished. Each needed to continue what had been started, openly sharing thoughts and feelings, clarifying what each believed, even if some resulting conflict then needed resolution. They needed to have a clearer picture of the attitudes and beliefs of the other, and of the issues between them brought up in counseling that were delicate ones and still unresolved. Marian and Paul left the counseling feeling closer than they had before, determined to continue on their own what they had started with the counselor. They still had differences and conflicts to resolve, but they felt now that they knew better what those differences were and how to start working on them.

❖❖❖

SUMMARY

Cohabitation, the living together of two unmarried adults of the opposite sex in a sexual relationship, has increased sharply in recent years among all age groups. Greater public acceptance of this phenomenon reflects changing public attitudes regarding sexual behavior among unmarried adults; increased availability and effectiveness of contraceptive devices; a greater demand for equal rights for women; efforts to abandon the "double standard"; a trend toward delayed marriages; and a new emphasis on the development of a meaningful relationship between a man and woman where both feel independent while relating to one another.

Cohabitation is not a unitary entity; it takes the form of a variety of relationships, some temporary or convenient, others more committed and permanent, some a "trial marriage," others a substitute for marriage. Moreover, it is entered into for a multitude of reasons, many frequently unknown to the partners, despite their stated motives. Cohabitation among college students, perhaps the most conspicuous participants, generally is of four types: the Linus Blanket type, where the primary quest on the part of one or both is for security and the satisfaction of dependency needs; the Emancipation type, where one or both are seeking freedom from parental or societal restraints; the Convenience type, usually of short duration, allowing a regular sexual outlet and domestic living without commitment; and the Testing type, where both are more mature and are seeking a satisfying intimate relationship while maintaining autonomy.

Counselors may need to help cohabiting couples deal with issues concerning commitment, social acceptance, relatives, the lack of legal safeguards, whether the relationship is to be monogamous, division of responsibilities, expectations about the future, and in many cases terminating the union.

Couples seeking premarital counseling either want to check on the state of their partnership in light of their forthcoming marriage, or are concerned that some underlying conflict may mar their future marriage. In the latter case, typically there is either an uncommitted partner, a passive-inactive partner, one who is unresponsive and insensitive, a partner who is apprehensive and pessimistic about the couple's future, or an angry or aggressive partner. In addition to focusing on key elements of their backgrounds and their current interaction patterns, the counselor often helps them examine their communication styles, their motivations, their attitudes regarding marital responsibilities, and their management of conflict. The purpose is less to resolve all conflict than to help the couple become aware of issues between them and learn some skills for resolving them. Four to six sessions are commonly required, with the counselor sometimes using assessment devices or test instruments as aids in the appraisal.

Chapter 7

◆◆◆

Counseling Gay and Lesbian Couples

Cohabiting **homosexuals**[1] have much in common with the cohabiting heterosexuals we considered in the previous chapter. Both are part of small social systems in which couples live together in an unorthodox living arrangement, usually but not necessarily without children, seeking satisfaction of their erotic and affectional needs. Both face stigmatization from the larger social system, often feeling a need to keep the sexual nature of

1 For the remainder of this chapter, we will use the popular terms *gay* and *lesbian* instead of the more common term *homosexual* for several reasons. The latter has a clinically negative connotation, suggesting either psychopathology or immoral behavior, or possibly both. By emphasizing sexuality, the term *homosexual* unfairly excludes or minimizes all other aspects of the gay lifestyle. The prejudice persists, in the use of the term, that interpersonal love, sensual pleasure, or erotic expressions of affection and intimacy must be achieved in a heterosexual form or they are unnatural, inferior, or sinful. *Gay* and *lesbian* are more neutral terms used by those persons themselves who are involved in a preferred erotic relationship with a member or members of the same sex.

their relationship secret from others whom they perceive as hostile and disapproving. Both lack most legal safeguards, since they are not considered by society to be part of a lawfully recognized marital union.

Similar as their situations may be, however, they differ in significant ways that the counselor must recognize before attempting to understand a gay male or **lesbian** couple seeking counseling. Despite the fact that homosexuality has existed throughout recorded history and is present in virtually every society in the world, the idea of two people of the same sex sharing an intimate erotic life together evokes a more negative reaction in most people than does the identical behavior between unmarried heterosexuals.

Thus, the counselor can expect same-sex couples not only to have experienced social prejudice imposed by a hostile and unaccepting society, but also to themselves share, consciously or unconsciously, many of these condemning attitudes as a result of having grown up in the same society. Weinberg (1972) has documented the ubiquitous nature of **homophobic** beliefs (excessive fears of homosexuality or homosexuals) within contemporary social mores and cultural attitudes. As Malyon (1982) points out in discussing some of the therapeutic issues involved in working with gay males, these clients have likely internalized these attitudes, contributing to a sense of guilt and desire to punish themselves. Thus, he argues, they require a gay-affirmative viewpoint from the counselor. This is in sharp contrast to what Harrison (1987) observes to have been the attitude of most counselors as recently as the early 1970s—namely, that they should attempt to change their gay clients' sexual orientation.

Homosexuality refers to a form of behavior—seeking sexual pleasures in an alternative way—and not to a clinical condition. Nevertheless, men or women suspected of engaging in such behavior typically are labeled as being a certain type of person. It is as though their sexual orientation alone described them fully. This is a mistaken idea, as mistaken as judging a person's entire life by the fact that he or she is heterosexual. Calling someone *heterosexual* or *homosexual* may say something about his or her sexual practices but little if anything about the broader issues of the person's personality, ways of relating to others, and so on. Still, the label *homosexual* taints the individual or the couple, arouses snickers as well as frequent public ridicule, and may instantly discredit the person(s) unless the stigma can be hidden. Until very recently, it was only by concealing his or her private life that the homosexual could hope to pass as normal, and thus not be open to scorn and ostracism.

That situation began to change in the last decade, as laws and public policies that discriminated on the basis of sexual preference were challenged successfully in the courts by gay rights advocates. As part of the gay rights movement's emphasis on gay pride, more and more gay persons opted to "come out" (of the closet) and assert their gay identity, insisting on greater social acceptance. However, the advent of AIDS (Acquired Immune

Deficiency Syndrome)—sometimes referred to as the "gay plague"—has once again had a disenfranchising effect on the homosexual population. In many cases, anti-gay heterosexuals have seized the AIDS scare to practice overt discrimination and even sexual violence and assault on homosexuals (Anderson, 1982; Harry, 1988).

SOME BASIC CONCEPTS AND TERMINOLOGY

Homosexual behavior can be found at all socioeconomic levels, among all racial and ethnic groups, and in rural as well as urban areas. According to best estimates (Marmor, 1980), the prevalence of exclusively homosexual behavior in Western culture ranges from 5 to 10 percent for adult males and from 3 to 5 percent for adult females. If **bisexual** behavior is included, these figures may be doubled. If these guesses are correct (if anything, they are likely to be underestimates, since many gays still avoid disclosure), homosexuality is a widespread phenomenon, even in a society such as ours that strongly discourages and may at times condemn the behavior.

Research on homosexuality—largely a taboo topic until Evelyn Hooker's (1957) pioneering studies—confirms that no essential difference exists in the incidence of mental problems between homosexual and heterosexual populations.[2] No single personality profile covers all gay persons (Bell & Weinberg, 1978), and the sexual orientation, once established, is not readily subject to change (Storms, 1986). As for etiology, Warren (1980) cites two opposing viewpoints: (1) homosexuality is an acquired taste (therefore "catching" and by implication, morally blameworthy); (2) it is inborn (therefore the gay person is not subject to blame). She notes that gays favor the inborn preference theory, while anti-gays tend to support the acquired taste explanation (thereby justifying firing of openly homosexual teachers, for example, because as role models they may unduly influence young people to make the arbitrary moral choice). Most psychiatric or psychological research (for example, Hooker, 1967) favors the view that the homosexual orientation is present at birth or that family factors operate early in their childhood to determine the ultimate homosexual predisposition.

Small communities typically present gay people with special problems regarding self-disclosure, often forcing them to pretend to others or even to themselves that they are heterosexual so they will be accepted in the nongay world. To remain exclusively gay in such communities is to live in

---

2 The American Psychiatric Association did not get around to declassifying homosexuality as a mental disorder until 1973. Even then, that decision was at least as much the result of political prodding from gay activists as it was the result of research such as Hooker's investigations. Prior to that decision, a man or woman whose sexual preference was not exclusively for a member of the opposite sex was diagnosed by psychiatric experts as abnormal. Until 1978, gay men were denied entry into military or government service on a routine basis. As recently as 1981, a U.S. congressman was forced to resign as a result of social pressure when it was discovered that he had engaged in a homosexual act.

daily fear of discovery, to secretly seek out other gay individuals or couples, and to remain segregated from heterosexual marrieds. Since the number of gays is usually limited, it is common to feel socially isolated and to solve the problem by moving on to larger communities such as San Francisco, the West Hollywood section of Los Angeles, or West Greenwich Village in New York City, if possible. Here gays are far more apt to meet other gays through homophile organizations, bars, or gay churches. As Harry (1988) observes, a number of gay and lesbian organizations devoted to socially integrating the newcomer into the gay world have sprung up in most large American cities within the last 15 years. Among other functions, these organizations provide a social network for meeting other gays, offering an alternative social setting to the often highly sexual context of the gay bar. The point, in keeping with the effort to make the gay life more than simply a sexual encounter or series of encounters, is to emphasize social and cultural, rather than predominantly erotic, opportunities.

The preceding is not to say that "gay scenes"—organized efforts to arrange erotic contact, often between strangers—do not exist. Casual sex has long been a part of gay life, at least for men, and, as Humphreys and Miller (1980) note, nearly all American towns have at least one homosexual scene. Bus terminals, freeway rest stops, isolated park bathrooms, stylish resorts or athletic clubs, all have served as places for men to establish contact for instant and impersonal sexual liaison.

"Cruising" in public parks or restrooms, far more frequent among gay males than lesbians, constitutes yet another form of searching for brief sexual activity with strangers where no interpersonal commitment, intimacy, or responsibility is required. However, the common belief that such promiscuous behavior characterizes all gay sexual unions is erroneous, according to Bell and Weinberg (1978). These researchers, studying 686 homosexual males and 293 homosexual females in the San Francisco area, found sexual activity in the privacy of homes to be far more common. Close to 40 percent of the respondents either did no cruising at all or did it no more than once per month. The risk of being arrested was an important deterrent to cruising in public places. Bath houses catering to homosexual clients, as well as the aforementioned gay bars, were more likely settings for casual sexual experiences.

The majority of gay men seek more extended relationships than those provided by casual sexual encounters. Although homosexual contacts can be had with relative ease, most gay men, as is true of most people in general, want something more, namely a more stable union with a loved partner. Typically, these "marriages" last up to three years or so, although, of course, there are exceptions, some extending over decades. Possibly these short-lived same-sex relationships, similar to cohabitant heterosexual unions, end more easily than do heterosexual marriages because no legal restraints bind the couple together, and no children keep them involved once problems between them develop.

BEING GAY IN A NONGAY WORLD—
THE "COMING OUT " PROCESS

On September 22, 1975, in San Francisco's Union Square, a woman moved out of the crowd, raised her arm, leveled a chrome-plated gun, and pulled the trigger. A man standing nearby saw the movement and pushed down on the gun barrel. The bullet missed its target by five feet. Oliver Sipple had just saved the life of the President of the United States. His quick action made him an instant hero. The President wrote him a letter thanking him. Over 1000 other people wrote to him praising him. It should have been a moment of triumph for Oliver. Instead it was a nightmare.

"Within 24 hours, reporters had also learned that the ex-Marine was involved in the San Francisco gay community, and the story became page one—and wire service—copy" (*The Advocate*, Oct. 22, 1975). The *Chicago Sun-Times* called him a "Homosexual Hero" in a headline. The *Denver Post* referred to him as a "Gay Vet." Oliver went into seclusion to avoid the media. He was so distressed at the prospect of his mother in Detroit reading about him as a gay hero that he all but declined to take credit for saving the life of the President of the United States! (Berzon, 1979, p. 88)

This excerpt poignantly illustrates not only what apprehension gay persons experience about the unintended discovery of their secret, but also how that fear of disclosure must permeate much of their daily behavior. As Berzon (1979) notes, nearly every gay person with a family is concerned about disclosure to his or her family. Since only about half the men in Bell and Weinberg's 1978 survey had told their parents of their gayness, the remainder attempted to conceal the fact by developing a series of obfuscating strategies. Gay lovers, especially in their 20s, may maintain separate residences, or, if they live together, may pose as roommates. They are likely to discourage parental visits, and, should a visit take place, will maintain the fiction that as roommates they sleep in separate rooms. Repeated visits, sometimes extending over several years, serve to reinforce the illusion that the two are simply very good friends who enjoy being together. Ultimately the pretense wears thin, though, and the parents become aware their child is gay. (In some cases, the parents continue to deceive themselves, even if they suspect, denying to themselves what their eyes tell them.) In either case, the term *gay* or *homosexual* is studiously avoided. The couple can never openly express physical affection toward one another in front of the parents and never make explicit reference to their union (Harry, 1988).

In another scenario, the couple may early on or later in the relationship decide to "come out" to their parents. Here they risk alienation or long-term, perhaps permanent, rejection. In the case of gay males, according to Bell and Weinberg's (1978) data, mothers are most often informed before fathers, presumably because, like most heterosexual males, fathers are more apt to be threatened and to refuse to accept the news. If the parents are strongly religious, both may find the revelation intolerable. If, as is happening increasingly, the parents learn simultaneously that their son is dying of

AIDS and has been living a gay life without their knowledge, the shock may be devastating.

"Coming out"—openly acknowledging and describing oneself as gay—is a process that occurs over time and in front of different audiences. "I came out with my parents" may be followed by "I told some of the nongay people at school" or perhaps "I finally came clean with the boss today." First, of course, the gay person must come out to himself or herself, establishing a positive self-definition. In the following case, a young adult struggles with his self-definition:

♦♦♦

Sheldon, 29, came to a counselor with a vague assortment of physical and psychological complaints. He reported experiencing anxiety attacks several times a week, without knowing what exactly was disturbing him. He felt dizzy at work and couldn't seem to concentrate on his job as a bookkeeper for a large furniture manufacturing firm. He had gone out with one woman for several weeks, but now found himself restless and not really interested in pursuing the relationship much further.

After two sessions of reporting a variety of symptoms of distress, he finally told the female counselor that he had something "awful to confess." He then proceeded to describe a series of experiences, beginning in high school, of visiting bath houses and public parks in a neighboring town in order to engage in impersonal sex with other men. However, he insisted to the counselor that he was not gay, that he actually disliked homosexuals and their "swishy" behavior, and that he wanted one day to marry and lead a conventional life. He had been sexually intimate with several women since high school, he contended, and while the experiences had ranged from neutral to unpleasant, he remained certain that through counseling he could learn to enjoy heterosexual relationships.

As Sheldon spoke of his growing-up years, the counselor recognized Sheldon's early patterns of difficulty with his family of origin. He was the youngest of four boys, living in a lower-middle-class family with what he described as a strong, domineering, and difficult mother and a weak, inadequate, and unconnected father. Sheldon felt disengaged from both parents, as well as from his brothers, growing up. The household was filled with tension among the family members, there was a great deal of confusion, and communication was poor or nonexistent.

The counselor recognized Sheldon's struggle over his gay identity, and consulted a gay psychologist from the local Gay Counseling Center over how best to help Sheldon resolve his conflicts over who he was. The consultant urged caution over helping Sheldon "come out," pointing out that the client was exhibiting distortions of reality as he fought to deny the object of his sexual urges. The counselor continued to explore Sheldon's past and present homosexual behavior, including an ongoing romance with an alcoholic young man that Sheldon insisted was not significant. She also continued to direct Sheldon's attention to family issues from the past as well as the present.

When Sheldon went back home to another state to visit his family, he was urged by the counselor to talk to his brothers about their sexual experiences. Not unexpectedly, it turned out that two of the three boys were gay but not openly so. The visit seemed to clarify a great deal to Sheldon regarding their upbringing, and he returned to counseling more accepting of himself, although not yet ready to reveal his gayness publicly.

When his parents came to town several weeks later, the counselor recommended that Sheldon invite them to join him in the next session. He expressed considerable discomfort over doing so, afraid something would slip out about his homosexual behavior. However, after the counselor reassured him that she would not reveal his secret, he finally consented to their presence. The mother's opening words, as she sat down, were "I wanted Sheldon to be a girl when he was born, since I already had three boys." By this statement she seemed to be acknowledging at some level that she understood why she had been called to the session, that Sheldon was struggling with his sexual identity. The counselor made no attempt to discuss homosexuality, but instead asked questions about the family's early years. Sheldon's father remained relatively quiet throughout the two-hour meeting, answering questions in a brief manner, and only when asked.

In subsequent sessions with Sheldon, the counselor helped him recognize that his parents "knew" and that he need not waste so much energy in hiding the truth from them. At first, of course, he needed to be truthful to himself, facing who and what he was. After two more meetings with the counselor, Sheldon terminated the sessions. He had accepted his gayness, and had "come out" on a limited basis, telling his woman friend and some colleagues at work. He never spoke of it with his parents, but he assumed they knew and were able to live with it without acknowledging it in so many words.

Most gay men, in spite of the popular stereotype, are not obviously effeminate in appearance or behavior. Since they pass as heterosexual, giving up the security of anonymity by coming out may be fraught with anxiety. As Harrison (1987) notes, "Every gay man, whatever his age, must decide when to stop asking permission to be himself and to go public about his sexual identity" (p. 226). As for lesbians, the secrecy may be somewhat easier to maintain, since society tolerates open physical affection between women far more readily than between men, and women living together generally raise fewer eyebrows than do cohabiting men. Both minority groups learn to avoid disclosure and to pass as "straight" within nongay settings by adopting the manner and dress of the majority. Part of that impression management is to remain silent in the face of jokes or other slanderous remarks about homosexuals if they wish to avoid drawing attention to their gay selves (Ponse, 1980).

The process of coming out has usually begun before the gay person contacts a counselor. That is, while no public disclosure has been made, the individual (young or old, single or married), has begun to acknowledge same-sex erotic feelings and fantasies to himself or herself. This self-recognition stage may last for a considerable period of time, during which the person may feel confused and may or may not act upon the feelings by having one or more homosexual experiences. In most cases this stage leads ultimately to the next stage of self-acceptance—risking rejection by telling carefully chosen others. (We saw in the case just presented that this may be a painful and drawn-out process.) As the individual sets about exploring his or her new sexual identity, there is increased mingling with others with similar sexual interests. (The amount of sexual experimentation differs between men and women, with men more likely to engage in one-time sexual contact, although this may occur with some lesbians also.) As the newly found freedom to sexually explore becomes less intriguing and the need for intimacy becomes stronger, a more stable and committed relationship with a single partner is likely to follow. As we observed earlier, the union may be short-lived, and may simply be the first of a number of such coupling experiences. In what Coleman (1982) calls the stage of integration, the gay person has forged a gay identity and incorporated both the public and private images into one unified self-presentation.

As for the counselor, it is essential to understand the signficance of these stages of the coming-out process. As with heterosexual clients, having relationships with a series of partners may well represent experimental dating and not necessarily failed relationships. We should note here too that the process is often sped up and made more complete by the inclusion in the counseling sessions of the client's current significant others, including, when appropriate, members of his or her family of origin. Exchanging feedback information, exposing family secrets, and dealing more effectively with interlocking problems often has a catalytic effect on hastening the emergence of a gay identity.

GAYS AND LESBIANS: SIMILARITIES AND DIFFERENCES

While we have for the most part written of gay male and lesbian couples as though they shared the same characteristics and concerns, the counselor must understand the ways in which these relationships also differ.

First the similarities: Both types of couples must face the choice of remaining hidden (denying their true identities to others, losing self-respect and a sense of control over their lives) or lifting the mask and revealing the secret (thereby risking loss of love and support from family and friends, forfeiting jobs or curtailing promotions, possibly facing police arrest) (Toder, 1979). In avoiding the disclosure of "the love that dare not speak its name," gay males and lesbians both frequently find themselves, in Rochlin's (1979) words, participating in the popular homophobic game of "I-know-they-know-and-they-know-I-know-they-know-but-let's-all-pretend-nobody-knows" (p. 162).

As we reported in the case of Sheldon, a gay male may engage in homosexual acts but deny to himself that he is gay, thus pretending that he measures up to the community standard of "maleness" and insuring that he will not be viewed by society as a lower-status female. Similarly, as Toder (1979, p. 45) reports, a woman in a same-sex love affair may fear being labeled homosexual by a rejecting society, and thus may deny the implications of the relationship ("I'm not a lesbian, I just happen to be in love with this person and this person just happens to be a woman").

Role playing in both gay and lesbian lifestyles may defy stereotypes. The popular "butch/femme" notion of a gay male couple emulating a traditional male-female married relationship (one partner masculine, dominant in sexual activity, providing the financial support; the other engaged in complementary household activity) is an improbable one. Rather, as Harry (1983) points out, gay relationships are more likely to be patterned after a best-friends/roommates model than a heterosexual role model. While "butch/femme" patterns do characterize some gay male relationships, especially those based on inequality, Harry (1983) contends that masculinity in appearance and behavior is likely to be highly valued in oneself and one's partner, suggesting a "butch/butch" pattern may be even more likely among gay male couples.

Homosexual women are more likely than their male counterparts to strive for stable, extended relationships (Saghir & Robins, 1980). While one-night stands or casual encounters do occur, they tend to be infrequent. Lesbians, much like their female heterosexual counterparts, are more likely to establish affectionate bonds with partners over a period of time before becoming sexually involved. In those same-sex love affairs, they tend to value equality, emotional expressiveness, and a similarity of attitudes between partners (Peplau & Amaro, 1982). Long-lasting relationships of more than a year's duration, with an emphasis on faithfulness, tend to be the rule. Thus, the total number of sexual partners is usually few compared to gay men. While sexual fidelity may be desired by gay male couples, it may also occasionally be breached by a casual sexual pickup experience by one or the other partner. Among homosexual women, casual or impersonal sex is the exception, although, once again as with heterosexual women, affairs may occur and may lead to a breakup of the relationship.

While a small minority of lesbians do engage in traditional gender roles (the "butch/femme" pattern), most are likely to divide household tasks and responsibilities according to talent and interest or by turns, since both are likely to be employed. Socializing is often done at home, usually with other lesbian couples or perhaps gay male pairs. In systems terms, as Rice and Kelly (1988) observe, it makes sense that a subsystem (the couple) trying to relate to a larger system (society) that either ignores or criticizes them, will attempt to tighten the partner boundaries, fusing with others like themselves and adopting a tight, self-protective posture against the outside world.

Generally speaking, according to Harry (1983), the social world of lesbians tends to be a world of couples whereas the world of gay men is one of singles and couples. As we just noted, among lesbians a sexual relationship may arise from an evolving affectionate relationship, while for gay men, in keeping with the socialization of men in general in our society, the sequence is likely to be reversed.

Evelyn, 24, and Anne Marie, 26, both assistant professors of music at neighboring universities in the same large western city, met at a music educator's conference and were immediately attracted to one another. They spent several days together, at mealtimes and between sessions, sharing work experiences and talking over their pasts. They found that they had lots in common—both were raised Catholic but no longer practiced their religion, both were brought up in small towns, both had had an early love of music—and when the conference ended they agreed to continue seeing each other. It was only after six months or so that their relationship became a physical one.

As they learned about one another, it turned out that Anne Marie had been a lesbian since her teenage years. A tomboy with an early aversion to girls' activities, she had had her first homosexual experience at 15 with another girl at a summer camp. Anne Marie had never been attracted to boys, or later to men. Instead she had had a number of romantic "crushes" on teachers growing up, and one long live-in arrangement with a woman when she was 21.

Evelyn, on the other hand, had had several love affairs with men, beginning during her adolescent years, but had found them unsatisfactory. For four years prior to meeting Anne Marie, she had not dated and had been celibate. Socially she was extremely shy, and felt inadequate at conventional feminine tasks, such as cooking, decorating, and choosing clothes. From the start she was fascinated by Anne Marie's sense of style as well as her confidence in social situations.

Together, the women bought a house and settled into a "married" lifestyle. They shared expenses, took turns cooking and doing various chores around the house, traveled to Europe on vacation together, and seemed in general to enjoy their life as a couple. Their friends were primarily people from work, mostly heterosexuals, although they also had gay male and lesbian couples to the house for parties. They were not obviously homosexual, nor did they ever bring the issue up before the university administrators, faculty, or students. While they did not deny their lesbian relationship, neither did they affirm or flaunt it publicly. Monogamous, they seemed to friends like a childless couple where both partners were oriented toward furthering their careers. As for family, Anne Marie, an only child, had been cut off from hers since she left home for college. Evelyn's parents were dead, and her two brothers rarely contacted her. When she did hear from them, they pretended Anne Marie did not exist.

After 14 years, Evelyn, now 38, and Anne Marie, 40, began to drift apart. They quarreled more often, seemed to have developed different interests from one another, found they had less and less to talk about, and finally decided to split up. Anne Marie revealed that she had found herself interested in a younger woman at her school, and wanted to be free to pursue that new relationship.

Since no strong family or social ties kept them together, they separated, with a counselor's help, without too much bitterness. Evelyn remained by herself in the house for several years, and then she too found a young woman of 26 who moved in with her as her lover. Both "married types" who needed the comfort, support, and intimacy of a coupled relationship, Evelyn and Anne Marie, after their "divorce," each ultimately sought and found another long-term relationship.

◆◆◆

ASSESSING GAY/LESBIAN COUPLES

Gay men and lesbians seek professional counseling at about the same rate as the general population (Woodman & Lenna, 1980). Although the problems inherent in being gay in a society rejecting of that sexual orientation may lead some to the counselor's office, it is more likely that they come looking for ways to combat external and internal stereotypes of homosexuals, and not for "treatment" for their homosexuality per se (Gartrell, 1983). All of us, those who grow up to become homosexual as well as those who become heterosexual, are exposed at an early age to myths that produce negative stereotypes, particularly about male homosexuality (see Box 7.1): they are sexual perverts, queers, sinners against the natural order of life, faggots, child molesters, possibly criminals. It is hardly any wonder that those who become gay are often filled with self-hatred. As Malyon (1982) points out, that negative self-image, along with an inevitable internalized homophobic attitude, is bound to have serious negative consequences for one's overall self-identity. A common solution is to develop a false identity by suppressing homoerotic promptings and taking on a heterosexual persona.

It is hardly surprising, then, to find gay persons who secretly struggle with themselves growing up, sometimes believing their sexual impulses mean they are mentally ill. For these individuals, accepting society's label that they are abnormal is often less painful than exploring the possibility of adopting a gay identity (Woodman & Lenna, 1980).

ACHIEVING A GAY IDENTITY

Closeting themselves helps homosexuals avoid facing the emotions of shame and guilt over who they are. Coming out, as we noted earlier, is risky, and often there is no turning back once a gay life is exposed. As

---

Box 7.1.   A Counselor Checklist of Common Myths Regarding Homosexuality

Do you believe these statements?

- Most gay men are effeminate and most lesbians are masculine in appearance and behavior.
- Most gay couples adopt male/female (active/passive) roles in their relationships.
- All gay men are sexually promiscuous.
- Gay men believe that they are women in men's bodies and gay women believe that they are men in women's bodies.
- Most gay people would have a sex-change operation if they could afford it.
- Most gay people are child molesters.
- People choose to become homosexual.
- Most gay people are unhappy with their sexual orientation and seek therapy to convert to heterosexuality.
- Counselors report high success rates in converting homosexuals to heterosexuals.
- Most gay people are easily identifiable by their dress and mannerisms.
- Homosexual behavior is unnatural because it does not occur in other species.
- Homosexuality is the result of an hereditary defect.
- Homosexuals have hormone abnormalities.
- All homosexual males have dominant, overbearing mothers and weak, passive fathers.
- Homosexuality threatens the continuity of the species.
- All male hairdressers, interior decorators, and ballet dancers are homosexuals.
- Homosexuality is an illness that can be cured.

Source: Gartrell, 1983, p. 396.

indicated in Box 7.2, the process of coming out is of major significance, not merely because of the public disclosure, but because it represents self-recognition and the start of gay self-identity. The counselor needs to assess how successfully and how fully this is accomplished, and should not be too surprised if further hesitation and stalling follow the initial disclosure to significant others. Also, the counselor should note in working with gay couples whether one of the partners is further along than the other in affirming his or her gayness, since greater concealment by one may have detrimental consequences for the relationship and the couple's social behavior with family and friends.

Estrangement from the family, emotionally, financially, and interpersonally, is especially painful. Gays sometimes report feeling like minority group members or second-class citizens in their own families, often feeling the need to explain, defend, apologize for, or hide their gayness, or else risk ridicule or ostracism. While some parents may ultimately accept their child's gayness, more are apt to be rejecting, especially on hearing the revelation, perhaps blaming themselves and wondering what they did wrong in raising their child. Some parents seize the opportunity to blame one another for the "aberration." In extreme cases, as Harry (1988) reports, more violent or forceful solutions are sought by despairing parents: kidnapping and homosexual deprogramming, usually of lesbians; pressures to seek psychotherapy in the hope of turning the person into a heterosexual; threats to cut off support, if their child is in college; and threats or attempts to take away a gay person's children, should they exist, unless the homosexual behavior ceases.

The person exposing his or her gayness is seeking external validation that he or she is a worthwhile, socially acceptable human being in the eyes

---

Box 7.2.   A Problem Appraisal Checklist for Gay\Lesbian Couples

Gay couples may experience problems in the following areas:

- Coming out—concealment vs. openness
- Self-acceptance of gay identity
- Family estrangement
- Church acceptance vs. condemnation
- Sexual exclusiveness vs. nonexclusiveness
- The AIDS crisis
- Long-term vs. short-term relationships
- Aging and later life problems
- Gay fatherhood and lesbian motherhood
- Lack of legal safeguards
- Gender role patterns in the relationship

of those individuals from whom such approbation is particularly important. In addition to family and friends, some gays may look to their church for affirmation that their sexual orientation need not be in conflict with their religious beliefs. Unfortunately, until recently, all American churches condemned homosexuality, causing a sense of alienation from organized religion on the part of most gays.

As McNaught (1979), himself a Catholic, reveals, growing up gay and Catholic may be akin to living in Northern Ireland with a Catholic mother and Protestant father. Loyalty to one seems to preclude loyalty to the other: the Catholic church censures homosexuality, while other gays castigate one for retaining ties to an oppressive church. The Judeo-Christian tradition throughout history has been highly critical of same-sex acts, assuming that heterosexuality is "natural" and that those who engage in homosexual activity do so willfully. While some conservative theologians continue to retain that viewpoint, others (for example, Nelson, 1982) believe that gays as well as the Church will benefit from the liberation of gays from oppression. Harry (1988) reports that in recent years a number of interdenominational churches for gays have sprung up in most large American cities, thus reducing some of the alienation many religious gays formerly felt. Moreover, some liberal churches, again in large cities, now permit affiliate fellowships for gay individuals and couples who prefer to remain in the church in which they were raised.

For the counselor, the therapeutic task may often include re-attaching an isolated gay client or gay couple to a larger system such as the Church, which in the past may have provided comfort and faith.

SEXUALITY AND THE AIDS EPIDEMIC

Coming to an agreement regarding the sexual exclusiveness of the relationship is often the single most important decision faced by gay couples (Silverstein, 1981). The point to look for here is not so much whether monogamy or nonmonogamy exists, but rather the extent to which the couple can agree on this point. Gay male relationships in particular lack the norms built into heterosexual marriage or other long-term male-female coupling, so that infidelity is not necessarily considered a serious offense or deviation. Since sex with a variety of partners is a fact of life in gay male relationships (Blasband & Peplau, 1985), the counselor should not apply heterosexual norms in evaluating the effect of such behavior on the couple's ability to stay together. Rather, it is important to determine if the casual pickup or affair has violated the couple's expectations, and, if so, the extent to which the violation impairs their future together.

Casual or impersonal sex has had to be reevaluated by gays (as well as nongays) in the light of the AIDS epidemic. AIDS is an infectious disease in which the body's immune system is damaged in varying, often progressive, degrees of severity, with the result that the body is vulnerable to fatal opportunistic infections and malignancies (Walker, 1987). Homosexual and bisexual men are among the highest-risk groups. By 1985, AIDS was the primary killer of men aged 20 to 50 in New York City and San Francisco (Fradkin, 1987).

Fear of AIDS has led to changing sex practices between long-term partners ("safe sex"), the closing of certain bathhouses, fewer casual pick-ups, and sometimes to celibacy in an effort by gays to protect themselves and their partners. For couples, the discovery by one person that he has AIDS not only is personally terrifying, but also leads to fear that he may become a dependent burden on his lover, or conversely, that the partner may reject him by leaving. Whatever that outcome, the infected person may have to reveal previously hidden casual experiences with other men to his unsuspecting partner, and also to face the disturbing possibility that he has transmitted the disease to his partner. Disclosure of AIDS may also lead to job loss, demands that he vacate an apartment, or rejection by family, friends, or work associates. Not surprisingly, the gay person may feel deserving of the AIDS disease, particularly if he still has not fully accepted his gay identity.

Counselors can also anticipate gay couples who seek help with problems concerning sexual intimacy, but who insist they are not frightened that one or the other partner may be HIV (human immunodeficiency virus)-positive (that is, infected by the virus that causes breakdowns in the immune system and ultimately leads to AIDS). Walker (1987) suggests that these individuals are likely practicing denial, and thus are seeking a less-threatening explanation for their current difficulties. She argues that unless the counselor working with the couple faces his or her own fear of AIDS and also is knowledgeable about the defense mechanism of denial occasioned by the threat of the disease, the counselor may unconsciously collude in the couple's denial and not raise the issue in assessing their presenting problem. (We'll return to the important topic of AIDS counseling for the entire family system of which the couple is one part later in this chapter.)

GAY PARENTING

Gay fathers and lesbian mothers, who number between 5 and 6 million in the United States, caring for some 12 to 15 million children ("Not All Parents Are Straight," 1987), require special assessment from the counselor. While the fact of being a parent may seem antagonistic to being gay, the facts are otherwise. Gay men marry for a variety of reasons: they may find their homosexuality personally unacceptable; they may use the marriage as a socially acceptable cover behind which to hide their gayness; they may marry to avoid continued family pressure. In addition, they may prefer male sexual partners but develop affectionate feelings for a particular woman. Compounding all these factors may be a genuine desire for children (Bozett, 1982). Lesbians too may marry and bear children because they wish to have them or because it is expected of them by society.

Bozett (1985) differentiates five marker events that typify a gay father's career: (1) a heterosexual dating period; (2) a marriage during which the man assumes the role of husband; (3) becoming a father; (4) alteration in the spousal relationship (usually separation and divorce); and (5) the activation of a gay lifestyle. Concurrent with these benchmarks, of course, is the man's growing awareness and acceptance of his own homosexuality.

Most gay males do not disclose their homosexuality to their prospective mates, although some do inform their future wives of their sexual orientation. In some cases, rather than being deceptive, it may be that these men do not consider themselves to really be gay, even if they have had one or more homosexual experiences. It may even be the case that the future wife, if informed, responds positively, perhaps because she believes the gay life is a thing of the past or, more rarely, she prefers nonheterosexual men (Bozett, 1982). Homosexual experiences during marriage may be hidden, or again may be tolerated by the spouse for reasons of her own (the couple has grown apart, she does not enjoy sex with him, she likes the social respectability of being married and wants to keep the marriage intact, she wants to protect the children from knowing, she too is having an affair, and so on).

Most marriages in which the husband is actively and openly gay will likely end in divorce, since the man will not be able to continue finding satisfaction in a heterosexual marriage and/or his wife will not be able to live with his homosexual patterns.

Premarital counseling with couples where past homosexual liaisons have been admitted needs to explore both the immediate and long-range effect this behavior is likely to have on the integrity of the future marriage. The counselor needs to help both persons honestly explore their abilities to sustain an intimate heterosexual relationship once united. If married, the couple needs help in exploring their options if they wish to continue together (for example, permitting the husband to continue periodic sexual liaisons with men). If children are involved, issues over informing them or of their custody require exploration.

Being a gay man does not preclude being a good husband and father. In the following case, a conventional middle-class professional man, married for twenty years and the father of three children, finally confronts his desire for a gay lifestyle:

Andrew S., M.D., was a practicing physician with an excellent reputation in the professional community. At 44, he was financially successful, had a happy marriage, and was the proud father of three children—all girls—whom he adored. But Andrew also harbored a secret: since high school he had engaged in a number of casual homosexual encounters in school restrooms and at public parks.

When he met Allison at college Andrew found her very attractive and dated her off and on for two years. After he graduated and before going on to medical school, they married. He never told her of his gay past, nor did he ever mention it to anyone else, including some gay friends he had known all his life. After twenty years of marriage, Andrew and Allison appeared to be the ideal couple: they were outgoing, intelligent, sophisticated, well travelled, excellent hosts, and they had three loving children to whom they appeared to be devoted. If Allison felt neglected at times and thought Andrew seemed less interested in sex than he should be, she concluded that he was busy with his career as a doctor and a member of the university hospital attending staff, rather than that anything was wrong between them.

Nevertheless, when Allison decided to return to graduate school after her children did not seem to need her as much as they had earlier, she met a young man 15 years her junior whose company she thoroughly enjoyed. Since her husband was away from home for long periods, she became more and more attached to her new friend, and soon they became sexually intimate. However, she soon felt guilty, knowing Andrew would not do such a thing to her, and she told her husband. At her insistence they decided to see a family counselor.

Andrew was surprisingly nonchalant about the affair. Although he stated that he himself would not do such a thing, he understood that perhaps he had neglected Allison too much recently. Between his practice, his hospital work, and his workouts at the men's gym at the university four nights a week, he recognized that he had not been available for her. They seemed to deal with what had happened in a way that appeared to be acceptable to both of them, and after three sessions they terminated counseling.

The male counselor did not hear from them for six months, at which time Andrew called for an individual appointment. He said Allison knew about the call, and accepted that there were some personal matters he wanted to explore with the counselor. Andrew began by saying that he had not been exactly honest in the joint sessions when he said he had been completely faithful. Actually, he now said, he had been sexually intimate with some female patients over the years. He seemed to gain some relief from this disclosure, especially from the counselor's apparent acceptance of his secret behavior. He did not make another appointment at the end of the session, but two weeks later he returned. This time, he appeared agitated, finally disclosing that he had lied during the previous meeting to test whether the counselor would be nonjudgmental. Now satisfied, he was prepared to tell the truth: he had been having impersonal homosexual experiences since early in their marriage. His workouts at the gym were really excuses to be with men, and to have homosexual contacts in the gym's shower room.

Andrew was now torn by his desire for a more open gay life and his responsibilities to his wife and children. He was certain that he was some kind of "freak" because married men should not feel or behave as he had. By coincidence, he spotted an ad in the college newspaper inviting married men who felt homoerotic feelings to join a weekly discussion group off campus. Thus reassured, and with the counselor's encouragement, he met with the group, feeling much relieved to find others in similar circumstances. With their support, and the support of the counselor, he finally told his wife, who seemed to accept the news with some understanding and acceptance. Next, he made plans to move into an apartment and begin to associate with openly gay men to see if indeed he preferred to live a gay lifestyle. To help him with his children, he sought out the local gay fathers' support group.[3]

Soon Andrew began to integrate a gay identity, feeling more whole and less fragmented than he had in twenty years. As he no longer felt torn by leading a double life, he now appeared more tranquil, and as a result more available to his children. Although they were rejecting at first, refusing to have anything to do with a gay father, they gradually learned to accept the truth of their father's sexual orientation. With the counselor's help, Andrew became more disclosing about his homosexuality to them, despite his fears of losing their love and respect. When he moved into a long-term relationship with Harold several months later, he did not introduce him to his daughters for a brief period of time. With support from his gay parents' support group, however, Andrew encouraged regular visits by his children, who now seem to appreciate their father's happy relationship.

Counselors assessing lesbian couples typically confront a different set of parenting problems, since such households are far more likely than those of gay men to contain children. Several factors probably are operating here: lesbians far more frequently have been married before turning to same-sex relationships; and they tend to come out later, increasing the likelihood of having borne children while married. Moreover, courts tend to award custody to a mother, particularly if her homosexuality has not been a contested issue in the divorce proceedings (Maddox, 1982).

It is not at all uncommon for one or both lesbian partners to have their children residing with them. Thus, they face many of the same problems of any blended family (see Chapter 5) where families with children from different households must reorganize their lives into a coherent new family unit. Here that reorganization is complicated by the fact that the union

3 The International Gay Fathers Coalition in Washington, D.C. maintains a list of support groups in various cities, along with the names of gay fathers in each area willing to offer assistance and guidance in dealing with children.

between parents may be temporary or short-lived, and may involve more than one such alliance during the children's growing-up years. Coparenting by two lesbians also must proceed without any legal safeguards, regarding custody for example, should the natural mother die, a further roadblock to involvement by the nonparent. Finally, family counselors may anticipate working with the children along with their parents, since living with openly gay parents is more likely than not to open children up to jeers and harassment from their peers (Moses & Hawkins, 1982).

SOME COUNSELING GUIDELINES

Most authorities (Harrison, 1987; Malyon, 1982; Woodman & Lenna, 1980) agree on the absolute necessity, as a minimum, of helping gay clients achieve, accept, and integrate a gay identity. Counselors who feel uncomfortable doing so, despite paying lip service to this goal, would do well to work through any internalized underlying, interfering homophobic feelings; if this is not possible, they should refer the client(s) to some other counselor or community group (for example, Gay Counseling Center) whose attitudes and outlooks are more consistent with facilitating a positive self-identity. To attempt to force gay clients to rid themselves of their homosexuality is a miscarriage of the counselor's mission.

In some cases, a gay person may insist on seeing a gay counselor, much like a woman client who may only feel comfortable with and understood by another woman, or perhaps a couple experiencing conflict with their children who are only willing to talk to a counselor who too is a parent. While such a request may mean nothing more than that the client wishes to speak to someone who has had similar experiences, it may also mean a great deal more. In the case of gay clients, it more probably reflects a distrust of "straight" counselors as members of a rejecting, oppressing group, or perhaps indicates incompletely worked-through feelings of self-acceptance on the part of the gay person. Fear of exposure of their secret, loss of privacy, concern that confidentiality might be broken also may play a part. In the situation where one member of a gay couple is far less open than the other about his or her sexual orientation, restricting social contacts primarily or even exclusively to other gays, distrust and suspicion may be so great that working with a nongay counselor is ruled out.

Regardless of the particular set of circumstances, the first phase of counseling gay or lesbian couples is to grapple with issues concerning trust. As Malyon (1982) contends, the client(s) must come to regard the counselor as a person of special knowledge, competence, and good will who cares about the client(s), if counseling is to proceed. Values must inevitably be addressed, including revelation of the counselor's therapeutic bias with respect to homosexuality along with goals of the treatment. For effective counseling to occur, counselor disclosure of attitudes is every bit as important as that same declaration by clients.

As we have observed a number of times, most gay couples who come for professional help are not there to seek guidance in changing their sexual orientation. Rather, for the most part they come with problems quite analogous to those presented by nongay couples: communication difficulties between partners, differences in commitment to the relationship, handling money, managing time together, dealing with children, infidelity, jealousy, sexual problems, intimacy concerns, breaking up, and so on. However, beyond these issues also common to opposite-sex partners are those unique to the experiences of gay persons in a coupled relationship. These include dealing with (1) their own overt or covert antihomosexual attitudes, leading to low self-esteem and lack of self-acceptance; (2) the degree to which as individuals and as a couple they are out in the open with both gay and nongay friends, family, employers, and colleagues; (3) the paucity of role models for their relationship, leading to uncertainty or to the adoption of inappropriate male-female patterns; and (4) communication difficulties, especially overcommunicating their feelings to one another, causing relationship fatigue and distress (McWhirter & Mattison, 1982).

In the following case, two men, both with previous gay experiences, turn a casual sexual encounter into a more extended relationship lasting five years. They contact a family counselor when that union develops signs of dysfunction.

Simon and Alf would probably seem to most casual observers to be mismatched. Simon, at 45, had established himself as an executive in a large pharmaceutical company, where he was considered to be among the three or four men likely to become chief executive officer in the near future. Alf, ten years younger, worked as a salesman for a small printing company, barely earning enough to support himself. They had met at a gay bar five years ago, and after some brief embracing had gone to Simon's house for what they both assumed would be a one-night stand. However, they found themselves attracted to one another and both wanted to continue the liaison. About three weeks into the relationship, Simon asked Alf to move in with him. Devoid of friends and looking for a safe place to live, Alf readily accepted.

Although their living together appeared to work reasonably well from the start, both were aware of major differences in background, education, and financial stability. Their social experiences and degree of gay identity also differed. Simon had a large social circle of prominent gay and nongay men and women. His homosexual behavior was whispered about at work, but neither denied nor admitted by him. He had had two previous live-in arrangements with men prior to living with Alf.

Alf, on the other hand, had had numerous recent homosexual bath-house experiences, but had not been in any but casual relationships until he met Simon. He had not attended college, but instead had joined a cult right after high school, probably in an effort to avoid dealing with his sexual urgings, particularly his homosexual feelings. When Alf's parents had had him kidnapped from the cult and deprogrammed, he had protested at first, but soon had submitted to their wishes. His impersonal sexual experiences with men began soon after returning home, and became a regular part of his weekly routine after work. He never discussed his homosexuality with anyone at work, and most of his co-workers thought of him as interested in women. Alf was essentially a loner before joining with Simon.

Not surprisingly, Simon dominated Alf, who took on his familiar passive role. The older man supplied most of the money, the friends, the travel opportunities. Alf was expected to cook, work in the garden, and in general take care of Simon after his hard day at the office. Their "butch/femme" pattern thus resembled a traditional male/female one. Simon was always the sexual aggressor, a role he demanded. Alf enjoyed being desired and valued, and felt safe and secure in the relationship.

Before living together, Simon had had extensive individual psycho-therapy, and as a result felt secure about his gay identity. Alf continued to struggle with his, and after they had been together for several years he too decided to seek individual therapeutic help. His "straight" counselor encouraged Alf to find new friends on his own, and to develop a stronger sense of self independent of Simon. In addition, Alf was urged to go through a "normal" adolescence, which he seemed to have skipped, includ-ing exploring other relationships in the gay community.

As a result of counseling, Alf got in touch with previously suppressed feelings of resentment over his subservient position with Simon. He recog-nized and became bitter over both his emotional and financial dependence on his lover. Alf did not own anything himself, he realized, and now he wanted something in his name from Simon. Also, he felt he had been taken advantage of long enough, having to go to bed when Simon decided, having to socialize when and with whom Simon decided, and so on. He now wanted to meet new men, something Simon opposed, ostensibly because of the danger of AIDS, but more personally because Simon feared Alf would leave him for a younger, more attractive partner.

The couple now was fighting more than ever before. Simon contended that Alf should either contribute more money or, if not, be more willing to contribute more toward housekeeping responsibilities. With increased struggles over sex outside their relationship, in addition to the conflicts over money, the two decided to seek counseling from a family counselor. Both preferred a woman counselor, because they felt there would likely be less prejudice against gay men. When Simon called her for an appointment, he said, "My friend and I are seeking couples therapy. *He's* free after 5 p.m. Are you interested?" Thus providing a clue that the counselor would be working with gays, Simon seemed to be asking whether, as a nongay, she was comfortable enough to work with them. Assured that she passed the initial test, they set up an appointment for the next day.

At the first session, both men presented, in graphic detail, a description of their favorite sex positions. Once again reassured that the female counselor did not appear startled or repelled, they went on in subsequent sessions to discuss relationship issues. For several weeks they discussed issues of power and control, in addition to their differing views of money. After this first phase of counseling, Simon put one-half ownership of their summer home in Alf's name, and agreed to a more equitable distribution of responsibilities at home. During this phase, the counselor helped Alf in particular work on his homophobic feelings, especially his concern that nobody in the nongay world could accept him.

As Alf developed a stronger sense of his gay identity, he was more willing to come out with his family as well as friends at work. In particular, the counselor helped both men assert their rights as a couple. Visiting Alf's parents, who knew they were both gay, they no longer pretended merely to be close acquaintances. When Alf's Aunt Georgia came to town, Simon was no longer identified as Alf's landlord, but rather as his gay partner.

The sexual issues were more difficult to resolve, and they took up most of the next phase of counseling, lasting two months. Despite Simon's expressed fear of AIDS, Alf continued his casual homosexual contacts. He did agree, however, to join a small discussion group, called "Safe Sex," where gay men frankly talked over their sex habits. While there was no sex per se in the group, Simon was alarmed, especially when he discovered that some group participants had tested HIV positive.

As Alf turned more and more to the group for role models, he began to question whether a woman counselor could really understand him or help him with his conflicts with Simon. Although Simon protested that they still needed to work on the issue of sexual exclusiveness, Alf insisted that he would no longer attend the sessions, and they terminated counseling.

Two years later, still fighting but still together, they once again briefly contacted their former counselor. They were at the point of separating, and asked for some guidance to make the final split-up as painless as possible. Alf now wanted to try living by himself, something he had never done before. Simon opposed the idea, but reconciled himself to remaining friends, to which Alf agreed. After five years as a couple, they let go of one another and went their separate ways.

As this case illustrates, working with gay couples does not call for any specific counseling techniques per se, but rather a set of attitudes and a level of knowledge toward homosexuality that help gay clients accept themselves and their life choices. Because internalized homophobic feelings are present in everyone, gays need help in uncovering and working through their own antihomosexual biases as a first step toward achieving a sense of self-worth and acceptance of a gay partner. Each partner may be at a different stage of self-acceptance as a gay person, and here the counselor can help bring previously hidden differences to the surface for clarification, reducing dissimilarity and conflict between the pair. As they achieve a better balance between their attitudes, underlying rejection of self and partner is minimized and resistance to coming out as a gay couple reduced.

Understanding how the couple define themselves and where they are in the coming out process is one of the counselor's first tasks. The issue of whether to make their gayness as a couple public may or may not be as important as their self-definition, which always requires counselor exploration, not merely counselor acceptance. As in most couple relationships, heterosexual or homosexual, the members' feelings regarding public exposure may differ, and these differences need examination and resolution.

The counselor needs to act as a facilitator, offering support and encouragement as gay clients affirm their gay identity. To be of maximum help, the counselor should be acquainted with community support systems and local resource services (mental health programs, health clinics, gay parents' groups, church programs, AIDS projects, gay newspapers, gay political organizations) available to gay clients.

Further, in assisting gays to affirm their sexuality, counselors may need to help them find ways to do so responsibly and safely. The emergence of the AIDS health crisis[4] demands the learning and practice of "safe sex." In most gay communities, casual encounters and oral sex have been discouraged, and the use of condoms, spermicidal jellies, and other safety measures undertaken, as awareness of the risk of AIDS has become more widespread. Most gays know all too well, by experiencing the death of many of their gay friends, the dangers to themselves and others involved in unsafe sexual practices. Some, however, may need help from the counselor in facing the risks, so that they do not simply deny or avoid possible consequences. It is vital here that the counselor too does not avoid discussing or deny the risk to one or both partners because of the counselor's own anxiety.

Counseling gays with ARC (AIDS Related Complex) or with full-blown cases of AIDS involves helping them deal with fears of all of the following: loss of independence, becoming helpless, rejection by a lover, financial problems, disclosure to family or others of being homosexual, punishment by society for being gay, contaminating partners, and their own ultimate death. Harrison (1987) urges counselors to empower gay clients in every possible way: to confront people who withdraw from them,

4   The crisis, of course, affects not only gays, but also heterosexuals, and therefore in no way should be considered an exclusively gay disease. However, gay males do make up the largest risk group (66 percent of all persons with diagnosed AIDS). Others at risk include intravenous drug abusers (17 percent), homosexual males who are also intravenous drug abusers (8 percent), persons with hemophilia or other coagulation disorders (1 percent), heterosexuals (4 percent), and recipients of blood transfusions (2 percent). Three percent of those with AIDS are in none of these groups (Harrison, 1987).

to affirm their right to receive support, to assert themselves in hospital settings, to demand being treated with respect and not as freaks or lepers, to express their anger and frustration, and so on. Even those persons who seem to have fully accepted their gay identity may regress, feel contaminated, become seriously depressed, or fear negative judgment from others. They may blame their illness on their sexual orientation, and thus feel deserving of the disease. The counselor may need to coordinate efforts with other health workers in monitoring the client's condition and in supporting increasingly direct discussions of death.

The family counselor needs to remain flexible, perhaps seeing the AIDS victim alone to explore feelings he is not yet ready to share, before bringing in the partner. Similarly, members of the family of origin may require separate sessions as preparation for a conjoint session with the AIDS patient alone or with his partner.

AIDS counseling also involves caring for survivors of the dying person, helping them grieve the loss. Not just gay partners, but also families of origin who have lost someone to AIDS may need help with bereavement. The social stigma attached to the disease may deprive them of the social supports they would normally expect to receive when a family member dies. As Walker (1987) notes, what individuals, couples, and families with AIDS problems have in common

> is that they all have a member who suffers a uniquely stigmatized fatal illness, one where issues of contagion reverberate through the family and into the larger culture. Most families and individuals are wrestling with issues of guilt and shame, blame and anger, betrayal and fear, helplessness and impotence. They are afraid of contagion, of social ostracism, of pain and death. They must care or be cared for in situations where they meet hostility, contempt, fear and inadequate care. They must fight endless red tape for potentially life saving medicine and perhaps be denied it. (p. 2)

Finally, the counselor must sort out and deal with his or her own feelings regarding death and dying. Attitudes toward sexuality in general and sexually transmitted diseases in particular require self-examination. Working with dying AIDS patients can be a devastating experience in itself, and it may be desirable to arrange for some supportive counseling or networking with other AIDS workers for assistance in mourning and to avoid counselor burnout.

SUMMARY

Gay couples have much in common with cohabiting heterosexual couples, but also some major differences: greater rejection by society, self-condemnation, more determined efforts at concealment, internalized homophobic feelings, and fear of disenfranchisement as a result of the AIDS health crisis.

Homosexuality is present in all societies, at all socioeconomic levels, and among all racial and ethnic groups, its prevalence ranging from 5 to 10 percent among males and 3 to 5 percent among females. Gays typically gravitate toward larger communities, from whatever place of origin, since meeting other gays is easier there and disclosure is less likely to lead to social ostracism. Gay subcultures exist in most large communities, easing entry into the gay lifestyle.

The majority of gay men seek extended relationships, but casual sexual encounters, particularly among younger gay men, are common. "Coming out" as a gay person can cause considerable apprehension, and typically is a process that extends over time and in front of different audiences. Lesbians are more likely than gay men to strive for stable, extended relationships.

All gays must struggle with achieving self-acceptance in a society in which homosexuality conjures up negative stereotypes and rejection from family, church, and nongay friends. Couples must reach an agreement on sexual exclusiveness, especially in light of the AIDS crisis. Gay fathers and lesbian mothers, who number approximately 5 to 6 million in the United States, must deal with integrating children into their gay lives; lesbians in particular often have their children residing with them and risk the loss of custody.

Counseling gays requires providing them with help in achieving a gay identity. In some cases, gays may insist on seeing a gay counselor, especially if they distrust a "straight" one or if they have not sufficiently accepted their own sexual orientation. Gay couples rarely come for counseling to change that orientation, but rather to deal with relationship issues much like their nongay counterparts. In addition, they typically attempt to grapple with such issues as their own homophobic feelings, problems with coming out, and the paucity of adequate role models. AIDS counseling may require teaching safe sex practices, and helping gay men, once infected, their partners, and their families of origin deal with the ultimate loss through death.

Chapter 8

✦✦✦

Counseling the Dual-Career Family

Two-paycheck families per se are hardly a new phenomenon, many wives having joined their husbands as breadwinners, largely out of economic necessity, throughout our country's history. Moreover, wives in low-income, immigrant, black, and farm families in particular always have contributed money, working at home or away, either supplementing a husband's income or in some cases providing sole support for their families (Aldous, 1982).

Two-person careers (Papanek, 1974) represent another familiar American phenomenon. Here the wife, often well educated but without employment outside the home, channels her talents and energies into performing an auxiliary role in her husband's high-achievement, high-commitment career rather than advancing her own occupational or professional development. She offers primarily emotional and practical support rather than household labor; the breadwinner-male/supportive-homemaker-female role structure goes largely unchallenged by the participants, both of whom appear to benefit from the arrangement. By freeing himself of family-based roles and domestic responsibilities, the man can pursue a productive public career. In this traditional "egalitarian" marriage, benefits also accrue to the domestically based wife. Her measure of success, however, comes from how successful her husband becomes, with the understanding that her help and support in furthering his career, while simultaneously managing family responsibilities and providing for their social lives, plays a key role in his attainments. According to a popular notion, "behind every successful man there is a [perhaps exhausted] woman," or possibly more accurately, "it takes two people to further one career."

The link between paid work for women outside the home and family processes did not gain the attention of social scientists until World War II, when married women left home in large numbers to seek employment in offices and factories. When it became clear in the postwar period that married women's role in the workplace was not merely a wartime phenomenon, "working wives" became the target of studies investigating the impact of a wife's work on her children and her marriage. Underlying these studies, as Walker and Wallston (1985) contend, was the assumption that the family's viability depended on sex-typed divisions of roles, and that therefore women pursuing careers were somehow entering into a deviant lifestyle that could threaten society's well-being.

As Hunt and Hunt (1977) note, the "two-person career" concept emphasizes the necessity of a second person's playing an emotionally supportive role to make a single career work. The liability carried by dual-careerists, these authors argue, is precisely in the lack of such a necessary auxiliary partner. In their view, the greatest challenge of two careers lies not in the required juggling of family and work responsibilities nor in the necessity for a new division of domestic labor between husband and wife, but in the lack of a "nonworking wife" at home they both require, symbolizing both support and success of the careerist.

FROM TWO-PERSON CAREER TO DUAL CAREERS[1]

The preceding brief background is important in understanding one of the most dramatic changes in family structure and relationship patterns to have occurred over the last two decades: the emergence of dual-career families in substantial numbers. In the 1960s, a period of heady optimism concern-

---

1 The terms *dual-worker* or *dual-earner* are sometimes used instead of *dual-career* to describe families today, presumably to eliminate any implied class bias inherent in the latter term. However, we believe *dual-worker* suggests that only income-producing efforts should be considered work, an affront to homemakers, volunteers, and other unpaid workers. In the same way, *dual-earner*, while cutting across all classes, fails to delineate the new phenomenon we wish to address in this chapter, namely the variation of a nuclear family in which both spouses simultaneously seek intellectual challenges from careers and emotional fulfillment from their family lives.

ing the possibilities for achieving significant changes in the structure of American life, many women, including those with young children, entered the professional work force. By 1974, according to Klein (1975), close to 5 million women were in career-level positions, a jump of 68 percent over the previous decade. Close to half were married and residing with their husbands (who themselves were likely to be pursuing careers).

By the mid-1980s—a time of swollen university enrollments with women pursuing career-oriented goals, greater career opportunities for women, two-career couples living together outside of marriage, as well as greater public acceptance of the two-career phenomenon—there were probably 5 million dual-career families (Goldenberg & Goldenberg, 1984). Half the married women in the work force today are mothers with children under the age of 5 (Gilbert, 1985), a growing trend that has widespread implications for marital and family living patterns.

Gilbert (1985) describes the changing attitudes and expectations of women in dual-career relationships over the past two decades. According to her studies, women of the 1960s, encouraged by the growing women's movement, could be characterized as being willing to continue traditional household and child-care responsibilities while adding the "opportunity" to have a career. As Hunt and Hunt (1982) point out in describing this earlier period, that work world largely excluded women but had special rules for those allowed to enter. Those rules permitted men in dual-career marriages to continue to lead lives similar to those of other career men, while women in dual-career marriages were expected to engage in a balancing act that allowed a measure of career involvement as long as it did not inconvenience the family.

Women in the 1980s, according to Gilbert (1985), are making a more conscious effort to share both home and work roles with their spouses. However, while both careerists may declare a willingness to share power and domestic responsibilities and to support their partner's career aspirations, in practice their efforts may frequently fall short of the mark. It is probably fair to say that while progress has been made in reaching truly egalitarian goals, women in general still are likely to assume a larger proportion of child and household responsibilities than their husbands, to defer career aspirations in favor of their mate's career advancement, and to cut back career activities during critical periods of family development (Farber, 1988).

Some of the attraction of pursuing a career while simultaneously maintaining a family has been replaced, for many women, by a greater awareness of problems stemming from the changing family lifestyle. Counselors can expect to see many dual-career couples seeking help with work-overload problems, role conflicts, and relationship difficulties. Achieving a workable balance—a more-or-less smoothly functioning interpersonal system in which each partner maintains a sense of independence, uniqueness, and wholeness, all within the context and security of the family relationship—is never an easy task for any couple. As Goldenberg (1986) observes, the task is made all the more difficult for contemporary dual-career couples by the lack of role models from the past from which to draw support. He argues that significant changes in the role structure between men and women are required to make a dual-career marriage work, and very few roadmaps for this journey presently exist.

CONCEPTUALIZING THE DUAL-CAREER LIFESTYLE

According to Rapoport and Rapoport (1969), themselves a two-career couple generally credited with coining the term "dual-career family," such a family structure involves both the husband's and the wife's pursuing active professional careers as well as active, involved family lives. By the term *career* they mean rather precisely, "those types of job sequences that require a high degree of commitment and that have a continuous developmental character" (Rapoport & Rapoport, 1976, p. 9).

Obviously, many noncareer jobs may be performed with considerable commitment, although they may bring little personal development or advancement in status or salary. These authors argue that careers typically have an intrinsically demanding character. They are likely to require educational preparation and related professional work experience. Gilbert (1985) emphasizes continuous, full-time commitment by both partners in her definition of a dual-career family as "a variation of the nuclear family in which both spouses pursue an uninterrupted lifelong career and also establish and develop a family life that often includes children" (p. 6). A less strict and probably more realistic definition is offered by a number of authors, including Shaevitz and Shaevitz (1980), who include couples as dual-careerists when both spouses have made a "significant commitment full or part time to a role outside of the home" (p. 12).

Unlike partners in a two-person career, one of whom (in most cases the wife) derives vicarious pleasure, achievement, and status from helping the other advance in a career, dual-careerists each pursue separate and distinct work roles, presumably offering support and encouragement to the career aspirations of one another. Ideally, the wife's career, no less than her husband's, is an integral part of her identity, representing a professional commitment that is more than a way to supplement the family income. Greater intellectual companionship, increased financial freedom, added stimulation, more opportunity for self-expression, an expanded sense of personal fulfillment, escape from household drudgery, and a possible closer relationship between father and children as a result of his greater participation in their upbringing are claimed as the potential benefits. The potential danger is in romantically overlooking the numerous sources of stress, and naively assuming dual-career families have the best of it all:

plenty of money, fulfilling family relationships, satisfying careers, an exciting and filled-to-the-brim lifestyle.

PROFESSIONAL WOMEN IN DUAL-CAREER MARRIAGES

Not all dual-career couples are the same. Some start out together at college preparing for careers that they then both pursue in an uninterrupted fashion. Some prepare together, but the woman stops to raise a family while her husband continues his career. Some women do not think of careers until later in life, perhaps when their children are grown or they have gotten divorced or been widowed. Some work part-time at their careers throughout the child-rearing years; others postpone any employment outside the home until their children are out of the house. The point is that no "one-size-fits-all" pattern exists, especially for women. Nor are all professionals, men or women, equally committed to their careers or equally involved with their families.

In a longitudinal study carried out over an eight-year period, Poloma, Pendleton, and Garland (1981) examined the consequences for a group of married professional women of having a dual-career marriage. In particular, they were interested in relating careers to stages in the family's life cycle. What effect does marriage and motherhood have on career development? How well are professional women able to coordinate their careers with those of their husbands? In the vast majority of cases, these researchers found that having children limited a woman's career involvement, causing her to turn down promotions with increased responsibilities and opt for part-time employment instead of full-time work, and limiting her geographic mobility.

For example, a female professor might turn down an opportunity for an administrative promotion (a demanding 11-month job) in favor of a more flexible teaching assignment geared to the normal academic year (hers and her children's). A woman physician choosing between work and family responsibilities might decide to work half-time. A woman attorney with a bright future in a prestigious law firm might find it necessary to relocate to another city to enhance her husband's career opportunities. In each case, career development is curtailed and possible marital and family tensions heightened. Most couples in Poloma, Pendleton, and Garland's (1981) sample chose to combine a career with child rearing, inevitably, depending upon age, stamina, and philosophy of child rearing, reducing career involvement.

These researchers were able to differentiate four major career types among professional women. The first, pursuing what is termed a *regular career*, begins her career right out of college or shortly thereafter, but before marriage, and may continue in her work with minimal interruption, possibly stopping for brief periods to bear children or to engage in part-time employment during early child-rearing years. While this career pattern resembles men's in the same profession, being a mother as well as a professional has its costs, especially when the children are younger (for example, allowing less evening work, less travel).

A woman's *interrupted career* begins as a regular career but is halted, possibly for several years, so she can be with her children, before resuming professional work. Thus, professional growth or opportunities for promotion may be reduced. On the other hand, there may well be a gain for some women who look forward to taking such a "sabbatical" from their careers. A brief hiatus after early career demands may be most welcome, although there is a risk of resentment from a husband not customarily granted such an opportunity for an interrupted career.

The woman with a *second career* usually receives her professional training near the time her children are grown or after they leave. Thus, the heaviest demands of early childbearing years are behind her before she embarks on professional training and a future career. Although she gets off to a late start and is likely to be behind age cohorts in income and status for a long time, in most cases she ultimately pursues a career pattern much like regular female careerists.

A *modified second career* begins earlier, with the woman obtaining training and subsequent career development after the last child is deemed no longer in need of full-time mothering (perhaps when entering kindergarten). Family demands are still present, so this woman may begin her career slowly, increasing the momentum of her work involvement step by step as her child-care responsibilities lessen over the years. Like the regular careerist, but with her childbearing years behind her, she may seek full-time or part-time work, but may need to be available for family demands for a period of time.

These data indicate that even with help from their husbands or live-in housekeepers, married career women with children have serious difficulty in following career lines like those of their male counterparts. Attempting to combine career and family is, of course, possible, but it is a pressure-prone situation that frequently leads to conflicts over the multiple and sometimes conflicting demands.

CHANGING DOMESTIC ROLE PATTERNS

Flexibility in defining and learning new roles and in accommodating family rule changes are essential elements in making a two-career relationship work. Establishing a new division of labor based on available time, interest, and skills is necessary if the couple is to avoid **role overload**, a frequent complaint of couples seriously trying to meet all work and family demands. Basic child care, meal preparation and cleanup, shopping, laundry, doctors' appointments, bill paying, arranging for maintenance of cars and household appliances, indoor and outdoor cleaning, travel planning, pet care, maintaining social relationships—these are just some of the tasks every couple must deal with that can become especially taxing when the couple is already overcommitted.

As we indicated earlier, at least some of these responsibilities ordinarily are handled by a wife at home, a key player lacking in a dual-career family. To some extent, relatively inexpensive female domestic help or cheap babysitting has been available in the past to help ease some of the burden, but as more women enter the workplace, fewer of them are willing to work at the low salaries these jobs command. Nor are female relatives as likely to be at home or nearby as in the past. To pay a housekeeper means the couple must work harder or more hours, increasing fatigue and reducing family time together.

What impact has the entry of women into employment had on their husbands' participation in household and family work? According to Walker and Wallston's (1985) survey, with some exceptions a nonegalitarian division of labor at home still tends to exist for families of professional women. However, husbands of employed wives do more family work than do husbands whose wives are not employed. Rapoport and Rapoport (1982) suggest that despite progress toward greater equity, the prevailing assumption remains that the major responsibility for domestic work, particularly child care, resides with women, even though their husbands might be willing to "help." Aldous (1981) contends that one reason for the imbalance in physical care for children extended by mothers and fathers may be that some women are loath to part with child-care responsibilities, often feeling guilt over time away from their children.

How much change has occurred in dividing responsibilities for household tasks in recent years, as two-career families have become more commonplace? Are husbands now more likely to increase their family work when their wives are employed? To what extent do women in particular continue to experience an inequitable amount of family-related work? Using data from two national studies concerned with how husbands and wives allocate time to household responsibilities, Pleck (1985) has determined that the nature of employed wives' overload and husbands' response to their wives' employment are both changing. While such overload for women still exists, it is declining as "men's time in the family is increasing while women's is decreasing" (p. 146). Moreover, according to this research, not only have husbands with employed wives increased their domestic involvements (child care, housework), but so have husbands whose wives do not work outside the home. Overall, Pleck concludes, a value shift in our society is occurring—no doubt stimulated in part by the surge of married women into the labor market—toward greater family involvement by husbands as well as a greater sharing of breadwinner responsibilities.

SOURCES OF STRESS IN DUAL-CAREER LIFESTYLES

Beyond changes in the division of labor, often calling for significant role restructuring within the family, all two-career couples must deal with a number of other issues that are potential sources of interpersonal conflict and family tension. Shaevitz and Shaevitz (1980) enumerate the following as a minimum list of such problems to be addressed: How will household tasks be assigned? Who will do what and according to whose standards? Should they have children? How many? Who will be responsible for their care? Who will be available in emergencies? Are child-care facilities available? Who controls the money? Separate or joint accounts? What are the rights of each in spending the money? How do they deal with job relocations? Is one partner's commuting to and from another city a realistic solution? What if one partner is significantly more successful in her or his career than the other? How can they learn to recognize and deal with overload or burnout? What special things must they do, as a dual-career couple, to enhance their relationship?

Frequently, the counselor's first task is to help two-career couples distinguish which of their problems are caused by the makeup of their specific marital relationship and which are problems inherent in a dual-career lifestyle. The issue is complex and the two clearly interrelated. Box 8.1 offers the counselor a list of strains that may result from the latter. Role overload, as we have noted, is a common complaint of dual-careerists, who assume responsibilities for multiple roles while lamenting the fatigue, the limited leisure time, and the drained energies caused by their chosen lifestyle. This is particularly true of those "superachievers," men or women, who insist on having it all—successful careers, fulfilling marriages, achieving children, glorious vacations, and elegant dinner parties.

Box 8.1. A Problem Appraisal Checklist for Dual-Career Couples

Dual-career couples may experience problems in the following areas:

- Role overload
- Career demands vs. personal and family demands
- Competition between spouses
- Achieving equity in their relationship
- Division of labor
- Job-related geographic mobility
- Child-care arrangements
- Time allocation
- Establishing social networks
- Maintaining a personal identity

Women, however, are more likely to experience role strain as they attempt to add career roles to their traditional gender-related roles. Who is more willing to stay home with a sick child, the mother or father? Which of the parents should defer the day's work plans to stay home if no trusted outside support (a housekeeper, a grandmother) is available? Most likely it is the woman—perhaps feeling guilty over failing to fulfill her traditional task with children, or perhaps unable to mobilize her husband to take over—who opts to remain at home. Her conflict, as a result of loyalties to work and family both, may lead to considerable strain and resentment toward her less-guilty spouse (not socialized to give child care his highest priority) and her children. Or, in some cases, she may try to deny the feeling of resentment at being primarily responsible for certain family activities. In such instances, some more traditional women may berate themselves that a "good" mother should be able to do whatever her family requires without complaining. Even those women less invested in motherhood may withhold any complaints, fearing that their husbands may suggest that if it is too difficult for them, then perhaps they should consider less involvement in their careers.

One common way for a woman to deal with career demands vs. tending to family needs is to adjust the former to accommodate the latter. As we noted in an earlier section, she may interrupt a career to have children, work part-time while her children are young, perhaps even delay starting a career until her children are self-sufficient or fully grown. She and her husband may, of course, choose not to have children. In some instances the couple may schedule work at different hours, so that they take turns caring for family responsibilities (although they may see each other only in passing, hardly conducive to a fulfilling relationship). Whose career is primary? Probably, although certainly not necessarily, the man's career takes precedence; he is probably the major breadwinner, and makes fewer adjustments to accommodate family needs than does his wife.

In the following case, both partners begin their relationship with high degrees of career involvement, but the situation changes:

Tony and Abby had each been married before when they met at a business conference. Tony, 45, had divorced four years earlier, having been married for 20 years to Florence, a homemaker. Their marriage had been unhappy for many years, and although both had agreed to stay together for the sake of the children, they had found it increasingly difficult to stick to their plan, and they had divorced as soon as their three children (Ben, 19; Howard, 18; Gillian, 16) were well into adolescence. Tony, a successful executive, had agreed to a generous alimony and child support settlement. After the "miserable" marriage and "painful" divorce, Tony had vowed not to remarry.

Abby, on the other hand, had been married three times, briefly each time, and at age 36 believed she did not want children and thus would have no reason to marry again. Because she was quite self-sufficient financially, as vice-president in charge of labor negotiations for a large firm, she had not sought nor did she receive any alimony from any of her failed marriages.

When they met, Tony was immediately smitten by Abby's intelligence and vivaciousness. She was extremely attractive, he thought, and her nonclinging behavior was a welcomed relief from Florence's overdependency. He respected her as an ambitious career woman, earning a good salary and eager to advance in her company. She too enjoyed his no-strings-attached attitude, and together they enjoyed travel, going to the theater, and socializing with friends. Except for the irritation of paying large amounts of money to his ex-wife, Tony was content, and Abby had never been happier.

After living together for three years without being married, the two needed to make a serious decision when Abby discovered she was pregnant. She now changed her mind and wanted to marry and have the baby. Although Tony was less than enthusiastic about the idea of marrying and especially of becoming a father again, he acquiesced on the condition that Abby take major responsibility for raising the child. He insisted that they hire a housekeeper to look after their child, so that their lives would be interrupted only minimally and they could enjoy their pleasurable life as before.

Tony and Abby married, and Abby continued to work while pregnant. However, toward the end of her pregnancy, her firm decided to cut back on personnel in her department, and she took that opportunity to resign but continue working for them as an independent consultant from her home. In addition to enabling her to work convenient hours, this seemed like a good opportunity to build a labor consulting business of her own at home while raising their child. The housekeeper she hired was helpful in freeing her from many domestic chores.

Unfortunately, soon after their son Donny was born, Abby's contract with the firm expired and she had trouble getting more accounts. With their combined income now seriously reduced, she fired the housekeeper, and while she enjoyed being with her child all day, the drop in income was troublesome to both Tony and Abby.

Abby now began to resent quite intensively the alimony and child support money they were sending to Florence and the children each month. Tony too was becoming more and more annoyed at Abby's loss of income, and especially with her requests that he do more with their child in the evenings and on weekends. Their relationship began to deteriorate, with a great deal of acrimony and blaming characterizing their time together.

Abby complained that he indulged his children with money and that it was unfair to her and would have to stop. He demanded she become more frugal, and began to control her expenditures. She claimed to have fired the housekeeper in an economy move, but kept secret from him her hiring of a cleaning woman on a once-per-week basis. When he asked her to get a babysitter and join him and his business associates for dinner at a gourmet restaurant one evening, she refused and instead showed up with her year-old son. The event turned out to be miserable for all concerned, and Abby swore she would not go out with him under those circumstances again.

When they contacted a counselor, it was readily apparent that both were misusing money to fight with each other. Each spouse was bitter and felt betrayed. The counselor chose not to deal with specific issues at first, but instead to focus on the inappropriateness of maintaining their premarital agreement on the kind of life they were to live. Abby in particular no longer believed in what she had agreed to before Donny was born, namely that she could handle matters at home, continue working, and not bother Tony with the day-to-day operations of the home. Tony remained angry at her because he believed she had reneged on her earlier promises in an unfair and uncaring way. Slowly they began to renegotiate a new "contract" based on a more realistic appraisal of their current situation and what each wanted from the relationship.

During counseling, Abby decided to return to full-time work, leaving their son, now 2, with an older neighborhood woman with whom she felt comfortable. The housekeeper had never been her idea, and the babysitter provided a more homelike atmosphere. Tony was persuaded to become more involved with Donny, who now was more responsive to his dad. The couple was encouraged by the counselor to return to many of the things they had enjoyed before, with recognition that the circumstances of having a child required some modification of earlier patterns. The parents began to take brief weekend vacations alone, leaving Donny with the babysitter, to whom he was now attached. Tony reported before counseling terminated that Abby had once again become more attractive to him, and that he was enjoying parenting for the first time in his life. Abby stated that being a successful working woman and a good mother did wonders for her self-esteem. She no longer felt she needed to be "supermom," able single-handedly to care for job, husband, and child without missing a step or experiencing exhaustion and occasional despondency.

Redistributing household and child-care responsibilities and renegotiating an outdated "contract" were key elements in making this marital system functional once again. However, successful counseling came about not so much from helping the couple achieve complete equality—an equal division of roles and work opportunities—but rather from accomplishing greater equity through a more flexible distribution of roles. The goal here is for each partner to experience, over time and across situations, a sense of fairness in trusting that both the role opportunities and constraints available to each will balance out. In our example, Abby felt better when she believed her needs were being heard and that she had some choices in the roles she chose to play. Even if a major portion of the responsibility for caring for her son, for example, fell on her, she came to feel her husband recognized her contribution, did what he could to help, and took greater responsibility in other areas, such as earning a living. Tony felt less exploited by becoming the single breadwinner for a time when he understood Abby's conflict between career and family demands. He also came to realize that she was committed to a career and not planning to change or renege on their premarital agreements. By resolving her dilemma over arranging satisfactory child care, something central to her sense of being a good mother, and no longer viewing the work role as incompatible with her maternal role, Abby was able to return to work and together they achieved a greater sense of equity.

The decision to have children is a key one for working parents. The birth of a child puts a strain on any marriage, changing the family system from a dyadic one to a far more intricate triadic one. Husband-wife relationships inevitably change as new forces operate within the system. In the case of dual-careerists, the presence of children further complicates their lives, especially if both are heavily committed to career development and advancement. Time allocations must be restructured, less leisure time for themselves is available, professional and domestic responsibilities need to be renegotiated. Juggling work and child care is rarely accomplished easily, and feelings of guilt and/or resentment are often the result. Some parents worry that being a good parent and being involved in a career are incompatible, and that choosing the latter may have a serious negative effect on the child's well-being. Other parents feel guilty over their resentment that the child has somehow infringed on their time, career, or marital relationship. In many cases, unable or unwilling to deal with the causes of increased pressures felt by one or both partners, they search for scapegoats to blame: overcommitment to friends and work, too much time spent with relatives (including, in the case of remarrieds, time spent with children from the previous marriage).

Working parents inevitably worry about whether they are providing proper parenting. For those who resume a career, quality day care for youngsters is essential if parental anxieties are to be kept in check. In the absence of high-quality, organized workplace facilities—still relatively rare—grandparents, neighborhood volunteer groups, trusted and dependable babysitters, and part-time or at-home work by one parent may fill the need. Each of these makeshift solutions carries positive and negative consequences. Parents who take turns in shifts caring for their children at home manage to provide them with at least one parent at home at all times, a definite plus, but often do so at the expense of feeling exhausted and of minimizing adult time together for the sake of the children, a negative result. By doing so, too, they deny the children the opportunity to experience parental interaction as well as interaction all together as a family unit.

Bringing children to a day class provides the stimulation of other children, a plus for the child, but often involves complicated pickup and drop-off arrangements, to say nothing of having to keep a sick child at home, for which stress-inducing last-minute adult plans must be made. Day classes also rob the child of a needed chance to be alone for periods of time. Hiring a full-time housekeeper can be more convenient and less disruptive, but it adds another person to the family system, changing possible alliances and coalitions. Grandparents, especially grandmothers, may help out, but their input regarding child care may introduce conflict; relinquishing a parental role to one's parent may reintroduce feelings on the part of adults of being children themselves. Besides, many grandparents themselves prefer to participate in the nonchild workplace.

Some child-care plans (for example, driving children to and from schools in a car pool with other parents) are usually easily worked out, although parents may run up against scheduling problems with other parents, or worse, people with whom it is difficult to be compatible. Nevertheless, barring unforeseen difficulties, such joint efforts are relatively anxiety-free for most working parents. The matter of caring for a sick child, on the other hand, is a far more difficult one to resolve, men in general being more willing to pick up and deliver than to stay home and minister to the sick. On the other hand, serving only as a backup parent for emergencies or routine activities (for example, chauffeuring children) may not feel right for some men, who may wish to be more central to their child's daily emotional life. This is especially so if their wives get to do the satisfying, fun things (for example, going to the school play, attending "Mommy and Me" classes).

Dual-career couples must be helped to work out an emergency backup system, a secondary group of caregivers who can be turned to when extraordinary events (a sick child, a school holiday) require a change of plans. Without such a secondary support system, stress on one or both dual-careerists is inevitable, and a frequent result is conflict and competition over whose work plans are more important and thus less subject to interruption.

Finally, one barrier to intimacy and marital harmony comes from feelings of competition between two high-achieving and ambitious people who happen to be married to each other. Even if one or both deny the feeling, insisting they are completely supportive of each other's career, some competition may lurk below the surface and intrude on the relationship. Especially if the two are in the same field or at the same career stage—or worse yet, both—comparisons of success and recognition are inevitable. While the competition need not be fierce, the counselor will need to explore its presence with the couple, attending specifically to when and under what circumstances it occurs. Even when couples generally are supportive of each other's professional strivings, feelings of competition may be exacerbated when supplies are limited (for example, when both spouses, just out of graduate school, apply for the one job opening). Competition over who earns more (presumably a measure of who is more successful) is ever-present, men in general still feeling their salary should exceed their spouse's (which in most cases it does). Competitive feelings need to be accepted by dual-career couples as a normal part of being high-achieving people and not necessarily as being destructive. Counselors might encourage each partner to voice, and thus help exorcise, any lingering guilt that might surround normal feelings of competition.

Whatever the sources of stress, the goal of equity based on mutual trust represents the ideal, if not the most easily achieved, solution for dual-career partners. As Hall and Hall (1979) point out, "One of the factors that strengthens a relationship is the feeling of equity for both parties—the feeling that each partner is benefitting from the relationship as much as he or she is contributing to it" (p. 154). The couple needs to bear in mind that equity is not achieved through a perfect 50–50 split in responsibility—never a real possibility—but rather is attainable only through a sense that they are striving toward a common goal, not reachable at the expense of one or the other partner.

COMMUTER MARRIAGES

For most people, intact marriages are assumed to involve two spouses sharing a single household. Yet, with the growth in the number of dual-career families today, it should not be surprising that an attractive job or career opportunity in another locale may lead one person to move away from his or her spouse and children without altering or upsetting the family's location. Known as **commuter marriages**, such arrangements entail the maintenance of separate residences by spouses who may live apart for periods ranging from several days per week to months at a time (Gerstel & Gross, 1983).

Needless to say, such an arrangement contains many built-in sources of stress, as couples strive to adjust to feelings of loneliness or mistrust, and learn to maintain intimacy and commitment on a long-distance basis. Couples who have a stronger and more established relationship, are older, and are free from child-rearing responsibilities are usually in the best position to deal with the tensions of the commuter lifestyle. According to Gerstel and Gross (1983), when at least one spouse's career is well established, the couple tends to fare better than when both partners must at the same time contend with the demands and uncertainties of new professional and marital identities. Older couples have a backlog of experiences together to better cushion the impact of separation; in some cases, where a husband's career has had priority in the past, both spouses accept the fact that it is now only fair and equitable that the wife have her turn.

Commuters—sometimes dubbed "married singles"—live apart precisely because each simultaneously wants to pursue a career, not because one or the other has an occupation that requires living separately for periods of time. (Examples of the latter include merchant marines, professional athletes, politicians, and entertainers.) Nor are they likely to commute for reasons of financial gain. While two active professional careers may yield high family income, that income often fails to compensate for the additional expense of maintaining two residences, travel, and telephone bills. Most often, commuter couples are people intensely committed to their careers, who at the same time value their marriage enough to be willing to put up with the hardship, cost, and effort involved in trying to make it all work.

While some couples manage to stay together precisely because they only see one another from time to time, most dual-career commuters are committed to their family and wish to keep their marriage strong. Both spouses are, at the same time, strongly committed to their professional identification. Most couples view the separation as a forced choice that benefits their sense of personal autonomy and work achievement, but that at the same time generates new tensions in the marital relationship (Walker & Wallston, 1985).

Most married commuters struggle to balance the tangible rewards of professional advancement—money, recognition, status—with the more intangible rewards of a continuing personal connection with spouse and children. Rather than requiring one partner to make a career sacrifice for the other, young professionals in particular may opt for a more equitable solution in which both are willing to give up time together now for the excitement and challenge of advancing their long-range individual careers (Winfield, 1985). While a commuter arrangement could loosen the marital bond, it might also have benefits for the commuter. He or she may welcome the freedom from family pressures and daily constraints, from having to accommodate to another's mealtime or bedtime patterns or be interrupted by child-care responsibilities. Kirschner and Wallum (1978) go so far as to suggest that the commuter may actually intensify his or her dedication to career, perhaps to justify having chosen such an unorthodox living arrangement.

Resolving issues involving job mobility is essential for many of today's young married couples. An attractive career opportunity, a chance for an advancement but in another town, perhaps offers to both spouses from different locales are common dilemmas in which difficult choices must be made. In some cases, a transfer within an organization for one leads to a predicament for others in the family, as they attempt to determine the wisdom of the other spouse's giving up a satisfying job, the children's changing schools in mid-year, selling the house, and uprooting everyone. Whose job is more important? Is disrupting a partner's promising career too much to ask for the sake of living together seven days a week? What stresses are really involved in relocating the family? What about living apart? For how long? How often and under what circumstances will they reunite? Can the marriage sustain the strain? What about the effect on the children? How will the family's familiar way of functioning change to adjust to the missing person?

In the following case, two young high-achievers, recently married and with a 2-year-old daughter, opt for living apart temporarily as the best solution in a tight job market:

Stacy and John met and married while both were attending graduate school. Both ambitious for careers, they loved the academic life and were certain that as professors they could have it all—intellectual stimulation, a social network of interesting friends, time off for travel, prestigious jobs, periodic sabbatical leaves, enough income to lead a comfortable life. Both also wanted what a family life would provide, and in her last year at the university Stacy got pregnant, as planned, gave birth to Robin, their daughter, during summer break, and without missing any school time received her Ph.D. in Greek literature on schedule. John, however, seemed to be less organized and became bogged down in his dissertation in psychology during his fourth year in graduate school. As a result, he found himself needing to return to the university for at least an additional year when she was ready to look for a university teaching job.

Finding a job proved to be more of a hurdle than Stacy had imagined. Only a handful of universities offered courses she was prepared to teach, and at those schools, teacher turnover was slow and job openings rare. After sending her resume to 150 colleges and universities, she discovered only 2 had openings, and there were eight applicants for each. Fortunately, her outstanding school performance plus strong letters of recommendation from her major advisor helped her land a two-year contract at one of these schools, a small university 600 miles away.

The job offer stirred up much soul searching in both Stacy and John. Should she take the one offer she had received or wait until a better one opened up later, perhaps next year, when, presumably, John would also enter the job market? What would she do in the meantime? What were the chances they could ever teach at the same or nearby schools? If she took the job, how often would they see one another? What about Robin?

These and other questions and uncertainties led them to make an appointment with a psychologist at the university's student health center. Both appeared very upset by the pending decision, blaming themselves for not having been realistic about poor job opportunities for Stacy when they planned their academic lives together. John also blamed his dissertation chairman for throwing what John considered to be needless roadblocks in his way, delaying progress in completing his study and thus not allowing him to follow Stacy. He admitted to feeling competitive with Stacy for the first time, envying the apparent ease with which she had completed her graduate work in four years. Stacy too admitted impatience with John's progress, criticizing him for taking on an impossible dissertation topic, choosing the wrong chairman, and in general not moving fast enough. Stacy talked of becoming a housewife and forgetting any academic aspirations, although she soon realized that such an act would be motivated by utter frustration and would ultimately be self-destructive. There was also the issue of money to be considered.

With the counselor's help over several sessions, they decided that Stacy would take the teaching post and that she would take Robin with her. Perhaps with fewer distractions at home, John could devote full time to finishing his dissertation and joining her. They believed their marriage could stand the necessary strain; in any case they had few choices and it would only be for a short period. They agreed to talk to each other at least five nights per week, after 11 p.m. to keep telephone costs at a minimum, and to plan reunions every two months.

Not surprisingly, the separation turned out to be more painful than either had thought. Both became lonely and depressed. In particular, they reported missing the small things that as a loving couple they had taken for granted—the daily exchange of small talk and gossip about school, the shared mealtimes when the three of them were alone together, even studying in silence next to one another in their bedroom. They missed their sexual intimacy, touching one another, being tender. John missed seeing Robin grow up.

Stacy did enjoy her students and colleagues, and had begun to make friends. She found a female undergraduate student to help babysit when necessary in the evenings, and a good day-care center near the university where she could leave Robin during the day. John did less well, gaining a great deal of weight, neglecting his household chores, too distracted to devote his limited energies to completing his dissertation. When they spoke on the phone, they frequently bickered, each feeling cheated by the separation. Their calls became less frequent, as each began to spend more (nonsexual) time with friends. When they did meet, usually at some half-way point, for the weekend, there was initial tension, and they invariably had a fight. Perhaps they expected too much or wanted to crowd too much into their brief reunion, but the feeling of awkwardness and discomfort with one another never left them.

Six months after their separation, John contacted the psychologist for additional counseling for himself. He expressed a deep longing to be with his wife and child, indicating he could not go on this way much longer. Continuing his systems view, although working with one member only, the psychologist focused on what John felt was happening to his family. Reviewing the family transactions within the last half year, John was asked to tally up the sacrifices and to see if any benefits might have accrued. He revealed that he was beginning to manage and to look at his manuscript again, but he was frustrated and lonely, and blamed Stacy for the decision that he realized they had made together. John was asked to clarify for himself how much of the current conflict with Stacy resulted from their present temporary situation, and how much represented previously unspoken but never resolved marital issues from the past. He confessed to resenting her apparent ease in graduate school when he was stumbling through, and her time away from him devoted to school at first and then the baby. He acknowledged that the friends they had together had tried to help after Stacy left, but he had failed to respond and soon they had stopped calling.

John was offered a number of techniques for allocating his time better. In particular, the psychologist urged him to focus on the primary goal— finishing his dissertation and getting back with his wife and child. While doing so, he needed to rebuild his social life, since friends were essential if he was to avoid feeling lonely and depressed. He needed to strengthen his sense of personal identity, and being by himself while Stacy and Robin were away was a good opportunity to work on that.

Stacy and John came to see the counselor together during her academic breaks and in the summer when she and Robin returned home. As the couple worked out some unfinished conflict from the past, their bond, weakened by the separation, seemed to grow stronger. John said he was proud of himself for learning to carry out domestic chores efficiently for the first time in his life. He still did not like to cook, relying too much on fast-food restaurants, but he was starting to watch his diet better. He said too that he was proud of Stacy's accomplishments and her independence, but he was afraid she no longer needed or wanted him. She reassured him that his fears were unfounded, and that she had begun making inquiries at her school about possible openings in psychology for him next year. For one week she went back to another state to visit some friends, leaving Robin with her father, a situation John enjoyed immensely.

During their second year of separation, John and Stacy talked less on the phone, saving money in order to meet more frequently. Each tried to make that meeting more relaxed, not expecting a two-day weekend would substitute for a month apart. They became physically closer than they had been all of the previous year, and each looked forward to their next rendezvous when parting. John finished his dissertation early in the second year and moved to be with his family. Together, he and Stacy sent applications for common employment to a large number of universities, hoping they might be able to teach at the same place. When they last sent a postcard to the counselor, it was to notify him of their new address at a university town in the Midwest, where both were getting ready to start teaching in the fall.

◆◆◆

ADAPTATIONAL STRATEGIES AND FAMILY SYSTEMS

It should be clear by now that there is more than one way to make a go of dual-career marriage. Hall and Hall (1979) offer a thumbnail sketch of several distinct patterns followed by effective career couples—couples satisfied in their homes, their family relationships, their lifestyles, their careers. From these authors' description it is clear that no single role structure is satisfactory to all dual-career pairs, each of which must forge an adaptational style that takes into account both work and family involvements and priorities. These authors distinguish four general types: accommodators, adversaries, allies, and acrobats.

Accommodators represent a marital relationship in which one partner is high in career involvement and low in home involvement while the second partner holds the opposite priorities. One assumes primary (but not total) responsibility for family-centered roles while the second takes major (but not sole) responsibility for career roles. More than likely this combination approximates gender-based roles in a traditional marriage. In most cases the main breadwinner is the professional man; it is the professional woman who involves herself more at home. If a move to another locale should become necessary, the family would likely follow him, since his career is paramount. Thus, a part-time or substitute teacher would accompany her computer-executive husband if he were transferred to another city.

Adversaries both are highly involved in their careers and only minimally involved in home, family, or parental roles. Each partner defines himself or herself primarily by career, while retaining an interest in maintaining a well-run home and smoothly functioning family life. Conflict in such an arrangement may arise over which of the two will perform noncareer-related tasks at home (for example, staying home from the office to wait for the repairman). While each wants the support of the other, neither is willing to make major career sacrifices to facilitate the other's career or fulfill family roles. Competition is probably more severe here than in the other transactional patterns (who won the grant, who got the promotion, who will follow whose job relocation). Children, if present, are a problem, since each partner prefers the other to assume major child-rearing responsibilities.

Allies are both either highly engrossed in their careers or in their home roles, but not in both areas. Their priorities are clear. They may view their roles as parents or as a couple as paramount, gaining satisfaction from home and family rather than from career advancement. Conflict tends to be low in this arrangement, since each is willing to support the other at home, and neither accedes to potentially stressful career demands. On the other hand, if both view their careers as all-important, conflict is kept low by minimizing domestic roles and the need for a well-organized home. Those who value careers often choose to be childless. Neither resents purchases by the other—they treasure each other's independence—and together they may rely on a housekeeper or dinner out instead of bothering with fixing meals at home. Commuting marriages for the sake of career advancement are more easily tolerated here than in other configurations.

Acrobats hope to have it all, since they both actively engage in careers and in home roles. That is, they seek satisfaction and fulfillment from playing all roles, juggling demanding career activities with performing family duties well. High achievement in their careers, a good marriage, happy children, a well-run home, exotic vacations, a reputation as top-notch host and hostess are all pursued, sometimes in a seemingly never-ending, frantic manner. Neither looks to the other to take over; both want to do it all themselves. No speaking engagement is turned down, no call for volunteers ignored, no office in a professional organization allowed to go unfilled, no child's birthday allowed to pass without a large, elaborate party, no soccer practice or musical recital by the children unattended. If conflict is experienced, it is apt to be internal (for example, work overload) rather than adversarial.

SOME COUNSELING GUIDELINES

Various counseling approaches, ranging from the problem-solving to the developmental to the interpersonal, have been proposed in dealing therapeutically with dual-careerists. For example, Sekaran (1986), a management and organizational authority, suggests ways in which counselors can help such couples identify and resolve conflict by providing them with better decision-making, stress-management, and time-management strategies. In addition to encouraging client couples to clarify (and perhaps reassess) their concepts of success, she offers suggestions for helping organizations change policies (offering parent leave, flexible work schedules, child-care assistance) so as to more effectively address the needs of employees from dual-career households.

Helping each partner confront and resolve his or her own unfinished developmental business has been suggested by Hall and Hall (1979) as a way of beginning to untangle current relationship conflicts. Glickauf-Hughes, Hughes, and Wells (1986) support this effort, arguing that while learning coping skills may help some dual-career couples, others may feel frustrated until more basic developmental issues (for example, trust, autonomy, intimacy) get resolved for each partner. For example, these authors contend that power conflicts (over household divisions of labor, career moves, use of leisure time, sex) may reflect each partner's childhood experience that others cannot be counted on to meet his or her needs, and that therefore he or she must "look out for number one." Until both spouses sufficiently master the developmental tasks of trust or autonomy (following the schema of Erik Erikson), their current ability to resolve power dilemmas and thus achieve equity will be seriously compromised.

A more interpersonal, systems-oriented view is offered by Goldenberg (1986). He maintains that to be effective, counseling for dual-career couples must be highly focused and must involve both partners conjointly. In his experience, their sessions together may well be the first time that one partner has been forced to attend to the other partner's agenda. When this happens, each partner may begin to become sensitized to the fact that more is happening interpersonally between the spouses than his or her individual unhappiness alone. According to Goldenberg (1986), such recognition is an essential first step in reorganizing the faulty relationship system.

Resistance to change, a factor operating in all therapeutic undertakings, may be especially pronounced in dual-career couples. By focusing on achievement and pursuing success, the busy dual-careerist may shield himself or herself from acknowledging marital or family strains until they are unavoidable, or an external event (such as, an extramarital affair) forces the couple to face their disintegrating relationship. With both accustomed to success in their professional lives, neither is eager to examine their failing marriage. As Price-Bonham and Murphy (1980) observe, dual-career couples often delay entering counseling until their relationship has deteriorated to an almost irreversible point.

Once in the counseling situation, it is essential that the couple be treated evenhandedly. The counselor's approach must not be tied to values and sex-role assignments of the traditional marriage. Counselors thus not only must be aware of the dynamic struggles within their client couples, but also must look for similar struggles within themselves that may be counterproductive to the counseling (Goldenberg & Goldenberg, 1984). The dual-careerist spouse who senses a bias in the counselor's attitude toward role stereotypes and gender-related domestic assignments "is likely to withdraw, feel ganged up on and probably pessimistic, if not despairing, about being understood" (Goldenberg, 1986, p. 4).

In the following case, we see two highly successful married individuals, at somewhat different stages of their careers, try to resolve pressing differences between them that add considerable stress to their already overburdened lives. At the wife's insistence, they contact a woman psychologist for counseling.

Marilyn and Frank, both physicians, met when she began her residency training to become a surgeon and Frank headed the Department of Surgery training program in a large city hospital. Although a mere five years older, at 35 Frank was considerably more advanced in his career than Marilyn, who had just finished her internship and begun her training under Frank to become a surgeon. They were attracted to one another from their first meeting, and soon began to date one another exclusively. Within a year of their meeting, they made plans to marry.

While their backgrounds seemed worlds apart—Frank came from a large working-class Mexican family, Marilyn from an upper-middle-class WASP upbringing—they felt confident that as intelligent people who had common values and career interests, they could make a go of marriage. Marilyn had been married before, to a man from an Armenian background, and had experienced no strain with his family or friends, so she believed she could overcome any social or cultural differences with Frank. He had been alienated from his family for some time, and although they lived in the same city, he saw them only rarely.

When Marilyn first met Frank, she was dazzled by his intelligence and clinical ability in surgery. While she was immediately attracted to him, she was at the same time taken aback by his reputation as a "womanizer." Within the hospital there was considerable gossip about his sexual promiscuity; he was known as someone who sought out all attractive nurses, as well as female medical students, interns, and residents. She thus distrusted his obvious interest in her, but as she got to know him this concern subsided somewhat, since he stopped pursuing anyone else. Besides, Marilyn was drawn to the combination of danger and romance he exuded. Frank, on the other hand, found her quick intelligence very appealing, and as he got to know Marilyn he realized and appreciated her steadying influence on him.

As they got to know one another better, they found they both came from hardworking, achieving families, each with a number of siblings and cousins with M.D.'s and Ph.D.'s. Moreover, they discovered that problems with alcoholism permeated both families, although neither Marilyn nor Frank had a particular drinking problem. Marilyn was the oldest sister in her family, accustomed to caring for her younger siblings. Frank was the youngest in his family, the baby everyone adored and wanted to indulge.

Even before they married, the couple quarreled a great deal. Marilyn was jealous and suspicious when she didn't know Frank's whereabouts for long periods of time, suspecting he was with another woman. Frank protested his innocence, but was frequently irritated by her lack of trust. He felt, too, that she never let anything pass, insisting that the smallest issue between them had to be examined and worked out in detail. In his family, he had been allowed considerable latitude—"space"—and he expected the same in this relationship. She had always been the "rescuer" in her family, and her close scrutiny of the basis for any tension between her and Frank was often done in the pursuit of clarification to reduce the stress and make things between them right again.

When they decided to marry, Marilyn persuaded Frank to see a professional for premarital counseling. In particular, she wanted them to see a married woman, whom she felt would understand the feelings and potential conflicts of a young professional woman in a dual-career marriage. Together they saw the counselor for six sessions. They seemed to benefit from the experience in that their communication patterns improved and they both felt more free to express to one another what they were experiencing in the relationship.

Frank and Marilyn married about a year after they met. After a brief honeymoon, both plunged back into extremely demanding work schedules. Marilyn was determined to be the best resident in the training program, a goal she seemed to reach. However, she was now aware that their unequal status bothered her; Frank seemed to her to be giving off a double message to her: "We are equal; I still am superior." She also became more sensitive to his behavior with the other residents, feeling that any decision he made that was not to someone's liking reflected poorly on her. He, on the other hand, felt her observing and evaluating him whenever he lectured, and he became very uncomfortable and defensive whenever he felt she was criticizing him or trying to "improve" him. Frank now found it harder and harder to maintain his position with Marilyn as her teacher, retaining her admiration and his superior status in her eyes. She still tended to put him on a pedestal, only to become disappointed when he didn't behave as she thought a concerned teacher should, or when he was not as interested in the evening in her cases as she felt he should be, tired or not.

As both devoted themselves to work and career advancement, their social contacts shrank, and their dependence on one another for stimulation and fulfillment deepened. More and more they behaved as "workaholics," childless, without many friends, their careers all-consuming. He no longer went to the gym after work, as he had done several nights each week before their marriage. She stopped seeing girlfriends for lunch or evenings out together.

After one year of this regime, both felt overburdened, put upon, and quarrelsome. Their "pressure cooker" lives now became further complicated when Marilyn was offered a chance to move to another, more prestigious surgery training at a university hospital in the same city. Both felt ambivalent about making the change: she was tempted to go but wanted Frank to insist she stay; he would miss her but felt some relief that he would be less open to her daily assessment of his job performance. They decided to schedule a new series of appointments with their counselor to work out some solutions.

The counselor immediately made them focus on exactly what a pressure-filled existence their lives had become. In their drive for success, she observed, they seemed to have neglected nourishing the intimate emotional bond that drew them together in the first place. The counselor suggested they now pause and make some decisions about what precisely they wanted out of their lives together. She stated her belief that they needed to reevaluate how they dealt with time demands, making certain that they left time and energy for fun, play, and relaxation together. They needed time too to dream and plan a little for their future. In addition, the counselor asked them to attend to their increasing social isolation, suggesting that a network of friends with whom to share work and marital experiences might prove to be a good antidote to becoming insular. Beyond those immediate goals, she indicated that they needed to reconsider the long-term effects of the lessening of differences in their professional status, since without doubt those differences would narrow in the future. By doing so, the counselor helped them focus and work through the issue of competitiveness between them. Could they imagine their lives together 15 or 20 years from now? Would they be together? Would there be children? How many? How far did each expect to advance in his or her career? How did they see the balance of family and career in their future together?

The couple had contracted for five sessions, and when the counseling series was completed they seemed to be in better contact with the unresolved issues between them. They agreed to work further on their own, and to see the counselor again in six months. When they did, it was clear that some progress had been made—in particular, they seemed to have achieved a better balance between career demands and time for one another—but significant problems remained between them. For example, there were the differences in cultural background. When Frank and Marilyn went together to the fiesta celebrating his mother's 65th birthday, there was open tension between them. She worried that he would behave in his old "macho" way in front of his cousins, appearing to ignore and thus dominate his Anglo wife. He worried that she would appear withdrawn, particularly if his family did not welcome her with open arms, a highly likely possibility.

Instead of denying dissimilarities in background, the counselor forced them to examine these past differences and to work through their impact on their present lives. The couple became aware that differences in social class and ethnic background led to basic differences in expectations regarding the role of women and the importance of family. The differences in their birth order—she the oldest child, he the youngest—also led to different expectations of roles and entitlements. These dissimilarities might or might not be significant, but they could not be buried or covered up.

The counselor also encouraged both spouses to separate their personal identities, in their case best accomplished by seeking separate work environments. In that way, competition between them would be minimized, although they needed to acknowledge it would not be eliminated completely. As they moved away from the teacher-student roles, each sought recognition in related, but not identical, fields in surgery. Frank remained primarily a teacher and trainer, Marilyn became a practitioner as a general surgeon.

The couple planned to have children within two years. They realized that the divisions of labor at home would have to be renegotiated when a child arrived, and they began now to plan to add on a nursery room to their house. They also began to discuss how their lives would change with the arrival of a baby, and how emergencies at home would be handled, since Marilyn intended to return to her career as soon as feasible. In the process, they started to socialize with other young couples from both their places of work, and talked with them at great length about family and career responsibilities.

Future sessions with the counselor were left open on an "as needed" basis. While Marilyn had learned to become less intrusive and Frank less withdrawn, they both knew more work on their communication patterns was necessary, and occasional backslides were probably inevitable. In all likelihood, they assured the counselor upon completing the current round of counseling sessions, they would be calling her again.

Many of the rewards and benefits of a dual-career marriage (an opportunity for self-fulfillment for both partners, greater intellectual stimulation, the chance to lead a more economically enriched life together) are seen in this case. At the same time, many of the common problems are also present (competition, restricted job mobility, difficulties with time allocations, work overload).

The counselor needs to help any dual-career couple understand that they are undertaking a marriage that may well give them both a sense of accomplishment, perhaps even elation, but often at the price of exhaustion and guilt over goals not achieved. To romanticize the dual-career family as "having it all" is to invite inevitable disappointment. Rather, the counselor must aid the couple in exploring their values and priorities, pursuing what is important to both partners, relinquishing experiences to which they assign less urgency, and accepting the limitations of their demanding lives.

SUMMARY

Working wives are a familiar phenomenon, but dual-career families have emerged in significant numbers only within the last 20 years. Such families contain husband and wife professionals both actively pursuing work requiring a high degree of career commitment, as well as involving themselves in their family lives.

Not all couples are necessarily equally committed to their careers or to their domestic roles. Women, depending on the stage of the family life cycle, may resolve the sometimes conflicting demands of the two roles by interrupting their careers for child rearing, by seeking part-time or temporary employment, or by restricting their geographic mobility in order to fulfill parental responsibilities. Some may postpone careers, or return to earlier careers only after their children no longer need them at home; others may return to the work force after becoming divorced or widowed.

To make a dual-career relationship work and to avoid role overload, especially for the woman, changes in who carries out domestic tasks, including child care, must be negotiated. Recent research data indicate that men's time engaging in family responsibilities is on the increase while women's is decreasing. Both a greater sharing of family involvement and of breadwinner responsibilities by both partners represents a value shift in today's society.

Beyond role overload, a number of stresses are potential sources of interpersonal conflict between dual-careerists. Clashes between career and family demands, competition between the spouses, and difficulties in making time available for all their work and family commitments are common. The presence of children may add to their responsibility overload, especially if adequate child care is unavailable or too costly. Whatever the sources of stress, the counselor needs to help the dual-career couple try to achieve the goal of equity: for each partner to feel that, overall, fairness exists both in their role opportunities as well as their constraints and responsibilities.

Commuter marriages, in which one adult moves away from spouse and child, usually for a job opportunity, place considerable strain on the marital bond, particularly among newly married couples with young children. Such "married singles" must often cope with feelings of loneliness and mistrust as they attempt to maintain intimacy and commitment to the marriage on a long-distance basis.

A number of alternative strategies are open to dual-careerists who attempt to find satisfaction at home and in their careers. Some may adapt to the situation by one partner's remaining high in career ambition but low in home involvement while the other partner adopts the reverse priorities. Others may become adversarial, both pursuing careers with only minimal attention to home, family, or their parental responsibilities. In another configuration, the two may become allies in their careers or their home life, but not in both. A final group may resemble acrobats who strive to have it all, seeking satisfaction from playing career and domestic roles fully, never missing an opportunity to add on another responsibility.

A number of approaches may be used in counseling dual-career families: helping them manage decision making and time allocation; having each partner separately resolve unfinished developmental issues from the past; or focusing conjointly on their interpersonal transactions. Whatever the counseling technique—and a combination is likely—the counselor must adopt an evenhanded approach to both careerists that is not bound by the values and sex-role assignments of the traditional marriage.

Glossary

AIDS Acquired Immune Deficiency Syndrome, an infectious disease in which the body's immune system is damaged, often in progressive degrees, making the person vulnerable to fatal opportunistic infections and malignancies; gay men and drug abusers are among the most likely victims.

anorexia nervosa Prolonged, severe diminution of appetite, particularly in adolescent females, to the point of becoming life-threatening.

behavioral The viewpoint that objective and experimentally verified procedures should be the basis for modifying maladaptive, undesired, or problematic behavior.

behaviorists Advocates of the behavioral view, in which tangible events and measurable data are sought rather than subjective reports or inferences.

binuclear family   A postdivorce family structure in which the ex-spouses reside in separate but interrelated households; the maternal and paternal households thus form one family system.

bisexual   An individual sexually attracted to both males and females.

boundaries   Abstract delineations between parts of a system or between systems, typically defined by implicit or explicit rules regarding who may participate and in what manner.

centrifugal   Tending to move outward or away from the center; within a family, forces that push the members apart.

centripetal   Tending to move toward the center; within a family, forces that keep the members together.

circular causality   The view that causality is nonlinear, occuring instead within a relationship context and by means of a network of interacting loops; any cause is thus seen as an effect of a prior cause, as in the interactions within families.

closed system   A system with impermeable boundaries, operating without interactions outside the system, and thus prone to increasing disorder.

community divorce   That stage in the divorce process in which each participant publicly redefines himself or herself to family members, friends, and the community at large as a divorced person.

commuter marriage   An intact marriage in which the partners maintain separate households, usually in distant cities, typically to pursue dual careers simultaneously.

coparental divorce   That stage in the divorce process in which issues surrounding child custody, visitation, and coparenting are resolved and arrangements defined.

crisis intervention   Brief, direct counseling focused on the here and now in response to an emergency situation.

custody   The assignment of children to one or both parents in a postdivorce family system, as well as the determination of the children's living arrangements. (See also **joint custody, joint physical custody, physical custody, sole custody, split custody.**)

cybernetics   The study of methods of feedback control within a system, especially the flow of information.

delinquency   Antisocial or illegal behavior by a minor.

disengagement   Family interaction in which members are isolated and feel unrelated to each other, each functioning separately and autonomously and without involvement in the day-to-day transactions within the family.

divorce mediation   A form of divorce arbitration in which the couple voluntarily learns to negotiate a mutually satisfactory settlement through brief, nonadversarial contact with a team knowledgeable in counseling and law.

dual-career marriage   A marriage in which husband and wife both pursue active professional careers as well as active, involved family lives.

economic divorce   That stage in the divorce process in which matters of money, property, and the redistribution of family assets are settled.

emotional divorce   That early stage in the divorce process in which both partners are forced to deal with their deteriorating marital relationship.

enmeshment   Family interaction in which boundaries between members are blurred and members are overconcerned and overinvolved in each other's lives.

entropy   The tendency of a system to go into disorder—that is, to reach a disorganized and undifferentiated state.

equifinality   In contrast to simple cause-and-effect explanations, the principle that similar outcomes may result from different origins.

family mapping   A symbolic representation of a family's organizational structure, particularly its boundaries and coalitions, used by structural counselors to plan their interventions.

feedback   A method of controlling a system by reinserting into it the results of its past performance.

feedback loops   Those circular mechanisms in which there is a continuous reintroduction of information about a system's output back into the system, initiating a chain of subsequent events.

gay couple   Partners of the same gender who develop and maintain a homosexual male or lesbian relationship.

genogram   A schematic diagram of a family's relationship system, in the form of a genetic tree, usually including at least three generations, often used by the counselor to trace recurring behavior patterns within the family.

homeostasis   A state of balance or equilibrium in a system, or a tendency toward this state.

homophobic   Excessively fearful of being homosexual oneself or of associating with homosexuals.

homosexual   A person of either sex with a sexual preference for, and sexual activity with, a person of his or her same sex.

identified patient   The family member with the presenting problem; thus, the person who initially seeks counseling, or for whom counseling is sought.

joint custody   A legal term denoting the right of both parents to share in certain major decisions (for example, religious upbringing, choice of schools) regarding their children.

joint physical custody   A shared legal arrangement between ex-spouses in which their children spend time on a regular basis with one and then the other parent.

legal divorce   That stage in the divorce process in which the judicial system becomes involved officially in ending the marriage; the marriage may be dissolved through civil annulment, no-fault divorce, or through a contested divorce hearing in court.

lesbian couple   A pair of females engaged in a sexual relationship.

linear causality   The view that a nonreciprocal relationship exists between events in a sequence, so that one event causes the next event, but not vice versa.

morphogenesis   A process by which a system changes its basic structure, typically in response to positive feedback, to adapt to changing environmental demands or conditions.

morphostasis   A process by which a system maintains constancy in its structure or organization, usually in response to negative feedback, in the face of environmental changes.

negative feedback   The flow of corrective information from the output of a system back into the system in order to attenuate deviation and keep the system functioning within prescribed limits.

negentropy   The tendency of a system to remain flexible and open to new input, necessary for change and survival of a system.

nonmarital cohabitation   An arrangement in which two unmarried adults of the opposite sex live together in a sexual relationship.

nuclear family   A family unit consisting of a husband, a wife, and their children.

open marriage   A nonexclusive marital arrangement in which extramarital sex by both partners is sanctioned; more broadly, a marriage where husband and wife are primarily concerned with autonomy and independence in intimate and marital relationships for both of them, and thus together work out marital rules that may or may not include sexual fidelity.

open system   A system with more-or-less permeable boundaries that permits interaction between component parts or subsystems, and is thus likely to function in an orderly manner.

parentified child   A child forced by his or her parents into a caretaking or nurturing parental role within a family; in extreme cases, the parents may abdicate the position of authority and assign the adult role to a child.

physical custody An arrangement, usually following divorce, in which a child lives with one parent, although visitation with the other is possible.

positive feedback The flow of information from the output of a system back into the system, in order to amplify deviation from the state of equilibrium, thus leading to instability and change.

prenuptial agreement A contract signed by a couple before marriage designed to modify certain legal repercussions, usually regarding money and property, that might otherwise occur, especially in the event the marriage ends in divorce.

prognosis A prediction or forecast about the outcome of a condition or disorder, including an indication of its probable duration and course.

psychic divorce The last stage in the divorce process, in which the ex-spouses must learn to accept the finality of their separation from one another, and commence regaining a sense of individual identity and autonomy.

psychoanalytic A viewpoint reflecting the theory of personality formation as well as the therapeutic approach developed by Sigmund Freud.

psychopathology Severe problematic, maladaptive, or dysfunctional behavior.

role overload Stress that occurs in a family when members, most likely one or both parents, attempt to fulfill a greater variety of roles than their energies or time will permit.

single parent A divorced person of either sex with whom the children of the marriage reside.

sole custody The award by the court of total physical and legal responsibility for the children to one of the parents in a divorcing couple.

split custody The award by the court of custody of one or more of the children to each of the parents in a divorcing couple.

stepfamily A linked family system created by the marriage of two persons, one or both of whom has been previously married, in which one or more children from the earlier marriages live with the remarried couple.

strategic family counseling A therapeutic approach in which the counselor develops a plan or strategy and designs interventions aimed at solving a specific problem.

structural family counseling An active, ahistorical therapeutic approach directed at changing or realigning the internal family organization or structure to alter transactional patterns among its members.

subsystems Organized, coexisting components within an overall system, each having its own autonomous functions as well as a specified role in the operation of the larger system; within families, a member can belong to a number of such units.

suprasystem   A higher-level system in which other systems represent component parts and play subsystem roles. Within a remarried family, the network of people (the former couple and their current family members, grandparents, aunts and uncles, cousins, and so on) who influence the remarried system.

system   A set of interacting units or component parts that together make up a whole arrangement or organization.

References

ABC News Closeup. (1986, August 1). After the sexual revolution [television documentary].

Ahrons, C. R., & Rodgers, R. H. (1987). *Divorced families: A multidisciplinary developmental view*. New York: W. W. Norton.

Aldous, J. (1981). From dual-earner to dual-career families and back again. *Journal of Family Issues, 2*, 115–125.

Aldous, J. (1982). *Two paychecks: Life in dual-earner families*. Newbury Park, CA: Sage Publications.

Anderson, C. L. (1982). Males as sexual assault victims: Multiple levels of trauma. In J. C. Gonsiorek (Ed.), *Homosexuality and psychotherapy: A practitioner's handbook of affirmative models*. New York: Haworth Press.

Andolfi, M. (1979). *Family therapy: An interactional approach*. New York: Plenum Press.

Bagarozzi, D. A. (1985). Dimensions of family evaluation. In L. L'Abate (Ed.), *The handbook of family psychology and therapy* (vol. II). Pacific Grove, CA: Brooks/Cole.

Barth, J. C. (1988). Family therapists' dilemma: Systems therapy with divorcing couples. *Journal of Family Psychology, 1,* 469–475.

Bateson, G. (1979). *Mind and nature.* New York: Dutton.

Beal, E. (1980). Separation, divorce, and single-parent families. In E. A. Carter & M. McGoldrick (Eds.), *The family life cycle: A framework for family therapy.* New York: Gardner Press.

Beavers, W. R. (1977). *Psychotherapy and growth.* New York: Brunner/Mazel.

Beavers, W. R. (1981). A systems model of family for family therapists. *Journal of Marriage and Family Therapy, 7,* 299–307.

Beavers, W. R. (1982). Healthy, midrange, and severely dysfunctional families. In F. Walsh (Ed.), *Normal family processes.* New York: Guilford Press.

Beavers, W. R. (1988). Attributes of the healthy couple. *Family Therapy Today, 3*(1), 1–4.

Beavers, W. R., & Voeller, M. N. (1983). Family models: Comparing and contrasting the Olson circumplex with the Beavers model. *Family Process, 22,* 85–98.

Bell, A. P., & Weinberg, M. S. (1978). *Homosexualities: A study of diversity among men and women.* New York: Simon & Schuster.

Belle, D. (Ed.). (1982). *Lives in stress: Women and depression.* Newbury Park, CA: Sage Publications.

Bernard, J. (1956). *Remarriage: A study of marriage.* New York: Dryden Press.

Bertalanffy, L von. (1968). *General systems theory: Foundation, development, applications.* New York: Braziller.

Berzon, B. (1979). *Positively gay.* Los Angeles: Mediamix Press.

Blasband, D., & Peplau, L. A. (1985). Sexual exclusivity versus openness in gay male couples. *Archives of Sexual Behavior, 14,* 395–412.

Bogdan, J. (1986, July-August). Do families really need problems? *The Family Therapy Networker,* pp. 30–35, 67–69.

Bohannan, P. (1970). *Divorce and after.* Garden City, NY: Doubleday.

Bohannan, P. (1984). *All the happy families: Exploring the varieties of family life.* New York: McGraw-Hill.

Bornstein, P. H., & Bornstein, M. T. (1986). *Marital therapy: A behavioral-communications approach.* New York: Pergamon Press.

Bould, S. (1977). Female-headed families: Personal fate control and the provider role. *Journal of Marriage and the Family, 39,* 339–349.

Bowen, M. (1978). *Family therapy in clinical practice.* New York: Aronson.

Bozett, F. W. (1982). Heterogeneous couples in heterosexual marriages: Gay men and straight women. *Journal of Marital and Family Therapy, 8,* 81–89.

Bozett, F. W. (1985). Gay men as fathers. In S. M. H. Hanson & F. W. Bozett (Eds.), *Dimensions of fatherhood.* Newbury Park, CA: Sage Publications.

Bradt, J. O., & Bradt, C. M. (1986). Resources in remarried families. In M. Karpel (Ed.), *Family resources: The hidden partner in family therapy.* New York: Guilford Press.

Brandwein, R., Brown, C., & Fox, E. (1974). Women and children last: The social situation of divorced mothers and their families. *Journal of Marriage and the Family, 36,* 498–514.

Bray, J. H. (1988). *What is in the best interest of the child? Custodial arrangements and visitation issues.* Unpublished manuscript.

Bray, J. H., & Anderson, H. (1984). Strategic interventions with single-parent families. *Psychotherapy, 21,* 101–109.

Caille, P. (1982). The evaluation phase of systemic family therapy. *Journal of Marital and Family Therapy, 8,* 29–39.

Carter, E. A., & McGoldrick, M. (Eds.). (1980). *The family life cycle.* New York: Gardner Press.

Carter, E. A., & McGoldrick, M. (1988). Overview: The changing family life cycle: A framework for family therapy. In B. Carter & M. McGoldrick (Eds.), *The changing family life cycle: A framework for family therapy* (2nd ed.). New York: Gardner Press.

Cherlin, A. J., & McCarthy, J. (1985). Remarried couples households: Data from the June 1980 current population survey. *Journal of Marriage and the Family, 47,* 23–30.

Clingempeel, A. J., Brand, E., & Ievoli, R. (1984). Stepparent-stepchild relationships in stepmother and stepfather families: A multimethod study. *Family Relations, 33,* 465–473.

Clingempeel, W. G., & Reppucci, N. D. (1982). Joint custody after divorce: Major issues and goals for research. *Psychological Bulletin, 91,* 102–127.

Cole, C. L. (1988). Family and couples therapy with nonmarital cohabiting couples: Treatment issues and case studies. In C. S. Chilman, E. W. Nunnally, & F. M. Cox (Eds.), *Variant family forms.* Newbury Park, CA: Sage Publications.

Coleman, E. (1982). Developmental stages of the coming out process. In J. C. Gonsiorek (Ed.), *Homosexuality and psychotherapy.* New York: Haworth Press.

Conger, J. J. (1981). Freedom and commitment: Families, youth, and social change. *American Psychologist, 36,* 1475–1484.

Constantine, L. L. (1986). *Family paradigms: The practice of theory in family therapy.* New York: Guilford Press.

Coogler, O. J. (1978). *Structured mediation in divorce settlement*. Lexington, MA: Lexington Books.

Crohn, H., Sager, C. J., Brown, H., Rodstein, E., & Walker, L. (1982). A basis for understanding and treating the remarried family. In J. C. Hansen & L. Messinger (Eds.), *Therapy with remarried families*. Rockville, MD: Aspen Systems.

Deceptive Picture: If you see families staging a comeback, it's probably a mirage. (1986, September 25). *The Wall Street Journal*.

Dell, P. (1982). Beyond homeostasis: Toward a concept of coherence. *Family Process, 21*, 21–41.

Derdeyn, A. P. (1976). Child custody contests in historical perspective. *American Journal of Psychiatry, 133*, 1369–1376.

deShazer, S. (1983). Diagnosing + researching + doing therapy. In B. Keeney (Ed.), *Diagnosis and assessment in family therapy*. Rockville, MD: Aspen Systems.

Doherty, W. J., & Baird, M. A. (1983). *Family therapy and family medicine: Toward the primary care of families*. New York: Guilford Press.

Duberman, L. (1975). *The reconstituted family: A study of remarried couples and their children*. Chicago: Nelson-Hall.

Duck, S. (1982). A topography of relationship disengagement and dissolution. In S. Duck (Ed.), *Personal relationships*. London: Academic Press.

Eidelson, R. J. (1983). Affiliation and independence issues in marriage. *Journal of Marriage and the Family, 45*, 683–688.

Einstein, E. (1982). *The stepfamily: Living, loving & learning*. Boston: Shambhala.

Epstein, N. B., Baldwin, L. M., & Bishop, D. S. (1983). The McMaster family assessment device. *Journal of Marital and Family Therapy, 9*, 171–180.

Epstein, N. B., Bishop, D. S., & Baldwin, L. M. (1982). McMaster model of family functioning: A view of the normal family. In F. Walsh (Ed.), *Normal family processes*. New York: Guilford Press.

Everett, C. A. (Ed.). (1987). *The divorce process: A handbook for clinicians*. New York: Haworth Press.

Farber, R. S. (1988). Integrated treatment of the dual-career couple. *American Journal of Family Therapy, 16*, 46–57.

Fishman, H. C. (1985). Diagnosis and context: An Alexandrian quartet. In R. L. Ziffer (Ed.), *Adjunctive techniques in family therapy*. New York: Grune & Stratton.

Folberg, J., & Milne, A. (Eds.). (1988). *Divorce mediation: Theory and practice*. New York: Guilford Press.

Fowers, B. J., & Olson, D. H. (1986). Predicting marital success with PRE-PARE: A predictive validity study. *Journal of Marital and Family Therapy, 12*, 403–413.

Fradkin, H. R. (1987). Counseling men in the AIDS crisis. In M. Scher, M. Stevens, G. Good, & G. A. Eichenfield (Eds.), *Handbook of counseling and psychotherapy with men*. Newbury Park, CA: Sage Publications.

Friesen, J. D. (1983). *Structural-strategic marriage and family therapy*. New York: Gardner Press.

Fulmer, R. H. (1983). A structural approach to unresolved mourning in single-parent family systems. *Journal of Marital and Family Therapy, 9*, 259–269.

Furstenberg, F. F. Jr. (1987). The new extended family: The experience of parents and children after remarriage. In K. Pasley & M. Ihinger-Tallman (Eds.), *Remarriage and stepparenting: Current research and theory*. New York: Guilford Press.

Furstenberg, F. F. Jr. (1980). Reflections on remarriage. *Journal of Family Issues, 1*, 443–453.

Ganong, L. H., & Coleman, M. (1987). Effects of parent remarriage on children: An updated comparison of theories, methods, and findings from clinical and empirical research. In K. Pasley & M. Ihinger-Tallman (Eds.), *Remarriage and stepparenting: Current research and theory*. New York: Guilford Press.

Gartrell, N. (1983). Gay patients in the medical setting. In C. C. Nadelson & D. B. Marcotte (Eds.), *Treatment interventions in human sexuality*. New York: Plenum Press.

Gerstel, N., & Gross, H. (1983). Commuter marriage: Couples who live apart. In E. D. Macklin & R. H. Rubin (Eds.), *Contemporary families and alternative lifestyles*. Newbury Park, CA: Sage Publications.

Getty, C. (1981). Considerations for working with single-parent families. In C. Getty & W. Humphreys (Eds.), *Understanding the family: Stress and change in American family life*. New York: Appleton-Century-Crofts.

Gilbert, L. A. (1985). *Men in dual-career families: Current realities and future prospects*. Hillsdale, NJ: Lawrence Erlbaum.

Glick, P. C. (1980). Remarriage: Some recent changes and variations. *Journal of Family Issues, 1*, 455–478.

Glick, P. C. (1984a). American household structure in transition. *Family Planning Perspectives, 16*, 205–211.

Glick, P. C. (1984b). How American families are changing. *American Demographics, 5*, 21–25.

Glick, P. C. (1984c). Marriage, divorce, and living arrangements: Prospective changes. *Journal of Family Issues, 5*, 7–26.

Glick, P. C., & Spanier, G. B. (1980). Married and unmarried cohabitation in the United States. *Journal of Marriage and the Family, 42*, 19–30.

Glickauf-Hughes, C. L., Hughes, G. B., & Wells, M. C. (1986). A developmental approach to treating dual-career couples. *American Journal of Family Therapy, 14*, 254–263.

Goldenberg, H. (1977). *Abnormal psychology: A social/community approach.* Pacific Grove, CA: Brooks/Cole.

Goldenberg, H. (1986). Treating contemporary couples in dual-career relationships. *Family Therapy Today, 1,* 1–7.

Goldenberg, I., & Goldenberg, H. (1984). Treating the dual-career couple. *American Journal of Family Therapy, 12,* 29–37.

Goldenberg, I., & Goldenberg, H. (1985). *Family therapy: An overview.* (2nd ed.). Pacific Grove, CA: Brooks/Cole.

Goldstein, J., Freud, A., & Solnit, A. (1979). *Beyond the best interests of the child.* New York: Free Press.

Granvold, D. K. (1983). Structured separation for marital treatment and decision-making. *Journal of Marital and Family Therapy, 9,* 403–412.

Green, R. G., Kolevzon, M. S., & Vosler, N. R. (1985). The Beavers-Timberlawn model of family competence and the Circumplex model of family adaptability and coherence: Separate, but equal? *Family Process, 24,* 385–398.

Greif, J. B. (1979). Fathers, children and joint custody. *American Journal of Orthopsychiatry, 49,* 311–319.

Greif, J. B. (1985). *Single fathers.* Lexington, MA: Lexington Books.

Gullotta, T. P., Adams, G. R., & Alexander, S. J. (1986). *Today's marriages and families: A wellness approach.* Pacific Grove, CA: Brooks/Cole.

Gwartney-Gibbs, P. A. (1986). The institutionalization of premarital cohabitation: Estimates from marriage license applications, 1970 to 1980. *Journal of Marriage and the Family, 48,* 423–434.

Haley, J. (1976). *Problem-solving therapy.* San Francisco: Jossey-Bass.

Hall, F. S., & Hall, D. T. (1979). *The two-career couple.* Reading, MA: Addison-Wesley.

Hansen, J. C. (1983). (Ed.). *Clinical implications of the family life cycle.* Rockville, MD: Aspen Systems.

Hareven, T. K. (1982). American families in transition: Historical perspectives on change. In F. Walsh (Ed.), *Normal family processes.* New York: Guilford Press.

Harrison, J. (1987). Counseling gay men. In M. Scher, M. Stevens, G. Good, & G. A. Eichenfield (Eds.), *Handbook of counseling and psychotherapy with men.* Newbury Park, CA: Sage Publications.

Harry, J. (1983). Gay male and lesbian relationships. In E. D. Macklin & R. H. Rubin (Eds.), *Contemporary families and alternative lifestyles.* Newbury Park, CA: Sage Publications.

Harry, J. (1988). Some problems of gay/lesbian families. In C. S. Chilman, E. W. Nunnally, & F. M. Cox (Eds.), *Variant family forms.* Newbury Park, CA: Sage Publications.

Hetherington, E. M. (1987). Family relations six years after divorce. In K. Pasley & M. Ihinger-Tallman (Eds.), *Remarriage and stepparenting: Current research and theory.* New York: Guilford Press.

Hetherington, E. M., Cox, M., & Cox, R. (1976). Divorced fathers. *Family Coordinator, 25,* 417–428.

Hetherington, E. M., Cox, M., & Cox, R. (1982). Effects of divorce on parents and children. In M. E. Lamb (Ed.), *Nontraditional families: Parenting and child development.* Hillsdale, NJ: Erlbaum.

Hill, R. (1986). Life cycle stages for types of single-parent families: Of family development theory. *Family Relations, 35,* 19–29.

Hoffman, L. (1981). *Foundations of family therapy.* New York: Basic Books.

Hooker, E. (1957). The adjustment of the male overt homosexual. *Journal of Projective Techniques, 21,* 18–31.

Hooker, E. (1967). The homosexual community. In J. H. Gagnon & W. Simon (Eds.), *Sexual deviance.* New York: Harper & Row.

Howell, R. J., & Toepke, K. E. (1984). Summary of the child custody laws for the fifty states. *American Journal of Family Therapy, 12,* 56–60.

Huber, C. H., & Baruth, L. G. (1987). *Ethical, legal, and professional issues in the practice of marriage and family therapy.* Columbus, OH: Merrill.

Humphreys, L., & Miller, B. (1980). Identities and the emerging gay culture. In J. Marmor (Ed.), *Homosexual behavior: A modern reappraisal.* New York: Basic Books.

Hunt, J. G., & Hunt, L. L. (1977). Dilemmas and contradictions of status: The case of the dual-career family. *Social Problems, 24,* 407–416.

Hunt, J. G., & Hunt, L. L. (1982). Dual-career families: Vanguards of the future or residue of the past? In J. Aldous (Ed.), *Two paychecks: Life in dual-earner families.* Newbury Park, CA: Sage Publications.

Ihinger-Tallman, M. (1987). Sibling and stepsibling bonding in stepfamilies. In K. Pasley & M. Ihinger-Tallman (Eds.), *Remarriage and stepparenting: Current research and theory.* New York: Guilford Press.

Ihinger-Tallman, M., & Pasley, K. (1987). Divorce and remarriage in the American family: A historical review. In K. Pasley & M. Ihinger-Tallman (Eds.), *Remarriage and stepparenting: Current research and theory.* New York: Guilford Press.

Isaacs, M. B. (1982). Facilitating family restructuring and relinkage. In J. C. Hansen & L. Messinger (Eds.), *Therapy with remarried families.* Rockville, MD: Aspen Systems.

Isaacs, M. B., Montalvo, B., & Abelsohn, D. (1986). *The difficult divorce: Therapy for children and families.* New York: Basic Books.

Jacobs, J. W. (1982). The effect of divorce on fathers: An overview of the literature. *American Journal of Psychiatry, 139,* 1235–1241.

Jacobson, D. S. (1987). Family type, visiting patterns, and children's behavior in the stepfamily: A linked family system. In K. Pasley & M. Ihinger-Tallman (Eds.), *Remarriage and stepparenting: Current research and theory*. New York: Guilford Press.

Kantor, D., & Lehr, W. (1975). *Inside the family: Toward a theory of family process*. San Francisco: Jossey-Bass.

Karpel, M. A. (Ed.) (1986). *Family resources: The hidden partner in family therapy*. New York: Guilford Press.

Karpel, M. A., & Strauss, E. S. (1983). *Family evaluation*. New York: Gardner Press.

Kaslow, F. W. (1988). The psychological dimensions of divorce mediation. In J. Folberg & A. Milne (Eds.), *Divorce mediation: Theory and practice*. New York: Guilford Press.

Kaslow, F. W., & Schwartz, L. L. (1987). *The dynamics of divorce: A life cycle perspective*. New York: Brunner/Mazel.

Keshet, J. K. (1980). From separation to stepfamily. *Journal of Family Issues, 1*, 517–531.

Kessler, S. (1975). *The American way of divorce: Prescriptions for change*. Chicago: Nelson-Hall.

Kirschner, B., & Wallum, L. (1978, November). Two-location families: Married singles. *Alternate Lifestyles, 1*, 513–525.

Klein, D. P. (1975, November). Women in the work force: The middle years. *Monthly Labor Review*, 10–16.

Kressel, K. (1985). *The process of divorce: How professionals and couples negotiate settlements*. New York: Basic Books.

Kurdek, L. A. (1981). An integrative perspective on children's divorce adjustment. *American Psychologist, 36*, 856–866.

Levant, R. F. (1988). Facilitating fathering skills through psychoeducational programs. *Family Therapy Today, 3* (12), 1–5.

Levinger, G. (1976). A social psychological perspective on divorce. *Journal of Social Issues, 32*, 21–47.

Lewis, J. M., Beavers, W. R., Gossett, J. T., & Phillips, V. A. (1976). *No single thread: Psychological health in family systems*. New York: Brunner/Mazel.

Lewis, R. A., & Spanier, G. B. (1979). Theorizing about the quality and stability of marriage. In W. R. Burr, R. Hill, F. I. Nye, & I. L. Reiss (Eds.), *Contemporary theories about the family*. New York: Macmillan.

Macklin, E. D. (1983). Nonmarital heterosexual cohabitation: An overview. In E. D. Macklin and R. H. Rubin (Eds.), *Contemporary families and alternative lifestyles*. Newbury Park, CA: Sage Publications.

Macklin, E. D. (1987). Non-marital heterosexual cohabitation: A review of research. *Marriage and Family Review, 1*, 1–12.

Macklin, E. D. (1988). Heterosexual couples who cohabit nonmaritally: Some common problems and issues. In C. S. Chilman, E. W. Nunnally, & F. M. Cox (Eds.), *Variant family forms*. Newbury Park, CA: Sage Publications.

Maddox, B. (1982). Homosexual parents. *Psychology Today, 16* (2), 62–69.

Makosky, V. P. (1982). Sources of stress: Events or conditions? In D. Belle (Ed.), *Lives in stress: Women and depression*. Newbury Park, CA: Sage Publications.

Malyon, A. K. (1982). Psychotherapeutic implications of internalized homophobia in gay men. In J. C. Gonsiorek (Ed.), *Homosexuality and psychotherapy: A practitioner's handbook of affirmative models*. New York: Haworth Press.

Marmor, J. (1980). Overview: The multiple roots of homosexual behavior. In J. Marmor (Ed.), *Homosexual behavior: A modern reappraisal*. New York: Basic Books.

Maruyama, M. (1968). The second cybernetics: Deviation-amplifying mutual causal process. In W. Buckley (Ed.), *Modern systems research for the behavioral scientist*. Chicago: Aldine.

Masnick, G., & Bane, M. J. (1980). *The nation's families: 1960–1990*. Boston: Auburn House.

McGoldrick, M., & Carter, B. (1988). Forming a remarried family. In B. Carter & M. McGoldrick (Eds.), *The changing family life cycle: A framework for family therapy* (2nd ed.). New York: Gardner Press.

McGoldrick, M., & Gerson, R. (1985). *Genograms in family assessment*. New York: W. W. Norton.

McNaught, B. (1979). Gay and Catholic. In B. Berzon (Ed.), *Positively gay*. Los Angeles: Mediamix Associates.

McWhirter, D. P., & Mattison, A. M. (1982). Psychotherapy for gay couples. In J. C. Gonsiorek (Ed.), *Homosexuality and psychotherapy*. New York: Haworth Press.

Mednick, M. T. (1987). Single mothers: A review and critique of current research. In S. Oskamp (Ed.), *Family processes and problems: Social psychological aspects*. Newbury Park, CA: Sage Publications.

Miller, J. G. (1978). *Living systems*. New York: McGraw-Hill.

Milne, A. (1988). The nature of divorce disputes. In J. Folberg & A. Milne (Eds.), *Divorce mediation: Theory and practice*. New York: Guilford Press.

Milne, A., & Folberg, J. (1988). The theory and practice of divorce mediation: An overview. In J. Folberg & A. Milne (Eds.), *Divorce mediation: Theory and practice*. New York: Guilford Press.

Minuchin, S. (1974). *Families and family therapy*. Cambridge, MA: Harvard University Press.

Morawetz, A., & Walker, G. (1984). *Brief therapy with single-parent families.* New York: Brunner/Mazel.

Morrison, P. A. (1986). *Changing family structure: Who cares for America's dependents?* Santa Monica, CA: Rand Corporation.

Moses, A., & Hawkins, R., Jr. (1982). *Counseling lesbian women and gay men: A life-issues appproach.* St. Louis: Mosby.

Napier, A. Y., & Whitaker, C. (1978). *The family crucible.* New York: Harper & Row.

National Center for Health Statistics. Annual summary of births, marriages, divorces, and deaths, United States, 1984. *Monthly Vital Statistics Report,* Vol. 33, No. 13. (DHHS Publication No. (PHS)85–1120). Public Health Service, Hyattsville, MD, September 26, 1985.

Nelson, J. B. (1982). Religious and moral issues in working with homosexual clients. In J. C. Gonsiorek (Ed.), *Homosexuality and psychotherapy.* New York: Haworth Press.

Newcomb, M. D. (1983). Relationship qualities of those who live together. *Alternative Lifestyles, 6,* 78–102.

Newcomb, M. D. (1987). Cohabitation and marriage: A quest for independence and relatedness. In S. Oskamp (Ed.), *Family processes and problems: Social psychological aspects.* Newbury Park, CA: Sage Publications.

Nichols, W. C., & Everett, C. A. (1986). *Systemic family therapy: An integrative approach.* New York: Guilford Press.

Norton, A. J., & Glick, P. C. (1986). One-parent families: A social and economic profile. *Family Relations, 35,* 9–17.

Not all parents are straight. (1987, July). KCET Television Production, Los Angeles, CA.

Olson, D. H. (1986). Circumplex model VII: Validation studies and FACES III. *Family Process, 26,* 337–351.

Olson, D. H., Fournier, D. G., & Druckman, J. M. (1986). *Prepare/Enrich counselor's manual.* Minneapolis: Prepare/Enrich, Inc.

Olson, D. H., Russell, C. S., & Sprenkle, D. H. (1983). Circumplex model of marital and family systems: VI. Theoretical update. *Family Process, 22,* 69–83.

Olson, D. H., Sprenkle, D. H., & Russell, C. S. (1979). Circumplex model of marital and family systems: I. Cohesion and adaptability dimensions, family types, and clinical applications. *Family Process, 18,* 3–28.

Papanek, H. (1974). Men, women, and work: Reflections on the two-person career. *American Journal of Sociology, 78,* 852–872.

Papp, P. (1983). *The process of change.* New York: Guilford Press.

Pasley, K. (1985). Stepfathers. In S. M. H. Hanson & F. W. Bozett (Eds.), *Dimensions of fatherhood.* Newbury Park, CA: Sage Publications.

Pasley, K., & Ihinger-Tallman, M. (1987). The evolution of a field of investigation: Issues and concerns. In K. Pasley & M. Ihinger-Tallman (Eds.), *Remarriage and stepparenting: Current research and theory*. New York: Guilford Press.

Pearce, D. (1978). The feminization of poverty: Women, work and welfare. *Urban and Social Change, 2*, 24–36.

Peplau, L. A., & Amaro, H. (1982). Understanding lesbian relationships. In J. Weinrich & W. Paul (Eds.), *Homosexuality: Social, psychological, and biological issues*. Newbury Park, CA: Sage Publications.

Peterman, D., Ridley, C., & Anderson, S. (1974). A comparison of cohabiting and noncohabiting college students. *Journal of Marriage and the Family, 36*, 344–354.

Pleck, J. H. (1985). *Working wives/working husbands*. Newbury Park, CA: Sage Publications.

Poloma, M. M., Pendleton, B. F., & Garland, T. N. (1981). Reconsidering the dual-career marriage: A longitudinal approach. *Journal of Family Issues, 2*, 205–224.

Ponse, B. (1980). Lesbians and their world. In J. Marmor (Ed.), *Homosexual behavior: A modern reappraisal*. New York: Basic Books.

Price-Bonham, S., & Murphy, D. C. (1980). Dual-career marriages: Implications for the clinician. *Journal of Marital and Family Therapy, 6*, 181–188.

Rapoport, R., & Rapoport, R. (1969). The dual-career family. *Human Relations, 22*, 3–30.

Rapoport, R., & Rapoport, R. (1976). *Dual-career families re-examined: New integration of work and family*. New York: Harper.

Rapoport, R., & Rapoport, R. (1982). The next generation in dual-career research. In J. Aldous (Ed.), *Two paychecks: Life in dual-career families*. Newbury Park, CA: Sage Publications.

Reiss, D. (1980). Pathways to assessing the family: Some choice points and a sample route. In C. K. Hofling & J. M. Lewis (Eds.), *The family: Evaluation and treatment*. New York: Brunner/Mazel.

Rice, D. G., & Rice, J. K. (1986a). Separation and divorce therapy. In N. S. Jacobson & A. S. Gurman (Eds.), *Clinical handbook of marital therapy*. New York: Guilford Press.

Rice, J. K., & Rice, D. G. (1986b). *Living through divorce: A developmental approach to divorce therapy*. New York: Guilford Press.

Rice, S., & Kelly, J. (1988). Choosing a gay/lesbian lifestyle: Related issues of treatment services. In C. S. Chilman, E. W. Nunnally, & F. M. Cox (Eds.), *Variant family forms*. Newbury Park, CA: Sage Publications.

Richards, C. A., & Goldenberg, I. (1985). Joint custody: Current issues and implications for treatment. *American Journal of Family Therapy, 4*, 33–40.

Ridley, C. A., Peterman, D. J., & Avery, A. W. (1978). Cohabitation: Does it make for a better marriage? *The Family Coordinator, 27,* 129–137.

Rochlin, M. (1979). Becoming a gay professional. In B. Berzon (Ed.), *Positively gay.* Los Angeles: Mediamix Associates.

Sager, C. J., Brown, H. S., Crohn, H., Engel, T., Rodstein, E., & Walker, L. (1983). *Treating the remarried family.* New York: Brunner/Mazel.

Sager, C. J., Walker, E., Brown, H. S., Crohn, H. M., & Rodstein, E. (1981). Improving functioning of the remarried family system. *Journal of Marital and Family Therapy, 7,* 3–13.

Saghir, M. T., & Robins, E. (1980). Clinical aspects of female homosexuality. In J. Marmor (Ed.), *Homosexual behavior: A modern reappraisal.* New York: Basic Books.

Sauber, S. R. (1983). *The human services delivery system.* New York: Columbia University Press.

Schoen, R., Urton, W., Woodrow, K., & Baj, J. (1985). Marriage and divorce in twentieth-century American cohorts. *Demography, 22,* 101–114.

Schwartz, L. L. (1987). Joint custody. *Journal of Family Psychology, 1,* 120–134.

Segal, L. (1987). What is a problem? A brief family therapist's view. *Family Therapy Today, 2* (7), 1–7.

Segal, L., & Bavelas, J. B. (1983). Human systems and communication theory. In B. B. Wolman & G. Stricker (Eds.), *Handbook of family and marital therapy.* New York: Plenum Press.

Sekaran, U. (1986). *Dual-career families: Contemporary organizational and counseling issues.* San Francisco: Jossey-Bass.

Seward, R. (1978). *The American family: A demographic history.* Newbury Park, CA: Sage Publications.

Shaevitz, M. H., & Shaevitz, H. J. (1980). *Making it together as a two-career couple.* Boston: Houghton Mifflin.

Silverstein, C. (1981). *Man to man: Gay couples in America.* New York: Morrow.

Spanier, G. B. (1983). Married and unmarried cohabitation in the United States: 1980. *Journal of Marriage and the Family, 45,* 277–288.

Sprenkle, D. H. (Ed.). (1985). *Divorce therapy.* New York: Haworth Press.

Stahmann, R. F., & Hiebert, W. J. (1987). *Premarital counseling: The professional's handbook.* Lexington, MA: Lexington Books.

Stier, S. (1986). Divorce mediation. *Family Therapy Today, 1* (3), 1–7.

Storms, M. (1986). *The development of sexual orientation.* Washington, DC: American Psychological Association.

Stuart, R. B. (1980). *Helping couples change: A social learning approach to marital therapy.* Champaign, IL: Research Press.

Taylor, A. (1988). A general theory of divorce mediation. In J. Folberg & A. Milne (Eds.), *Divorce mediation: Theory and practice.* New York: Guilford Press.

Thompson, E. H., Jr., & Gongla, P. A. (1983). Single-parent families: In the mainstream of American society. In E. D. Macklin & R. H. Rubin (Eds.), *Contemporary families and alternative lifestyles.* Newbury Park, CA: Sage Publications.

Toder, N. (1979). Lesbian couples: Special issues. In B. Berzon (Ed.), *Positively gay.* Los Angeles: Mediamix Associates.

Turner, N. W. (1985). Divorce: Dynamics of decision therapy. In D. H. Sprenkle (Ed.), *Divorce therapy.* New York: Haworth Press.

Umbarger, C. C. (1983). *Structural family therapy.* New York: Grune & Stratton.

U. S. Bureau of the Census. (1980). *Current population reports,* series P-20, No. 352. Washington, DC: U. S. Bureau of the Census.

U.S. Bureau of the Census. (1986). Households, families, marital status and living arrangements: March 1986. *Current population reports,* series P-20, No. 412. Washington, D.C.: U.S. Government Printing Office.

Visher, E. B., & Visher, J. S. (1979). *Stepfamilies: A guide to working with stepparents and stepchildren.* New York: Brunner/Mazel.

Visher, E. B., & Visher, J. S. (1982). Stepfamilies in the 1980s. In J. C. Hansen & L. Messinger (Eds.), *Therapy with remarried families.* Rockville, MD: Aspen Systems.

Visher, E. B., & Visher, J. S. (1986). *Stepfamily workbook manual.* Baltimore, MD: Stepfamily Association of America.

Visher, E. B., & Visher, J. S. (1988). *Old loyalties, new ties: Therapeutic strategies with stepfamilies.* New York: Brunner/Mazel.

Visher, J. S., & Visher, E. B. (1981). Common problems in stepfamilies. In A. S. Gurman (Ed.), *Questions and answers in the practice of family therapy* (vol. 1). New York: Brunner/Mazel.

Wachtel, E. F., & Wachtel, P. L. (1986). *Family dynamics in individual psychotherapy: A guide to clinical strategies.* New York: Guilford Press.

Walker, G. (1987, April and June). AIDS and family therapy. *Family Therapy Today, 2,* 1–7.

Walker, L. S., & Wallston, B. S. (1985). Social adaptation: A review of dual-earner family literature. In L. L'Abate (Ed.), *The handbook of family psychology and therapy.* Pacific Grove, CA: Brooks/Cole.

Wallerstein, J. S. (1986). Women after divorce: Preliminary report from a ten-year follow-up. *American Journal of Orthopsychiatry, 56,* 65–77.

Wallerstein, J. S. (1988). Children of divorce: The dilemma of a decade. In E. W. Nunnally, C. S. Chilman, & F. M. Cox (Eds.), *Troubled relationships.* Newbury Park, CA: Sage Publications.

Wallerstein, J. S., & Kelly, J. B. (1974). The effects of parental divorce: The adolescent experience. In E. J. Anthony & C. Koupernik (Eds.), *The child in his family: Children at psychiatric risk.* New York: Wiley.

Wallerstein, J. S., & Kelly, J. B. (1975). The effects of parental divorce: Experiences of the preschool child. *Journal of the American Academy of Child Psychiatry, 14,* 600–616.

Wallerstein, J. S., & Kelly, J. B. (1976). The effects of parental divorce: Experiences of the child in later latency. *American Journal of Orthopsychiatry, 46,* 256–269.

Wallerstein, J. S., & Kelly, J. B. (1980a). Effects of divorce on the visiting father-child relationship. *American Journal of Psychiatry, 137,* 1534–1539.

Wallerstein, J. S., & Kelly, J. B. (1980b). *Surviving the breakup: How parents and children cope with divorce.* New York: Basic Books.

Walsh, F. (1985). The timing of symptoms and critical events in the family life cycle. In J. C. Hansen (Ed.), *Clinical implications of the family life cycle.* Rockville, MD: Aspen Systems.

Warren, C. (1980). Homosexuality and stigma. In J. Marmor (Ed.), *Homosexual behavior: A modern reappraisal.* New York: Basic Books.

Weber, T., McKeever, J. E., & McDaniel, S. H. (1985). A beginner's guide to the problem-oriented first family interview. *Family Process, 24,* 356–364.

Weed, J. A. (1980). National estimates of marriage dissolution and survivorship: United States. *Vital and Health Statistics:* Series 3, Analytic Statistics: No. 19. DHHS Publication No. PHS 81–1403. Hyattsville, MD: National Center for Health Statistics.

Weinberg, G. (1972). *Society and the healthy homosexual.* New York: St. Martin's Press.

Weiss, R. S. (1975). *Marital separation.* New York: Basic Books.

Weiss, R. S. (1979). *Going it alone: The family life and social situation of the single parent.* New York: Basic Books.

Weltner, J. S. (1982). A structural approach to the single-parent family. *Family Process, 21,* 203–210.

Westley, W. A., & Epstein, N. B. (1969). *The silent majority.* San Francisco: Jossey-Bass.

Westoff, L. (1977). *The second time around: Remarriage in America.* New York: Viking Press.

Whitaker, C. A. (1977). Process techniques of family therapy. *Interaction, 1,* 4–19.

White, S. L. (1978). Family therapy according to the Cambridge Model. *Journal of Marriage and Family Counseling, 4,* 91–100.

Whiteside, M. F. (1983). Families of remarriage: The weaving of many life cycles. In J. C. Hansen & H. A. Liddle (Eds.), *Clinical implications of the family life cycle.* Rockville, MD: Aspen Systems.

Wiener, N. (1967). *The human use of human beings: Cybernetics and society* (2nd ed.). New York: Avon.

Winfield, F. E. (1985). *Commuter marriage: Living together, apart.* New York: Columbia University Press.

Woodman, N. J., & Lenna, H. R. (1980). *Counseling with gay men and women: A guide for facilitating positive life-styles.* San Francisco: Jossey-Bass.

Woody, J. D. (1983). Sexuality in divorce and remarriage. In J. C. Hansen, J. D. Woody, & R. H. Woody (Eds.), *Sexual issues in family therapy.* Rockville, MD: Aspen Systems.

Name Index

Subject Index

362.8286
G618

84819

LINCOLN CHRISTIAN COLLEGE AND SEMINARY

362.8286Goldenberg, Herbert.
G618   Counseling
          today's families

                    84819

DEMCO